Secondary School Reading

FRIDAY

Secondary School Reading

What Research Reveals for Classroom Practice

Edited by

Allen Berger
University of Pittsburgh

H. Alan Robinson
Hofstra University

National Conference on Research in English

ERIC Clearinghouse on Reading and Communication Skills
National Institute of Education

This book is dedicated to the many devoted teachers and administrators in secondary schools. Their commitment is part of the promise for a better world.

Grateful acknowledgement is made for permission to reprint from Louise M. Rosenblatt's "A Way of Happening." From *Educational Record*, Summer 1968. © American Council on Education, Washington, D. C. Used by permission.

Book Design: Tom Kovacs

NCTE Stock Number 42958

Published 1982 by the ERIC Clearinghouse on Reading and Communication Skills, 1111 Kenyon Road, Urbana, Illinois 61801, and the National Conference on Research in English.

This publication was prepared with funding from the National Institute of Education, U.S. Department of Education, under contract no. 400-78-0026. Contractors undertaking such projects under government sponsorship are encouraged to express freely their judgment in professional and technical matters. Prior to publication, the manuscript was submitted to the National Conference on Research in English for critical review and determination of professional competence. This publication has met such standards. Points of view or opinions, however, do not necessarily represent the official view or opinions of either the National Conference on Research in English or the National Institute of Education.

Library of Congress Catalog Card Number: 82-61719

Contents

Foreword

The Educational Resources Information Center (ERIC) is a national information system developed by the U.S. Office of Education and now sponsored by the National Institute of Education (NIE). It provides ready access to descriptions of exemplary programs, research and development efforts, and related information useful in developing more effective educational programs.

Through its network of specialized centers or clearinghouses, each of which is responsible for a particular educational area, ERIC acquires, evaluates, abstracts, and indexes current significant information and lists this information in its reference publications.

ERIC/RCS, the ERIC Clearinghouse on Reading and Communication Skills, disseminates educational information related to research, instruction, and personnel preparation at all levels and in all institutions. The scope of interest of the clearinghouse includes relevant research reports, literature reviews, curriculum guides and descriptions, conference papers, project or program reviews, and other print materials related to all aspects of reading, English, educational journalism, and speech communication.

The ERIC system has already made available—through the ERIC Document Reproduction Service—much informative data. However, if the findings of specific educational research are to be intelligible to teachers and applicable to teaching, considerable bodies of data must be reevaluated, focused, translated, and molded into an essentially different context. Rather than resting at the point of making research reports readily accessible, NIE has directed the separate clearinghouses to work with professional organizations in developing information analysis papers in specific areas within the scope of the clearinghouses.

ERIC/RCS is pleased to cooperate with the National Conference on Research in English and the Commission on Reading of the National Council of Teachers of English in making *Secondary School Reading: What Research Reveals for Classroom Practice* available.

Bernard O'Donnell
Director, ERIC/RCS

Acknowledgments

Researchers and teachers have infrequently followed a common path in examining and analyzing reading phenomena in secondary classrooms. It is therefore timely and fitting that the National Conference on Research in English and the Commission on Reading of the National Council of Teachers of English should collaborate in developing a volume that unites reading research and secondary teaching perspectives. A major goal of this project has been to prepare a volume on research in secondary reading that speaks to teachers, providing them with information enabling them to increase their effectiveness. This project also has aimed to advance knowledge and stimulate other researchers in secondary reading.

The accomplishment of these goals is evident, but it has been achieved only through the splendid collaborative efforts of the editors, the contributors, the publishers, and the members of both organizations. Both organizations are indebted to the ERIC Clearinghouse on Reading and Communication Skills for its many services in the production of this professional title. Thanks are due also to those members of NCRE and the Commission on Reading who helped with encouragement and specific suggestions at various stages in the project. Thanks are due, of course, to the dedicated professionals who contributed the insightful chapters that comprise this book. We offer thanks also to the publishers for timely publication. But the greatest appreciation must be reserved for the hard-working editors from the Commission on Reading, Allen Berger and H. Alan Robinson. Editing a volume such as this requires vision, tact, and tenacity—all qualities that our editors possess in abundance. The volume itself stands as an emblem of their success in attracting an exceptional range of inspired contributions.

James Squire, President
National Conference on Research in English, 1982

Leo Ruth, Director
Commission on Reading
National Council of Teachers of English, 1982

Preface

In these troubled times it is encouraging to see signs of cooperation. It has been through the cooperation and good will of many people and groups that this book has come into being. Even with all this cooperation, it has taken three years.

The original idea for this project—to provide to teachers a second updated version of *What We Know about High School Reading*—was generated at the Commission on Reading meeting of the National Council of Teachers of English Annual Convention in San Francisco (November 1979). The original publication, composed of four articles, appeared during the 1957–58 academic year. The first revision, composed of eight articles, appeared in 1969. Both publications were edited by M. Agnella Gunn and published under the auspices of the National Conference on Research in English (NCRE) and the National Council of Teachers of English (NCTE).

During the year following the NCTE convention in San Francisco we engaged in extensive correspondence with representatives of the National Conference on Research in English and the National Council of Teachers of English. The end result of the communications was that we were asked to produce this updated version with the involvement of NCRE, the NCTE Commission on Reading, NCTE, and the ERIC Clearinghouse on Reading and Communication Skills. We prepared sample tables of contents and presented them for critical examination at the Commission on Reading meeting at the NCTE Annual Convention in Cincinnati (November 1980). Contributors were asked to take as broad a view as possible and to relate reading to the content areas wherever appropriate to their themes.

Many people cooperated in the creation of this publication. Leo Ruth of the University of California, Berkeley, chaired the Commission on Reading meeting at which the idea emerged. At that meeting was commission member P. David Pearson of the Center for the Study of Reading who was also president-elect of the National Conference on Research in English. He was a key pivotal person through his involvement with these two organizations. NCRE provided continuing support and voted to defray expenses for the typing of the final manuscript at a meeting chaired by then NCRE President Roy C. O'Donnell of the University of Georgia. Paul O'Dea and Bernard O'Donnell provided support, respectively, as director of NCTE Publications and director of the ERIC Clearinghouse for Reading and Communication Skills. The contributors deserve credit for sharing their expertise, with special thanks to Margaret Early who has been an author in each of the three editions. We are grateful also to the teachers and administrators who took time from their busy schedules to read this publication. They, too, became a part of this cooperative venture.

                                        Allen Berger
                                        University of Pittsburgh

Secondary School Reading

Prologue

H. Alan Robinson
Hofstra University

The objective in this collection is to help the classroom teacher in the secondary school make use of some of the current research related to reading instruction. Each of the twelve chapters begins with an introduction to set the stage and ends with a conclusion to put the ideas into perspective. At times the conclusions are classroom applications; frequently, classroom applications are stressed in other parts of the chapters. As is often true of research, all of it is not immediately functional; in such cases the authors have tried to help the reader develop insights which can lead to creative classroom strategies. Should the reader "miss" some of these insights, Margaret Early has discussed and listed many of them in her valuable epilogue.

The language of the authors reflects the language of the researchers; and, of course, the authors in this collection are often the researchers themselves. At every opportunity authors have attempted to define and explain terminology which may be new or used in ways that differ from readers' anticipated meanings. Much of the terminology and the ideas behind the terms are new to educators, coming to us from cognitive psychology, information processing, psycholinguistics, and sociolinguistics. Some the reader will recognize as familiar concepts with new labels.

Several overriding research-related conclusions appear throughout the volume. They are stated in many different ways and are exemplified in different contexts. Early discusses several of them in her epilogue. They are stated here, however, as a conceptual preorganizer for the reader.

1. High school students can read with some degree of understanding, but their responses to what they read are generally superficial, abstract formulas. They rarely return to text and use it for explaining and supporting their interpretations.

Such behavior may be an outcome of the way they have been taught.

2. The tests we use to assess reading ability are inadequate. They do not measure prior knowledge of the students; they do not present tasks similar to classroom tasks; they do not provide for opportunity to respond to what has been read through explanation and evaluation (since responses are normally multiple-choice or filling-in-the-blanks).

3. The organization of prior knowledge in the heads of readers (schemata) needs to be activated and/or developed if reading comprehension is to take place. Readers cannot interact with authors adequately if they do not have some prior knowledge to bring to the reading task.

4. The contexts of reading impinge on reading performance. Readers need to be aware of *what, why,* and *how* they are reading in relation to given tasks and given situations. Teachers need to help students develop strategies over time to cope with the large variety of reading tasks within and outside of the classroom setting—textbooks, magazines, newspapers, trade books, standardized tests, informal tests, home assignments, library work, reference materials, laboratory work, and so forth.

5. Students must have guidance in self-regulating their learning through text. Important strategies are (a) defining their own reading tasks, (b) setting their own reading purposes, and (c) planning their own learning.

6. Teachers should insist that publishers present them with textbooks that not only meet the content needs but that also demonstrate superior organization of those content ideas. Students may be helped to bring organization to their reading as a means of improving comprehension; authors can contribute to improved comprehension by presenting information in a carefully structured, coherent manner.

7. Reading comprehension needs to be considered within the contexts of reading. The teacher does not always know "the correct response." At times the teacher and the student will anticipate general agreement; at other times the learning experience will be enriched by the difference.

8. Reading and writing (plus discussion) are closely related tools of learning. Attention needs to be paid to having these communicative partners taught and used in an integrated fashion.

9. An old cry: All content-area teachers should take responsibility for teaching the reading and writing strategies essential in their classrooms. Reading and writing success depends on a total commitment across the curriculum. Such a comprehensive program needs the full and active backing of the school administrators.

10. Specialized reading services, usually reading labs or remedial reading situations, should only be organized as supplements to a comprehensive reading and writing program across the curriculum.

The ten points listed above may serve as a rough outline as the reader studies each chapter. Undoubtedly the reader will discover many other important conclusions not listed here.

1 Reading Achievement

Anthony R. Petrosky
University of Pittsburgh

This review of reading achievement in the secondary schools is based on the 1979–80 assessment of reading and literature conducted by the National Assessment of Educational Progress (NAEP). The assessment was designed to find out what students at three age levels know and can do in a specific academic area. It surveyed the attainments of nine year olds, thirteen year olds, and seventeen year olds to provide a broad portrait of students' reading skills and attitudes toward reading. A variety of item formats, passage types, and levels of difficulty were deliberately included to assess the extent to which such variations might interact with student performance.

As all other NAEP assessments, this one was the product of several years of work by many educators, scholars, and lay persons from all over the nation. Initially, these people designed reading and literature objectives by proposing goals they felt Americans should be achieving in the course of their education. After careful review, the objectives were turned over to writers, whose task it was to create exercises (items) appropriate to the objectives. Once the exercises passed extensive reviews by subject-area specialists, measurement experts, and lay people, they were administered to a probability sample. These samples were chosen in such a way that the results of the assessment could be generalized to an entire national population. That is, on the basis of the performance of about 2,500 seventeen year olds on a given exercise, generalizations could be made about the probable performance of all seventeen year olds in the nation.

Unlike other testing programs, NAEP does not report scores on individuals. In addition to the national results for three age groups, NAEP provides results for groups of respondents. Respondents are classified by sex, race, region of the country, level of parents' education, grade, community size and type, and achievement class. Results are presented for males and females enrolled in school at the time of the assessment; for black students and white students (Hispanic students are included along with white students); for the Northeastern, Southeastern, Central, and Western regions of the country; for (1) students whose parents have not graduated from high school, (2) students who have at least one parent who has graduated from high school, and (3) students who have at least one parent who has had some education beyond high school. Results are also presented by type of community—advantaged urban, disadvantaged urban, and rural; and size of community—big cities, fringes around big cities, medium cities, and small places. In addition, results are presented in four ranges of achievement or performance: the first achievement level represents the lowest one-fourth of the national sample and the fourth represents the highest one-fourth of the national sample. After assessment data have been collected, scored, and analyzed, the National Assessment publishes reports and disseminates the results as widely as possible.

This discussion of students' achievement in reading is based on the most recent NAEP reading report, *Reading, Thinking, and Writing: Results from the 1979–80 National Assessment of Reading and Literature.* While the report presents findings for all three age groups, this chapter focuses mainly on the achievements of seventeen year olds.

What We Know

A substantial part of the NAEP reading and literature assessment was devoted to surveying students' attitudes, habits, and practices in reading. Students were asked, for instance, "What kind of a reader are you?" Only 6.2 percent claimed they were poor readers while 62.4 percent thought they were good readers, and 28.9 percent responded that they saw themselves as very good readers. Large percentages of students reported that it was usually easy for them to keep their mind on their reading (63.1%), read long sentences (81%), finish silent reading in class in the amount of time given (68.6%), read a story with new words (51.2%), finish books they have started (71.4%), read books with small print (71%), find a book that interests them (54.8%), read very long books (41.5%), and find a book on a subject that is easy for them to read (81.6%). Almost all students thought it was very important to be able to read, but the picture was somewhat less positive when we looked at how much they said they enjoyed reading. At age nine, 80.9 percent of the students said they enjoyed reading very much; at age seventeen, 42.4 percent said they enjoyed reading very much. At age nine, 3.2 percent responded that they did not enjoy reading at all, while at age seventeen, 5.3 percent responded that they did not enjoy reading at all.

When asked how often they read for enjoyment during their spare time, 53.6 percent of the nine year olds said they read almost every day and 32.7 percent of the seventeen year olds claimed they read almost every day. Of the seventeen year olds, 32.3 percent claimed they read once or twice a week for enjoyment while 26.7 percent reported that they read less than once a week and 7.9 percent said they never read for enjoyment.

When we examine the frequency of seventeen year olds reading in the context of how long they read, we find that most read for less than an hour (75.9%) and only 19.5 percent read for one or two hours while 4.2 percent read for three or more hours. When we look at these figures in comparison with how much television they reported they "watched yesterday," only 38.8 percent said they watched none or less than an hour while 60.8 percent reported watching one to three plus hours. Most (63.6%) would rather spend their free time going to a movie, and only 13.4 percent would spend that time reading a book. When asked which of a group of activities they would enjoy doing the least, 46 percent responded with reading a book.

The picture that emerges from these survey questions is not a very bright or encouraging one. While most students think it is important to read, few read for enjoyment and even fewer would choose to read a book in their spare time. When these teens do read, they read for short periods of time. It is not so much the case that they cannot read, but that they choose not to, especially when given the opportunity to do other things like watch television or go to a movie. When students give reading such a low priority and so little time, we must begin to wonder about their involvement in reading and, consequently, the quality and depth of their reading.

When asked what kind of materials they like to read, the seventeen year olds gave the following order of genres: short stories (42%), fiction books (38%), current news magazines (37%), nonfiction (25%), poetry (17%), editorials (12%), plays (11%), and literary criticism (3%). In addition to asking questions about the kinds of materials they read, we surveyed their values for reading.

The results indicated they knew they could read for a number of reasons, but they preferred to read for practical reasons rather than for personal growth or pleasure. And although almost half of the students reported that they read daily newspapers, most reported they learned about current events from television and radio.

Although these survey results paint only the broadest picture of seventeen year olds' reading attitudes, habits, and practices, we get a definite sense of these teens as people who think they are good readers, but in fact read very little, and not much at all for enjoyment. While large percentages report they do not have problems with their reading, a third to half report problems finishing inclass reading and finding books that interest them. They watch television more than they read and they prefer going to a movie in their spare time rather than reading. When they do read on their own, it is for very short periods of time. Generally, they value reading most for its presentation of information, not for personal growth or pleasure. In short, these are people who understand the value of reading, but choose not to read very much. When given the opportunity to read, most of them would rather not.

Now that we have a sense of seventeen year olds' general orientation toward reading, we can take a closer look at how well they read. In designing assessment items and interpreting the results, a four-step model of the comprehension process evolved:

1. initial comprehension
2. preliminary inferences and judgments
3. a reexamination of the text in light of these interpretations
4. richer and possibly more accurate comprehension of the text as a whole

Looking at results across a wide range of multiple-choice and open-ended items, the major conclusion must be that American schools have been reasonably successful in teaching the majority of students to complete the first two steps in the process, but have failed to teach more than 5 to 10 percent to move beyond their initial interpretations of texts. As the final NAEP report concluded,

> Students seem satisfied with their initial interpretations of what they have read and seem genuinely puzzled at requests to explain or defend their points of view. As a result, responses to assessment items requiring explanations of criteria, analysis of text, defense of judgments, or points of view were in general disappointing. Few students could provide more than superficial responses to such tasks, and even the better responses

showed little evidence of well-developed problem-solving strategies or critical-thinking skills. (p. 2)

In order to understand the grounds for the conclusions, we need
to delve into students' performance on the various items that
indicated student achievement in terms of our four-step model.
These include, in addition to the general survey items, items
clustered in three groups: explaining responses to written works,
evaluating written works, and general responding.

Explaining Responses to Written Works

The first group of exercises included multiple-choice items that
asked students to identify the mood of a piece, a character trait, an
emotion, or a theme. Then they were directed to explain and
substantiate in writing their answers to a question that involved
them in making an inference about one of the aspects (mood,
character, theme, or emotion) of the selection. Another exercise in
this group asked students to identify and explain, using text-based
evidence, an important theme or idea they saw in the selection.
Since theme is a relatively abstract notion, the question-stems for
these exercises were very specific, pointing students toward such
things as plot, character, setting, images, language, and structure
as possible approaches to analyzing the selection. Results for all
items (including unreleased selections) are summarized in table 1.

Table 1

Explaining Responses

	Adequate	Barely adequate	Inadequate	Unrateable
Theme				
"i was you" (poem)	4.6%	19.0%	70.3%	6.1%
Unreleased narrative	9.7	20.2	61.6	8.6
Character				
"Somebody's Son" (story)	41.4	42.4	13.6	2.5
Unreleased description*	38.3	43.1	16.3	2.3
Mood				
"Rodeo" (poem)	41.2	37.9	16.6	4.3
Unreleased narrative*	37.8	26.6	32.2	3.4
Emotion				
"Good Dog" (story)	57.7	22.9	11.7	7.7

*Nonfiction

Overall, the results suggested that seventeen year olds are not used to explaining the meaning they draw from texts. Although a reasonably high percentage wrote explanations of their assertions about mood and characterization, the degree of their success (41%) was far below their success (75%) on the inferential multiple-choice items that preceded the open-ended explanatory tasks. Even when students performed adequately, the majority of their explanations turned to summary or synopsis rather than to some systematic analysis of the text or their own ideas and values.

When we look at the results for these open-ended explanatory tasks by race and community, we see that blacks performed 15 to 20 percent below their white counterparts and students from disadvantaged-urban communities performed 11 to 26 percentage points below students from advantaged-urban communities. Students from rural areas performed considerably above students from disadvantaged communities but 10 to 15 percentage points below students from advantaged-urban communities.

Evaluating Written Works

Two sets of exercises were developed to assess students' evaluative skills. The first set focused on the criteria students bring to reading; it asked them to list three things that make a good story (or poem). The second set focused on students' evaluations of stories and poems by first asking, in a multiple-choice question, if a specific story or poem was good, and then directing them to go on and explain what in the passage had led them to that judgment.

Results from the first set of items revealed that 43 percent of seventeen year olds cited aspects of content as their evaluative criteria for stories, while 46 percent gave subjective reactions such as "interesting," "funny," or "adventurous," and 16 percent cited form. The picture changed somewhat with the evaluative criteria they used for poems. Unlike their reactions to stories, 62.4 percent cited form as an aspect of their evaluative criteria for poems, and only 31.2 percent cited content, while 43.9 percent gave subjective reactions. Generally, students' criteria indicated that they operated on the level of the text as a whole, rather than on individual aspects of the text such as characters, setting, or believability.

Although it is interesting to see how students say they evaluate their reading by looking at their ability to formulate evaluative criteria, the results tell us nothing about their ability to apply these criteria to written works in reasoned ways. The second set of evaluative exercises asked students to explain their evaluations of texts. The results are summarized in table 2.

Table 2

Evaluating Written Works

	No evaluation	Brief list of assertions	Content, details or summary	Evaluation with evidence
Story—Fable	5.1%	36.8%	38.2%	19.8%
Story—African folk tale (unreleased)	10.1	44.8	24.6	20.6
Poem—"Mother to Son"	6.3	28.1	57.5	8.1
Poem (unreleased)	15.7	54.6	25.6	4.1
Story—"One of These Days"	12.2	48.1	29.9	9.8
Averages	9.9	42.5	35.2	12.5

The majority of the evaluative responses fell into two broad response patterns. Most of the students simply listed vague assertions or observations about the passages. Some of these responses contained references to the text, but most of them were unsupported statements. The second response pattern was a synopsis or summary of the story or poem. Though the evaluative criteria were not explicitly stated in these responses, the students seemed to be singling out the content of the work as their reason for liking or disliking it. Very few of the students wrote evaluations with supporting evidence.

What is most striking and alarming about these responses, besides their quick and easy nature, is their vague almost universal applicability. Many of the responses could be interchanged across stories and poems and seem to indicate, as the following representative examples do, that even the very best students do not know how to compose specific, successful evaluations.

> It was a very good story because the main points were easily to follow. The theme was very evident, although it did seem a little weak. In addition, the story had much action which kept the reader interested.

> The story was full of suspense and kept the reading [sic] in
> doubt as to the outcome. The author uses much description in
> revealing the characters and the setting. There is a hidden
> meaning running throughout the story and this definitely
> intrigues the reader. Together with the suspense, the extra-
> ordinary description, and the underlying motive, the author
> has created an interesting story.

When we look at the results for these evaluative tasks by race
and community, we see that blacks performed 2.2 to 8.9 percentage
points below their white counterparts on the open-ended tasks, and
that students from disadvantaged-urban communities performed
2.7 to 13.1 percentage points lower than their counterparts from
advantaged-urban communities. Students from rural areas performed from slightly above to 10.3 percentage points above their
counterparts from disadvantaged-urban communities, while performing slightly below to 5 percentage points below students from
advantaged-urban communities.

General Responding

For these exercises, students were given stories and poems they
had never seen before and asked to "write down your thoughts and
feelings" or to "write a composition" about the story or poem.
Responses to four poems and one story were analyzed using a
content analysis scheme that first showed the primary response
category a response fell into and then showed additional response
categories as they appeared in the same response. This approach
focused on the main thrust of each response, while also tabulating
instances of other aspects of the response.

Students read and responded to "Somebody's Son," a brief characterization of a son and his letter to his mother in which he
discusses his leaving home; to A. E. Housman's poem, "Into My
Heart"; and to "Check," a poem by James Stephens. They also
responded to two other poems, but these are unreleased and will be
used to assess change in the next reading and literature assessment.

The response categories (Egocentric, Retelling, Emotional,
Personal-global, Personal-analytic, Evaluation, Reference to other
works—general, Reference to other works—specific, Analysis—
superficial, Analysis—elaborated, Inferencing, and Generalization)
were defined well enough to yield high percentages (all over 90%)
of agreement among raters who scored each response for the
appearance of any one of the twelve categories and for predominant mode. Since the definitions of these categories are lengthy
and accompanied by specific examples, it would be best if readers

interested in their specific qualities referred to the complete NAEP report.

Instead of reporting the detailed results of these exercises, let us take a look at the larger picture to get a glimpse of what happens when students are asked to read and respond to a work they have never seen before. First, nearly all (97%) of the responses were rateable; when presented with these selections and only a limited time to develop a response, most seventeen year olds at all ability levels were able to say something. Their responses indicated they had read the selections and understood them well enough to make some kind of appropriate response.

Second, selection overwhelmingly determined the type of response. In regard to predominant response mode, "Into My Heart" generated 71.1 percent inferencing responses, while "Somebody's Son" produced 67.2 percent personal–analytic responses. This trend was apparent for all selections and, furthermore, no other response mode accounted for even half as many responses to any one passage. It seemed that the characteristics of the selections determine the kind of response students produce.

Third, although each reponse produced a predominant response mode, there were some commonalities running across the responses. For instance, it was not at all uncommon to find retellings, evaluations, emotions, and inferencing in individual responses. There was a low incidence of egocentric, personal–global, other works general and specific, and either superficial or elaborated analysis in the responses.

And fourth, no matter how sophisticated the responses appeared they were generally superficial and abstract. Like the evaluative responses, they seldom included specifics and are best characterized as series of assertions loosely developed at an abstract level around a single point. And while they were coherent enough, they were, at the same time, underdeveloped. Most were not the careful reasoned responses we might expect from students trained and practiced in writing about their reading.

Conclusion

As stated in the final NAEP report: "The most significant finding from this assessment is that while students learn to read a wide range of material, they develop very few skills for examining the nature of the ideas that they take away from their reading. Though most have learned to make simple inferences about such things as a character's behavior and motivation, for example, and can express their own judgments of a work as 'good' or 'bad,' they cannot return to the passage to explain the interpretations they have made" (p. 2).

These findings seem to be a direct reflection of current practices in testing and instruction. When multiple-choice testing and quick easy discussions dominate the curriculum, how can we expect anything but the most basic performance from students? When reading and writing are separated in the curriculum and when students are not encouraged to discuss or write about their reading in any extended, reasoned way, is it such a surprise that they then lack the more comprehensive thinking and analytic skills?

Sophisticated skills such as analysis, inference, generalizing, evaluating, and theorizing are best, and perhaps only, assessed and taught through extended discourse—speaking and writing. It seems clear that speaking and writing tasks are necessary for the development of these critical thinking skills so absent from students' performance on this assessment. Although there are aspects of reading and literature like literal recall that are perhaps best assessed and taught through multiple-choice exercises and quick classroom discussions, there are other aspects of reading and literature, such as critical thinking skills, that can only be assessed and taught through writing or discussion tasks because they require explanation, elaboration, and documentation.

Simply put, students seem not to have learned the problem-solving strategies and critical thinking skills by which to look for evidence to support their interpretations and judgments. A large proportion (75%) have mastered initial literal and inferential skills, but very few (22%) have learned to use evidence. In addition, almost none of the seventeen year olds demonstrated any knowledge or use of techniques for analyzing a passage. Hardly any of them approached a text through such conventional procedures as paragraph by paragraph (or stanza by stanza) analysis, or by using elements of the passage to comment on such things as setting or character development, or by following a theme or idea through its progression in the text.

While these findings are discouraging, it is encouraging that a large proportion of students were able to make literal and inferential interpretations, and they were able to write summaries and synopses. It seems clear that what these students need most is the training and practice in critical thinking skills that would enable them to go beyond what they already do well.

Two other findings are worth mentioning for both their testing and instructional implications. First, throughout the assessment, text passages played a role. Clearly, the nature of the passage has a strong, shaping influence on students' responses. Second, it seemed equally clear that the variety of item types—multiple-choice and open-ended—showed what neither type alone could. By using both types of exercises, students' skills were viewed along a continuum ranging from literal and inferential comprehension to the more complex critical thinking skills. Either type of exercises alone would have given only a partial, incomplete picture of students' performance.

What Can Be Done?

Now that we know what students can do, we need to ask ourselves what we can do to help them overcome the shortcomings that are so evident in this assessment. One of the most important things administrators and teachers can do is look closely at the kinds of testing used in their schools and classes. Do multiple-choice and quick, easy answer formats dominate the curriculum? If they do, the chances are very high that they are directing instruction along the lines of lower-level skills—the kind assessed by multiple-choice tests. Students need to be tested with the kinds of exercises that encourage the use of critical thinking skills if these skills are to be an important part of the curriculum. This means that we need to create assessments that ask students to write about their reading— assessments that ask them to use their knowledge and conceptual strategies to make interpretations that they substantiate with evidence from texts and their own values and ideas. At the same time, instruction should focus more on the integration of reading and writing, especially by teaching students how to write about their reading. It is not enough to test and instruct people in quick, easy answer approaches to texts.

Second, these critical thinking skills cannot be left to reading and English teachers alone. They are part and parcel of learning in all academic areas and should, as such, be stressed across the content areas. Students in science classes, for instance, can be taught to write lab reports the way scientists write them rather than relying on workbooks and fill-in-the-blanks to report their experiments. Students in social science classes can be taught to read and write about their content-area material so they get practice in forming interpretations and evaluations that they substantiate with evidence.

Third, these critical thinking skills cannot be left to writing alone, even though writing is critical to their development. Teachers need to examine their classroom practices to see if they are giving students the opportunities to engage in meaningful discussions where points of view are aired and defended. All too often, classroom discussions are dominated by quick, easy answers and teachers with predetermined answers and hidden agendas. Students need to be involved in genuine problem-solving discussions that focus on their interpretations and their use of evidence to support and criticize their interpretations.

Fourth, institutional support for this kind of systematic reading and writing instruction across the content areas must come from informed administrators working closely with teachers. Together administrators and teachers can organize summer workshops and inservice training to build the kind of integrated reading, writing, and discussing curriculum that will foster the growth of critical thinking skills. We need to recognize that a large proportion of teachers were never taught how to teach these higher order critical thinking skills; consequently, we face a massive inservice need. Initiation for inservice must come from both teachers and administrators, but it will not work unless administrators understand what teachers need and, then, make it possible for them to get it. In short, teachers and administrators need to work for inservice training in writing, question-asking techniques, group discussion strategies, and the integration of reading and writing. We must also face the fact that very little of this inservice training will be effective unless teachers are given opportunities to implement what they have learned in settings conducive to instruction in critical thinking skills. This means smaller classes and teacher aides who either free teachers from the mundane administrative chores or aid them in leading class discussions, writing workshops, and student conferences. These important higher order skills cannot be taught in crowded classes where it is near to impossible to carry on extended discussions and systematic writing assignments.

And fifth, teachers and administrators need to work together to examine the kinds of textbooks they are using in their schools and classes. Do they encourage the quick, easy answer type of discussion, or do they provide opportunities for students to engage in extended discussions and writing tasks? Too many of the textbooks in use are nothing more than quick answer workbooks and as such they cannot foster critical thinking skills.

In our time of diminishing resources for education, it will be extremely difficult for teachers to receive the training and support they need to effectively teach the higher order critical thinking skills in reading, literature, and writing, especially given the fact that they must be stretched-out across the curriculum into all content areas. The findings of this national assessment are clear: the nation's seventeen year olds cannot go beyond initial comprehension to extend and defend their readings of texts. If we are going to change this disheartening trend, then we need to make the commitment to teaching critical thinking skills. This inevitably means investments of time and money from the public who must support the educational system for there are no quick, easy, or cheap ways to teach these higher order skills. If students are to learn them, they must engage in genuine problem-solving discussions, and they must talk and write about what they read.

Reference

Reading, thinking, and writing: Results from the 1979–80 National Assessment of Reading and Literature (Report No. 11-L-01). Denver, Colo.: National Assessment of Educational Progress, 1981. (ERIC Document Reproduction Service No. ED 209 641; 82p.)

2 The Contexts of Reading

Sharon L. Smith, Robert F. Carey, Jerome C. Harste
Indiana University

Not long ago, a freshman at our university asked this question: "Why is it so easy for me to read a sports article and so difficult to read my economics text?" To answer this question, one hardly need apply a readability formula, perform a conceptual analysis on the two selections, or check the student's reading level. The difference is because the student is an experienced reader of sports material but inexperienced in economics. From his statement we can safely infer that sports play a role in his life; formal economics do not. He can relate sports to his own interest and knowledge, easily compare this information with other information at his disposal, and evaluate the worth of the article according to criteria about which he feels confident. In short, he can create a true mental text from the graphic display.

What the student might have asked was why he was a competent reader in one situation and a less competent reader in another. An economics professor with no interest in sports might have the same experience, but with the selections switched. When a reader attempts to create a text from material in which he or she has little interest or background, reading is difficult, though rarely fruitless.

Most teachers know that much class-assigned reading is often boring or baffling to students because it does not relate naturally to the students' own interests and experiences. It is not helpful to say "stop stripping text of context," because it is not the teacher's intention to do so. Rather, teachers often find, to their own bafflement, that for many students the context of interest and experience is simply not there. In this chapter, therefore, we do not belabor the obvious—that meaningful reading cannot occur in a vacuum—but rather look at the evidence for and the implications of this statement for secondary teachers. In this attempt we first set up a framework for thinking about various kinds of contexts that pertain to reading. Then we discuss the reading process in relation to context. Next, we report on some research concerning contextual issues that have yielded useful insights into the experience of readers. And finally we bring this analysis to bear upon classroom instruction, addressing the question of how teachers can apply their understanding of context to their work with students.

Context Defined

Three kinds of context in reading can be defined operationally as follows:

> Linguistic context is the written text per se, that which appears visually on the page.
>
> Situational context, a concept akin to Malinowski's (1923) "context-of-situation," is the setting in which a reading-event occurs; it includes the linguistic text, the individuals involved (e.g., a student and a teacher), the location (e.g., in a classroom or at home), the expectations (e.g., that a recall test will be given over the material), and all such other factors impinging immediately on the event.
>
> Cultural context is the social/political matrix in which the situation of reading has come about.

Linguistic context, then, is one aspect of situational context, from which it derives its vitality. The situational context, in turn, exists within and depends upon cultural context. In a diagram of embedded circles, we could envision cultural context as a great circle containing the other two. This is the context that is least clearly defined but most powerful, as becomes evident in studies exploring differences in literacy-related behaviors among cultural groups.

Because cultural context exerts a strong influence of which we may not be consciously aware, it is worthwhile to consider it here in some detail. Two facts seem especially salient. One is that print has played a crucial role in the development of western civilization, pervading virtually all aspects of our experience. We live in a "print environment" (Harste, Burke, and Woodward, 1982). The other is that the preeminence of print is being challenged by electronic media, notably television and computers, resulting in what we might call an explosion of information production and processing.

Our schools, however, remain centered in the print culture, and we seem far from the day when print will not be the major repository of knowledge at least for the common reader, even though younger generations are increasingly immersed in other forms of communications. Without question, the dominance of print has influenced our attitudes toward and uses of language. In our culture, great value is placed upon what Scallon and Scallon (1979) described as the English-essay style, a discursive, elaborative use of language to fully probe a topic or express a point of view. Especially in academic settings, our communications are well grounded in language, and we place great importance upon the ability to use language for argumentative, explanatory, or rhetorical purposes.

This emphasis on elaborative language bears a close relationship to the development of writing and the print media in our culture— to what Olson (1975) called the phenomenon of the "autonomous text." Books and other printed materials are regarded as having an existence of their own, separate from that of either the reader or the writer. This is a peculiarity of our highly literate culture we may take for granted, not realizing that because of it the integrity of the text sometimes takes precedence over the integrity of the reader.

It is at this point that the competition of other media becomes problematic for the print culture of the schools. Whatever else we may say about television programming, for example, most of it does not challenge the integrity of the viewer in the sense of which we are speaking here. On the contrary, television programmers are clever at devising ways of enhancing viewers' integrity. They do this by relying heavily on a narrative mode familiar from early childhood, by breaking up expository material such as news reports into short chunks that do not tax the attention span or reasoning process, and even by interspersing commercials which feature artifacts of daily life. Moreover, television programs are ephemeral, which means that they do not assume the character of autonomy that books and other solid matter appear to have. Experience with television, then, is bound to affect the young reader's experience with books.

Yet it remains important for the maturing reader to learn to deal with and control rather large amounts of printed material. For while television seems to be simplifying the task of comprehension, the concomitant rise of computers is more certainly complicating it. Due largely to the powerful processing capacities of computers, we live in an information-saturated culture in which the business of codifying, storing, and reporting information, largely in print, is all-consuming. What happens to the personal dimension in this milieu is a primary concern of educators. In sum, television over-accommodates while electronic information processing overwhelms. Within that context, we must place the enduring print media and the role of reading.

Contexts and Schemata

Taking a retrospective glance over developments in language over the last two decades, what seems most striking is the emergence of both cognitive and social perspectives for the study of language. Reading, as a language activity, has been involved in this development. In both language study in general, and reading in particular, theory has evolved from a focus on the mechanical act of decoding to a broader view: namely its role in cognitive development and social learning.

To be sure, there are real problems connected with such a change of perspective. It is much easier to understand and explain a machine than a living thing. But any machine is only a model of what occurs in nature, so it is good to go beyond the relative simplicity and sureness of mechanistic functions to language as it occurs in a natural human setting—classroom, library, living room, or street—and see how it works as a system within innumerable systems of meaning.

Recently a number of researchers (cf. Anderson, Spiro, and Montague, 1977) have made use of the concept of schema (pl., schemata) to explain comprehension in reading. A schema can be explained as a pattern of knowledge formed from experience that enables the individual to make sense of what he or she perceives. It is something like a concept, but usually more complex, being composed of a cluster of relatable concepts—a cluster moreover that tends to be changing most of the time. For example, an individual who has always lived in Buffalo, New York, will have a different schema for "snowstorm" from that of someone who has always lived on the Oregon coast. A person who has lived in a number of climates will probably have a more flexible schema. It is a matter of experience with snow and of what one considers worthy of being called a storm. As you read this chapter or this book, or anything else, pay attention to terms or phrases that seem to draw a blank in your thinking, and you will realize the importance of having schemata for understanding. Schemata form a mental context important for finding meaning. Learning involves building up a repertoire of useful schemata for understanding new information. In short, what we comprehend depends in an important way on what we already know.

To return to our opening example of the student who was a good reader of sports but a poor reader of economics, we now have a bit of jargon to explain his plight. He had a well-developed set of schemata for reading his sports articles, but a sparse one for economics. This notion of schemata being more or less well developed for particular subjects also reminds us that teachers and textbooks are schema-rich in areas where students are schema-poor. Once one has formed a schema for understanding something, it is hard to imagine its not being there, and one might wonder at a student's inability to understand what is obvious (to the teacher) and presented in plain English (plain to the writer of the text).

Or a student may evoke a schema that seems inadequate or inappropriate, resulting in an alternate interpretation. This is where situational context can play a vital role, for the situation determines whether, or to what degree, such alterations are seen as socially acceptable. A classroom where a premium is placed on verbatim textual recall may lead the students to shrink back from their own knowledge contexts and embrace the linguistic context so earnestly that reasoning is inhibited.

In developmental reading materials, for example, a common format is a series of short passages with comprehension questions at the end. The passages are discrete and the questions imply that all readers are supposed to find the same meaning in them. Readers are encouraged therefore to cling to the language of the text, to try to memorize it, because that is the safest way to be sure that the teacher's assumptions are not violated. Of course, the task becomes awesome or impossible when there is so much language one cannot manage it all, as is the case when one goes from short passages to whole texts. When the texts also become more abstract and conceptually dense, the linguistic context by itself may not be sufficient to represent the meaning.

To mature as a reader, a student must learn to go beyond the text, to use the words given as a jumping off place for individually-based thought. This is the goal in reading development, but it is not easy to encourage in exercises designed to build up comprehension skills. One must soften the boundaries between the language of the text and the language of the environment. Through discussion in which textual information is related to other experiences and the reader's own ideas, students can be prompted to react, to speculate, to consider what the message of any text means to them. They should be posing the questions as well as answering them. This can be done even with very short passages or single sentences, as long as this principle is observed: the reader develops meaning by bringing in context outside the text. When the boundaries between the text and the environment are regarded as permeable, the meaning can flow in two directions. The text will have a greater impact, not a weaker one, at the same time that its message is being affected by what the reader already knows.

Context of Situation and of Culture

As outlined by Chomsky (1957) among others (virtually all of whom are echoing nineteenth-century linguist Ferdinand de Saussure), the broad notions of competence and performance have been central to the scientific study of language for a number of years. *Competence* is the underlying system of language rules mastered by all members of any speech community. Competence, naturally, is an abstraction, an idealization. It is the aspect of language that provides for our awareness of the difference between grammatically acceptable and unacceptable sentences, for example. *Performance*, on the other hand, is not an abstraction or idealization at all. It is comprised of the actual utterances of people, including any and all "pragmatic" aspects of authentic speech. These would include hesitations, pauses, redundancies, and so on. Even a brief reading of the notorious "Watergate" tapes, for example, provides one with data for suggesting that even allegedly educated persons frequently speak in other-than-acceptable (i.e., nonstandard dialect) fashion.

While these two concepts have played some role in the development of transformational-generative grammars, we suggest (following Halliday, 1978, as well as a number of other sociolinguists) that it is no longer a useful distinction. To speak of linguistic (or, as does Hymes, 1972, "communicative") competence is to attempt to "decontextualize" meaning. We suggest that language can be defined effectively only through its use, that is, its meaning in context. The same may be said for any instance of language use—including reading. Neither the reader nor the text can be studied profitably in isolation (Rosenblatt, 1978). Each is an integral element of the other's environment and neither is a meaningful entity, at least in analytic terms, in a vacuum.

Bartlett's (1932) work on memory, for example, showed that Britishers will comprehend an American Indian folktale within a framework that makes sense in terms of their own literary tradition. Such findings have been replicated by Kintsch and Vipond (1977) with middle-class Anglo-Americans and American Indians. Related research was conducted by Scallon and Scallon (1979) in which data supported the conclusion that Alaskan (Athabaskan) Indians were being asked to accommodate a European literary tradition. Even in public school settings, this tradition proved to be formidably alien to native conceptions of the cosmos. What the researchers called the European "essay" tradition was clearly not a *form* which had any substantive meaning within the conventions of Athabaskan culture.

Another example of how situational context can affect language processing and language understanding in ways we might not anticipate emerged in Donaldson's (1978) work using Piagetian measures to determine children's stages of cognitive development. One task involved showing children two sticks of the same length, first together and then apart, to determine whether they could "conserve" the equality of length when the original context was changed. Generally it has been found that young children tend to respond differently when the placement of the sticks is changed, indicating a lack of conservation. Donaldson, however, found evidence that children might be responding to social rather than to perceptual or cognitive factors. That is, children may learn early that, when adults repeat questions, they have found the first response unsatisfactory, and so, being very sensitive language users, they change the answer. In so doing, they have examined the kinds of constraints operating in this setting, and, realizing that authority lies with the adult, they try to oblige. Donaldson tested her hypothesis by presenting a jack-in-the-box and saying it might leap out and spoil things, requiring that the same question be asked again. In this setting, when they were no longer responsible for the repetition of the question, even very young children were significantly more likely to say that the sticks were the same length after they had been moved.

These observations raise the question of how much of our developmental data are contaminated by the unnatural or unexamined pragmatic constraints that are operating. Clearly, much of the behavior that has been identified as evidence of a certain level of thinking in some "pure" sense may actually be responses to particular constraints that we, as teachers or researchers, impose upon the situation. This point was underscored by the work of Sebeok (in press) and others regarding the contextual constraints inherent in virtually any experimental design. This problem is most commonly labeled the "Clever Hans" phenomenon, after the notorious nineteenth-century horse which apparently had the remarkable ability to do arithmetic. But it was really his master who was doing the sums, while the horse was stamping out answers in response to the man's exceedingly subtle and often unwitting signals.

Bates (1979) used the term *pragmatics*, by which she meant awareness of the social rules that pertain in a particular situation. She distinguished pragmatics from sociolinguistics in this way: sociolinguistics is concerned with generalized kinds of rules that operate to affect the way we use language, and pragmatics is concerned with particular kinds of constraints operating in a given situation. Harste, Burke, and Woodward (1982) clarified the dimensions of situational pragmatics with children as young as three years. Even at this age, their subjects responded differently to requests for writing or drawing according to the tools they were given. One youngster, indeed, refused to write with a crayon and requested a pen instead. Here we see social constraints (the request of an adult) mediated by other situational constraints (the proper function of the tool given) and the resulting problem-solving response of the child as she endeavored to make sense of the situational requirements.

It may seem a long speculative leap to relate the behavior of preschool children to the responses of adolescents in a secondary school classroom, but we can reasonably assume that early childhood sophistication in interpreting the contextual implications of a task has been raised to the level of an art by mid-adolescence. Secondary school students are still responding primarily to the situational implications of the task rather than simply to the task itself. A major difference between the preschoolers and the high schoolers, perhaps, is that the latter have undergone so many differentiating experiences that they vary a great deal more among themselves in how they identify and interpret the salient features of a situation.

We are always responding to signs in our environment. In this semiotic sense (cf. Halliday, 1978; Halliday and Hasan, 1980), signs are the cues we detect for interpreting underlying significance in a phenomenon or situation. When we say we cannot see the forest for the trees, we mean that we are ignoring this sign potential while observing many trees together. In terms of the notion of schema discussed earlier, we may say that we are not evoking a schema for forest, so we are missing an important *gestalt*—the whole that is greater than its parts. Now suppose, by some peculiarity of the light, we can see only one tree at a time. Then the experience of the forest, its complexity as a whole ecology, may elude us. The whole configuration is a sign which cannot be derived logically from the parts we are shown. In this image it is also important to note that the trees themselves do not constitute the forest. They are part of it, and they signal its presence to us, but a forest is a great deal more than a collection of trees, and the trees themselves assume various meanings depending on how we are regarding the forest. In short, the more context we take into account, the more powerful and the more variable the signs we perceive for detecting meaning.

From a semiotic perspective, then, it is probably the broad-based kinds of schema-accessing potentials that make readers confident of the meaning they have gained, or, in the event that schemata have not been accessed, make them perplexed or discouraged in their ability to read a given text. Clearly, this dynamic sign-response interaction is an important part of the comprehending process, not just a component but integral and central to the whole effort to acquire meaning.

Speech-act theory (Searle, 1975) is relevant to this consideration of how language is used in the constructive activity of comprehending. In this framework, language is viewed as a social action, which functions in a socially significant way, rather than as a linguistic form. This perspective includes the intent of language— its connection with events that go beyond its own form—and exposes the illusion that we control the variables in situations that we manage according to some plan. For example, in a naturalistic study of student/teacher interactions McDermott (1977) observed how a bilingual child with reading difficulties used certain behaviors, such as turning to the wrong page, to keep her teacher from calling upon her in a reading group. The teacher believed she was managing the group in a humanistic way, which meant not embarrassing the child. In many secondary classrooms, students exert pressure on the teacher to explain the material in the book, giving them exactly what they need to know for a test. This is a way of managing the teacher's high priority on accurate mastery of specific content. What is common to these examples is that, in both, the students avoid reading by tuning into the teacher's management system and making direct use of that.

Carey, Harste, and Smith (1981) found that college students were also monitoring the situation in which ambiguous texts were encountered and responding to that. In many instances, they preserved the ambiguity, and some commented on the oddness of a text written to be ambiguous, showing their awareness of the experimental nature of the setting. That put the ball back into the researchers' court. In a classroom situation where grades or other rewards were at stake, they might have been more circumspect in their response. The problem would be to figure out how the teacher wanted them to interpret the passage. As noted earlier, we often impose our own constraints upon research and learning situations and then examine the results as if they had nothing to do with us.

Consider the strategies that students apply to standardized reading tests, which are presumed to measure levels of comprehension. These strategies call for almost exclusive attention to linguistic context. A test-wise student will study the questions carefully and then scan the passage for answers. We even teach such strategies in study skills instruction, showing students how to define the task as a problem of matching certain elements in the question to certain elements in the text. We teach them to pick the answer the examiner intended, even if this means ignoring alternative answers which, though they are logically justifiable, aren't going to ring true for the machine that grades their answer sheets. Thus we define the situational context in the most cynical way, while the cultural context is reduced to the looming spectre of permanent records and the role that a handful of test scores plays in our lives. The test-taker is well advised, if possible, to dispense with real mental and cultural experience and attend to these puzzles, which often call upon values and suppositions peculiar to classroom testing.

What a comprehension test measures, mainly, is the reader's ability to pick up on a very limited set of cues, to stay very close to the text, and to select the test writer's inferences. What it does not measure, or reveal in any way, is how the reader has reconstructed the message of the text, related it to his or her prior knowledge, synthesized this information with other information, or thought critically about it. Indeed it is unlikely that much of this kind of thinking went into the test-taking effort. If it did, the reader wouldn't go fast enough to make a good score on the test.

Test score statistics aren't telling us what we need to know. Students who look all right on these measures may still be in serious difficulty. We need to get away from such distractors and form a view of reading that has real potential payoff for classroom learning. Daigon (1980) described "rhetorically based and rhetorically deficient" tasks and made the point that many school tasks are rhetorically deficient in that they don't have authentic elements of context available to provide real language situations. Standard comprehension tests are an example of this.

Our best strategy is to provide as rich and as natural a language environment as possible, one in which students are encouraged to select signs that have meaning for them and to respond to these signs in ways that make sense according to the students' knowledge and experience. When we abstract language we are in effect altering the importance of some potential signs. There is a danger in excluding signs that could help students access what they already knew. We may make language-based learning more difficult through proscribing signs that could bring out relationships to various levels of context—not only linguistic but also situational and cultural. Potential signs are always abundant, but they are also dependent on individual experience and past encounters with language. The challenge is to determine which are the important ones to select for a given case.

A major value of the research on sign potential is the framework it provides for relating linguistic context to more general contexts. We have been able to identify many more possible signs, all with the potential of altering comprehension and the long-term synthesis of comprehension that we call learning. That is, the theory of context has given us a theory of comprehension and a theory of text. We used to think of reading as an information transfer process. Then we began to think of reading as an interaction. What we are now finding is that it is a transaction (Rosenblatt, 1978); a truly dynamic interrelationship is in fact a function of signs being used by language learners. This perspective can get us out of the notion that someone did a "good" reading or a "bad" reading of a particular text. We can look instead at what signs were or were not used, how, and with what finesse. We may find that much of what we have considered poor comprehension is in fact a very good use of the sign potential we, as teachers, have provided.

Applications to Teaching

From the perspective discussed, it becomes clear how important the teacher's concept of comprehension is to students' reading and learning behaviors. Many teachers may not have thought specifically about this issue and would have difficulty explaining exactly what comprehension is. Generally, teachers appear to view comprehension in one of two ways: (1) as "meaning maintenance," with emphasis on understanding, preserving, and storing meaning as given in a text or lecture; or (2) as "meaning generation," with emphasis on constructing meaning that goes beyond the text. If we regard comprehension as primarily "meaning maintenance," we are directing students to consider mainly the linguistic aspects of what they read. This restriction closes down meaning options and affects the kind of processing that takes place.

Teachers can predefine the limits of cognitive processing by the way they decide to organize and present their materials. Students who assume a restrictive model of text interaction from instructional cues may become dull comprehenders even while flourishing in their ability to answer certain kinds of questions about the text (as evidenced by Petrosky's report in chapter 1). It is not uncommon for students to be bewildered by the sudden inadequacy of such a model when they go from high school to college, where the emphasis is shifted from accuracy of memory to problem-solving abilities. It is also clear that some students may become so dependent on teacher organization of meaning that they may have difficulty learning to learn for themselves after high school.

Throughout the formal educational process, beginning with the first classroom experience and continuing for as long as the individual participates in any kind of instructional situation, the development of control over printed language is a crucial ability. To the extent that the teacher maintains a tight control, the student may be kept in an unproductive dependency, which can result in a kind of learned helplessness that surfaces when the external control is absent. In high school, when print becomes a primary source of information, the emphasis should be on guiding students to independent control. This means that the learner assumes equal integrity with both the teacher and the text. Traditionally, the teacher is the authority in the classroom, with the text and the student subordinate to that authority. Such a model, however, does not accommodate the long-term needs of the student as a comprehender and learner from print (Bresnahan, 1981).

In practical terms, assignments and projects should be designed that call for the use of information rather than merely the storage and regurgitation of it. These projects should be set up in a way that leaves much of the specific definition and planning of activities to the students themselves, so that they help to create the situational contexts in which reading will occur. Many students will resist and demand to be told exactly what to do. The teacher must then resist them, at least to the extent of providing only as much guidance as is truly necessary, leaving the student some responsibility for designing the task. There is nothing more devastating to a teacher's ego than a student's quizzical look and complaint that "this assignment isn't organized." The teacher must respond by showing students how to organize tasks for themselves, calling upon resources they can contribute from their own experience and ideas.

It is generally a mistake to rely on one textbook as the sole provider of information in any subject. This gives one text entirely too much authority. Alternative sources of information should be provided in the library or in the classroom. Reading, as much as possible, should be embedded in a context of locating, synthesizing, and producing knowledge.

Earlier, the importance of a natural and rich language environment was stressed. One way to achieve this is to fill the classroom with good, interesting books in the specific content area and make it possible for students to browse among them and read them. Another is to encourage students to talk and share ideas in class discussion and small groups. The teacher should monitor the amount of talk that goes on in the classroom and who does it. It is important for students to be prime contributors to this talk.

If students are slow to respond to attempts to get them to participate in the creation of a "live" situation, it may help to orient them to productions that have meaning for them: the composing of alternate texts with their own articles and interpretations of the subject matter, magazine or newsletter style publications, bookmaking—any kind of written production intended for an audience besides just the teacher. As a general rule, collaborative learning activites have greater long-term benefits than competitive ones, such as taking tests.

This is not to say that no conventional study requirements should be made. On the contrary, we would be doing students a grave disservice to send them out of our classrooms with no experience in studying textbooks or in demonstrating what they learn on tests. But this should not be the only activity, or even the primary one. It is important to show students how to learn from texts. Learning, as has been noted, requires putting oneself into the text as well as taking the text information into one's head. Within a content area, the teacher can tone down a text's mystique by showing students how to survey and question the text. The teacher can have students ask and answer questions concerning the organization of the text, the author's point of view, and the content as represented in the table of contents. Students can skim through a whole chapter or even a whole book to find something that looks interesting, then stop and consider that for a while. The class can talk about where the book came from, who wrote it and when, and speculate on the reasons why (Smith, Smith, and Mikulecky, 1978). This approach broadens the situation and elevates the status of the reader.

Teachers can help students become aware of the contributions they make to their own learning. For example, they can devise demonstrations in which the class starts with a very small amount of information and gradually expands it, changing the linguistic context in ways that call for varying uses of other contexts. To illustrate, suppose you as a reader are given a single letter, the consonant *C*. There is not a great deal of information here if you confine yourself to this text; as a speaker of English you know that it is the third letter of the alphabet and has a certain range of possible phonetic representations in our language. Beyond this, however, you may bring your own associations to bear—perhaps *C* is your initial, or perhaps it is a grade you don't want in a graduate course, or perhaps you remember that it is the Roman numeral for 100. If you cared to take the time, you might find you could produce a whole dissertation on the possible meanings of the letter *C* by drawing freely on situational and cultural contexts.

Suppose the letter is placed within a word, say *Change*. Now you must discard most of the elaboration of meaning you produced for the letter *C*, but you can go through the same exercise with the word, which is likely to have so many potential situational and cultural associations that you would have to be very selective to confine yourself to a dissertation. Next, imagine the word set in a sentence, for example, *Change is the only evidence of life.* Again you must discard some meaning, but at the same time a great deal more is evoked; once you have such a whole proposition you can begin judging its truth value and all the contexts in which that must be considered.

The point is that as we extend linguistic text, we are expanding context geometrically. We can make letters into syllables, syllables into words, words into sentences, and eventually create a book. Furthermore, we must look not only at the covers of the book but also at where it should be placed for the student to find—in a library or a classroom bookcart. We can see how reading is surrounded by an awesome environment of meanings that are both internal and external to the individual reader. It is this environment of meanings that enriches (or impoverishes) the experience and ultimately the learning that will evolve from interracting with the text. This exercise can be used as presented with a class, or it can provide a pattern for a lesson centered in particular course content.

The secondary teacher may ask students to consider their own varied experiences with language. Some field work might be appropriate: have students attend closely to the way people talk in different situations. Many students will not of course respond immediately to the teacher's efforts to get them to become "natural language users" in the classroom. Some may never respond. A frequent problem with reading and language instruction in early grades is that language is treated out of context as a linguistic system unto itself. This is artificial and boring and may lead to personal disaffection with written language long before the student reaches high school. We are bored by that which excludes us. Long-term boredom may be a malaise that is difficult to cure. But we can *begin* the process, at least, by encouraging students to bring their own personalities into their reading, by having them use their own language as much as possible, and by setting up situations in which they learn from themselves and each other along with their teachers and their books.

Conclusion

We turn to literature for a summary that sheds a different light on the fundamental issue. In "Funes the Memorious," the South American writer Jorges Luis Borges (1962) tells the story of a young man whose memory was awesomely perfect. Borges wrote:

> He knew by heart the forms of the southern clouds at dawn on the 30th day of April, 1882, and could compare them in his memory with mottled streaks on a book in Spanish binding he had only seen once and with the outlines of foam raised by an oar in the Rio Niger the night before the Quebracho uprising. (p. 152)

As fascinating as such a mental feat is, we may sense at once something peculiar about a mind that stores images intact and manipulates them like objects on a shelf. We inspect the workings of our own memories and how they contribute to the development of what we call knowledge, and we find that it is the exception, not the rule, that events or objects will retain perfect integrity over time. What happens to most of what we comprehend at a given moment is that it loses its own distinctive features and becomes a part of something else.

Not so for Funes the Memorious. He kept each image intact, indefinitely, with the result that he accumulated a heap of separate memories that did not blend into larger entities. Thus he had no systems, no categories, no general concepts for operating upon the data that he acquired through his remarkable perception.

Funes did not make meaning that went, in Bruner's (1973) phrase, "beyond the information given"; that is, he did not form higher level concepts that would provide a framework for connecting individual perceptions into complex entities that endured through changes in space and time. His own face was new to him whenever he saw it at a new angle. "I suspect," says the narrator, "that he was not very capable of thought. To think is to forget differences, generalize, make abstractions. In the teeming world of Funes, there were only details, almost immediate in their presence" (p. 154). Details themselves, we recognize, are worthless unless they relate to something larger than themselves.

To strip text of context is to ask students to operate in the manner of Funes, that is, to deal with signs as they are given rather than as they can be made to function through the more powerful systems of interpretation available through knowledge of situation and culture. The incredible precision of Funes' memory was, in fact, possible because of the absence or suppression of this other kind of functioning. But he did not think, and he had no use for the information he acquired. To avoid this result is the real point of emphasizing the larger contexts of reading.

References

Anderson, R. C., Reynolds, R. C., Schallert, D. L., and Geotz, E. T. Frameworks for comprehending discourse. *American Educational Research Journal*, 1977, *14*(4), 367–381. (ERIC No. EJ 184 138)

Anderson, R. C., Spiro, R. J., and Montague, W. C. (Eds.). *Schooling and the acquisition of knowledge*. Hillsdale, N.J.: Lawrence Erlbaum, 1977.

Bartlett, F. C. *Remembering: A study in experimental and social psychology*. Cambridge: Cambridge University Press, 1932.

Bates, E. Pragmatics and sociolinguistics in child language. In D. M. Morehead and E. E. Morehead (Eds.), *Normal and deficient child language*. Baltimore: University Park Press, 1979.

Borges, J. L. Funes the memorious. *Labyrinths: Selected short stories and other writings*. New York: New Directions, 1962.

Bresnahan, R. *Feed the naked, clothe the hungry: Short and long term views of student needs*. Paper presented at the Lilly Conference on College Learning: Problems in Reading and Writing, Indiana University, Bloomington, February 1981.

Bruner, J. Going beyond the information given. In J. Anglin (Ed.), *Beyond the information given*. New York: W. W. Norton, 1973.

Carey, R. F., Harste, J. C., and Smith, S. L. Contextual constraints and discourse processes: A replication study. *Reading Research Quarterly*, 1981, *16*(2), 201–212. (ERIC No. EJ 240 384)

Chomsky, N. *Syntactic structures.* The Hague: Mouton Press, 1957.

Daigon, A. Rhetorically-based and rhetorically deficient tasks: An explanation. In J. Meagher and W. Page (Eds.), *Language centered reading instruction.* Storrs: University of Connecticut, Reading-Language Arts Center, 1980.

Donaldson, M. *Children's minds.* Glasgow: William Collins and Son, 1978.

Halliday, M. A. K. *Language as social semiotic.* Baltimore: University Park Press, 1978.

Halliday, M. A. K., and Hasan, R. *Text and context.* Tokyo: Sophia University, 1980.

Harste, J., Burke, C., and Woodward, V. Children's language and world: Initial encounters with print. In J. Langer and M. Smith-Burke (Eds.), *Reader meets author/bridging the gap: A psycholinguistic and sociolinguistic perspective.* Newark, Del.: International Reading Association, 1982.

Hymes, D. H. Models of interaction and social setting. In J. J. Gumperz and D. H. Hymes (Eds.), *Directions in sociolinguistics.* New York: Holt, Rinehart and Winston, 1972.

Kintsch, W., and Vipond, D. Reading comprehension and readability in educational practice and psychological theory. In L. Nillson (Ed.), *Proceedings of the conference on memory.* Hillsdale, N.J.: Lawrence Erlbaum, 1977.

McDermott, R. P. Social relations as contexts for learning in school. *Harvard Educational Review*, 1977, *47*(2), 498–513. (ERIC No. EJ 163 585)

Malinowski, B. The problem of meaning in primitive languages. Supplement to C. K. Ogden and I. A. Richards, *The meaning of meaning.* London: Routledge and Kegan Paul, 1923.

Olson, D. R. Review of *Toward a literate society*, J. B. Carroll and J. Chall (Eds.). *The Proceedings of the National Academy of Education* (Vol. 2), 1975.

Rosenblatt, L. *The reader, the text, the poem.* Carbondale: Southern Illinois University Press, 1978.

Scallon, T., and Scallon, A. *Literacy as cultural exchange: An Athabaskan case study.* La Jolla, Calif.: Laboratory for Comparative Human Cognition, University of California at San Diego, 1979. (Mimeograph)

Searle, J. R. A taxonomy of illocutionary acts. In K. Gunderson (Ed.), *Minnesota studies in the philosophy of language.* Minneapolis: University of Minnesota Press, 1975.

Sebeok, T. A. *A perfusion of signs.* Bloomington: Indiana University Press, 1977.

Sebeok, T. A. Dialogue with a Nobel laureate. *Semiotica*, in press.

Smith, C., Smith, S. L., and Mikulecky, L. *Teaching reading in secondary school content subjects.* New York: Holt, Rinehart and Winston, 1978.

3 The Reading Process

Judith A. Langer
University of California—Berkeley

Many of us have been trained to focus on what students do; we look at test results, work sheets, and exercises in order to understand our students' reading achievement, the skills they have acquired, and the skills which still need to be learned. However, much of the reading research during the past fifteen years has added another dimension particularly useful for helping students learn to read better—a focus on *how* rather than on *what* students do. Although "process" and "product" are far from new concepts, our expanded knowledge about the reading process can make a difference in the goals of our lessons, in the way we interact with students as we help them learn, and in the manner in which we assess needs and evaluate growth.

Research into the reading process has shaped our understanding of how readers "make meaning" when they are engaged in a reading activity. This research has highlighted a learning triad: the reader, the text, and the context (or learning environment) as they interactively affect the manner in which a student comprehends a particular text. Smith, Carey, and Harste illuminated context and, of necessity, touched on the other components in chapter 2. In this chapter, three aspects of recent research are described and then related to the learning triad. They are (1) the constructive nature of reading, (2) the influence of background knowledge, and (3) the use of metacomprehension or self-monitoring when reading. After reviewing aspects of this research which are particularly pertinent to the instructional setting, instructional activities useful for the secondary school are described.

The Constructive Nature of Reading

Reading is interactive because it requires coordination between the reader's background knowledge and the reader's use of actual

39

text (Rumelhart, 1977). At times, the construction of meaning tends to be more idea- or concept-driven (Bobrow and Norman, 1975), and to rely less on cues from the text itself. At other times, readers tend to pay more attention to details of the text and to concentrate on smaller units of language.

Remember the many instances when we've seen our students "figure out" the words or "say the sentences right" without any idea of what it all meant; they had started with the words and sentences but had little sense of the more global meaning of the passage. Processing the text by focusing on bits of meaning is slow, takes space in memory, and may interfere with the reader's interpretation of what the author is saying. On the other hand, when the process focuses too heavily on overall concepts, readers sometimes emerge with a general idea of what a passage is about but lack the specifics. The result is imprecise perception of meaning with too many reader-made assumptions. It is important that we (1) be aware of possible overreliance on one strategy or the other; (2) focus our instruction on the flexible use of cueing systems intext, context, and within the reader; and (3) encourage our students to make decisions about the strategies which are most helpful in comprehending a particular text in a given situation. Asking students such questions as "Did you get that from the text?" "Did you think of that yourself?" or "Is that helpful in understanding this text?" may help both student and teacher evaluate comprehension strategies for a particular portion of a particular text.

To understand the many variables which affect the compehension process, we also need to look beyond text- or concept-driven strategies. The notion that the development of meaning is a constructive process draws upon the works of such diverse people as R. Anderson (1977), Bartlett (1932), Goodman and Goodman (1978), Polanyi (1966), Rosenblatt (1978), and Rumelhart (1977). The constructive process includes the following as constraints on reading: (1) the reader's general knowledge, language patterns, and attitudes; (2) the language and content of the text; (3) the demands and goals of the specific reading task; and (4) the instructional environment and general climate for learning as they all interact (Cook-Gumperz, Gumperz, and Simons, 1979; Harste, Burke, and Woodward, 1982; and Langer, 1980a). These constraints provide a broad view of what influences an individual student in processing and comprehending a particular text.

Comprehension is not a simple text-based process in which readers piece together what the words, sentences, or paragraphs "say"—as if words themselves have some inherent meaning. Nor is it simply a concept-driven process in which readers begin with a global notion of what the text will be about, and anticipate the larger meanings the text will convey. Rather, comprehension is a process which requires *readers*—real live readers with ideas and attitudes of their own—to interpret what the author is saying. From this point of view, the text is merely a blueprint using a linguistic code; readers must use the blueprint to stimulate their own ideas and create their own meanings. This is not to suggest that readers go off into an idiosyncratic world of fanciful meaning but that they alone have the power to create meaning—their meaning that is closer to or further from the meaning that the author intended, but reader-generated nonetheless. Once teachers accept this notion of meaning construction, it permits instruction to focus on *why* a certain interpretation was or was not made.

As a passage develops, ideas are introduced, refined, and integrated. Meaning cannot be derived from a sentence or text segment alone. It must be considered as part of the reader's growing vision of what the entire passage is about. Therefore, meaning derived from a particular portion of the text will be shaped by how earlier segments were interpreted and will continue to develop and change in the light of later segments. In addition, interpretations of passages will change based on the context or purpose for reading.

As teachers we need to help students use an appropriate mix of reading strategies. At this time we do not know a better-worse or first-second sequence of strategies. Poor readers tend to be those who become overly reliant on one strategy (Spiro, 1980). Readers must use the words and sentences in a text as well as their personal language, knowledge, and experience to create a changing and growing meaning. As readers progress through a text, their vision grows; ideas develop; and with appropriate guidance they start to utilize a fluid range of strategies and cueing systems.

Secondary teachers should bear in mind that as readers engage in each new reading task, they already have important knowledge to use in striving to generate meaning. Students generally have a good hunch about the genre of the passage (newspaper article, worksheet with passage and fill-in questions, social studies text, biography); about the general topic; about the language and tone of the passage; and about the information they will need when they finish reading (for multiple-choice questions, class discussion, research paper). By being aware of these factors (all of which affect the manner in which the student processes the text), teachers can assist students to develop more efficient and more effective comprehension strategies. Students should always know why they are reading the text (quiz, report, literary discussion) and be helped to think in advance about the kind of information to focus on. Discussions focusing on what students already know about the topic and the genre, and suggestions about how these might be dealt with in the text, are rich ways of developing expectations which are helpful for comprehension.

The Influence of Background Knowledge

In this chapter *background information* refers to explicit "facts" which are specifically related to the topic; *background knowledge* is used in a more discursive sense to describe both specific "background information" and all other usefully-related knowledge, however tangential it might be. Just about everyone agrees that in some critical way background information plays an important role in how a student comprehends a passage. Frequently this generalization has been intuitive; teachers are often aware of a knowledge gap between the text and the reader (especially in subject-area textbooks). In recent years, there has been a good deal of research into the question of prior knowledge and how it affects comprehension. Researchers now know empirically what teachers have suspected—cultural background, personal world knowledge, and first-hand experiences with related topics all affect (1) the manner in which readers organize information in memory (Pichert and R. Anderson, 1976; Reynolds et al., 1981; Rumelhart and Ortony, 1977; Steffensen, Jogdeo, and R. Anderson, 1978); (2) what text-related information will be brought to mind in reading about a given topic (R. Anderson, Spiro, and M. Anderson, 1978; Langer, 1980b; Langer and Nicolich, 1981; Spiro, 1980); (3) what associations readers will make based on personal experiences and background knowledge (Langer, 1981a, b, 1982); and (4) what language or vocabulary they will marshall based on their perspectives of the reading tasks (R. Anderson and Pichert, 1977; R. Anderson, Pichert, and Shirey, 1979).

It is now known that in order to comprehend a text students need to relate the vocabulary and concepts in the text to some background knowledge they already have stored in memory (Rumelhart and Ortony, 1977; R. Anderson, 1977). If a reader has poorly-organized or weakly-developed understandings of a particular concept, comprehension becomes difficult (Pearson, Hansen, Gordon, 1979).

One aspect of this problem that teachers must seriously consider involves student/teacher communication (Langer, 1982; Y. Goodman, 1978). Does the teacher really *know* that a student lacks background knowledge about a specific topic, or has the student simply used language which the teacher did not believe was related to the topic? Did the student introduce information which the teacher felt to be tangential because it did not fit with the language and ideas the teacher expected to be expressed? We must consider not only the language and content which is presented in the text but also differences between the language and background knowledge of teacher and student. Because of differing life experiences, people organize their knowledge in different ways, and these may differ from student to student as well as from student to teacher. We must remember too that there is an "academic" language—a way of organizing and retrieving information and a way of discussing ideas which may simply not be in the realm of a student's experience. In such situations, the student may have a store of useful and related knowledge—if only he or she could verbalize it and the teacher use it as an aid in developing comprehension.

When students begin to read about a topic, or when there is a class discussion, language or ideas may seem fuzzy, irrelevant, or tangential. It is the teacher's role to help students make links between what they know and what they read. Most students know *something* about what they read or discuss in school. To help students become aware of what they do know that is useful for comprehension, we might ask them why they thought of certain ideas and why they gave the responses they did. This will help us focus on the kind of thinking the student did and the kind of reasoning that took place when the response was made. Teacher and student may then discuss what could have been done differently, which bit of information may have been more appropriate than another, and why.

Before textbooks are assigned, teachers should first check to see what background knowledge their students have—student knowledge in student language. This background knowledge can then be related to the vocabulary and concepts which are in the text—moving from what is known to the new. Although some students will undoubtedly need some direct instruction in new concepts, others will be able to read and comprehend the text with greater success if they are given the opportunity to begin with the background knowledge *they* relate to the reading task, to judge for themselves how this might help them better understand the text information, to think about what else they know that might be helpful, and to use their own concepts to help them understand less familiar vocabulary. Starting with the student's language and background knowledge rather than that of the teacher or the text may make all the difference in the manner in which a text is processed and the degree to which it is understood.

Metacomprehension and Reading

More efficient readers are those who have some sort of control over their own reading strategies (Brown, 1982; Paris and Lindauer, in press; Garner and Reis, 1981). This control of strategies is called metacomprehension. Metacomprehension refers to a monitoring system which involves self-reflection and awareness of what we know or need to know in a particular reading situation, and what needs to be done if things go wrong (Brown, 1982). Metacomprehension can be thought of as having two separate components: awareness and action. "Awareness" is the self-reflection people do when "watching" their own cognitive behavior as they read. This includes (1) awareness of the goal of the reading assignment, (2) awareness of what is known about the topic and the reading task, (3) awareness of what needs to be known, and (4) awareness of the strategies which facilitate or impede the gaining of meaning from reading. "Action" is the self-regulatory activity people engage in as a response to their self-monitoring. When things go wrong, regulatory mechanisms help readers (1) to relate the reading problem to similar problems, (2) to engage in strategy changes, (3) to check to see if their problem-solving attempts have been successful, and (4) to anticipate what to do next.

Metacomprehension activities serve as a "third eye" permitting a reader to check that ideas in the text make sense and are consistent with one another (Baker and Brown, in press). Because there are varying levels of "how much you need to understand," readers must make this judgment based on their purposes for reading. Poor readers are less aware than good readers of the strategies they use during reading (so too for young as compared to older readers), and they are also less aware when things go wrong. Similarly, young readers do not seem to notice inconsistencies even when they are capable of doing so (Markman, 1979); therefore, young (or poor readers) are less likely to seek clarification of poorly understood material. What this means to the classroom teacher is that we cannot expect students to "read more carefully," "figure things out for themselves," "look it up," or "ask someone for help" when so often the student is unaware that something has "gone wrong" in the first place.

Results from research on metacomprehension can help teachers focus on the fundamental processes their students use when they do or do not comprehend a text. In most classroom environments, the teacher rather than the students makes the decisions about what the students are to *do* and what they need to *know*. Learning to choose which strategies to use is excluded from instructional activities because appropriate teaching procedures may have been too vaguely defined. However, some instructional strategies have recently been suggested that can easily be incorporated into instructional programs. Brown, Campione, and Day (1981) developed a technique for helping students reflect on their own comprehension through internalizing and monitoring certain rules for summarizing passages. Their rules are (1) delete trivial material; (2) delete redundant material; (3) substitute a superordinate term for a list of items; (4) substitute a superordinate event for a list of actions; (5) select a topic sentence, if any; and (6) if there is no topic sentence, make it up. It is not merely the presentation of rules which makes this activity different from most summarizing activities, but the fact that the rules require decision making and judgment on the part of the students. The students are also encouraged to understand the significance of their decisions and to anticipate the outcome of their actions. Students and teacher work closely together to help gain the strategies and the self-reflection necessary to become more efficient learners in general.

Similarly, T. Anderson (1978a) developed self-questioning techniques to improve students' comprehension and retention. Students are encouraged to generate questions before reading (for anticipation), during reading (for focus), and/or after reading (for studying and remembering) based on items in the text being read. Teachers might use such student-generated questions as an interim activity to facilitate comprehension or recall, or as an evaluative index of what the student learned from the text. Some of the activities Anderson suggested were (1) when reading silently, students can generate questions about material to be learned; (2) students can initially study the text material without generating questions, and

then question one another in "study pairs"; and (3) for test preparation, students can develop a master list of questions which can
be evaluated by the group and used by class members as a study
aid.

Baker and Brown (in press) made the distinction between metacomprehension (keeping track of comprehending) and reading for
remembering or studying. The latter involves identification of
important ideas, testing one's own mastery of the material, allo-
cating study time effectively, and developing effective study strategies. The more explicit that teachers are in helping students
understand and use the rules (as well as monitor the effectiveness
of their use), the more successful instruction will be.

Two general kinds of problems that impede successful comprehension are inefficient or inappropriate application of rules and
strategies and lack of background knowledge. The activities suggested here for studying and remembering can help students
not only learn the specific rules or skills but also learn self-
management, self-regulation, and self-monitoring in other learning
situations.

Process Strategies

Although reading is in many ways a recursive activity in which
the mind races ahead to anticipate what will come next and skips
backward to review and revise interpretations that have already
been made, it is helpful to focus on three stages of reading: before
the text is read, while the text is being read, and after the eyes
have left the page (Robinson, 1978). Using such a paradigm we
can consider such prereading characteristics as the role of background knowledge; reader/text interaction during reading; and
the review, recall, and student response activities which occur
after the text has been read (Tierney and Cunningham, in press).
Instructional activities *before* reading might focus on the vocabulary and conceptual knowledge appropriate for a specific task.
They would surely also include prequestions (T. Anderson, 1978b),
analogy (Hayes and Tierney, 1980; Rumelhart and Ortony, 1977)
and the idiosyncratic associations students tend to make in an
attempt to relate what they already know to what will be contained
in the text (Langer, 1980b, 1982). *During*-reading activities might
focus on helping the reader develop self-questions or respond to
inserted questions (André and T. Anderson, 1978). Anticipation of
large structural, organizational, or rhetorical elements might also

be developed, Interventions *after* reading might focus on postquestions (R. Anderson and Biddle, 1975), student responses (Gagné, 1978) and textually-based recollections (Pearson and Johnson, 1978).

We have segmented the forces which constrain reading comprehension in order to gain a clearer view of the nature of the constraints. However, comprehension, in reality, is multidimensional and the multiple constraints described must be considered simultaneously and perceived in their naturally interwoven textures to be useful in secondary schools. When instruction focuses on strategies—on *how* a student interpreted a certain idea or arrived at a certain response—then students will learn to cope more effec-·tively with a wide variety of reading tasks, on their own, as independent readers.

The following chart suggests some of the strategies teachers might consider when they are planning instructional activities. The list is by no means complete; it merely serves as the beginning of a guide which teachers can develop further in their daily work. Although the division of strategies into before, during, and after the reading experience has been provided for purposes of clarity, most of the strategies are used throughout the reading process and can be used for instructional purposes in a variety of combinations.

Process Strategies

Before Reading	During Reading	After Reading
content-related background knowledge (concepts)	predicting what comes next	organization of recall (hierarchical)
text-related knowledge (format, text structure)	integrating (constructive aspects)	organization of text (recall of structure as well as recall of details)
specific vocabulary knowledge	using self-questions	postquestions (textually-and-scriptally-based)
understanding the purpose for reading	knowing when additional information is needed and how to get it	long and short term recall of understanding of task
familiarity with style, genre	keeping purpose for reading in mind	knowing when being uncertain is okay
knowing what one knows and needs to know	monitoring inconsistencies	judging if information gained is sufficient (based on purpose)

Conclusion

Three major areas of research related to the reading process have
been reviewed briefly in this chapter: how readers construct
meaning, the relevance of background knowledge, and the use of
metacomprehension (or self-monitoring) when reading. These have
been related to aspects of the reader, the text, and the context (or
environment) that influence every reading experience. For instructional purposes, it is helpful to consider each of these factors as it
contributes to the shape of each new reading situation. The cited
research suggests that instruction should

1. encourage students to be flexible in their use of text and
   personal knowledge;

2. make students aware of what they already know about a topic
   and how that knowledge relates to what they will read;

3. focus on texts that are read for a variety of meaningful
   purposes;

4. use instructional dialogue to help both teacher and student
   reflect upon particular interpretations and responses;

5. foster students' development of a "third eye" to notice when
   things go wrong and to evaluate strategies to use in particular
   reading situations; and

6. lead students to trust in their abilities as makers of meaning.

References

Anderson, R. C. The notion of schemata and the educational enterprise. In
R. C. Anderson, R. J. Spiro, and W. E. Montague (Eds.), *Schooling and
the acquisition of knowledge.* Hillsdale, N.J.: Lawrence Erlbaum, 1977.

Anderson, R. C., and Biddle, B. W. On asking people questions about what
they are reading. In G. Brown (Ed.), *Psychology of learning and motivation* (Vol. 9). New York: Academic Press, 1975.

Anderson, R. C., and Pichert, J. W. *Recall of previously unrecallable information following a shift in perspective* (Technical Report No. 41).
Champaign: University of Illinois, Center for the Study of Reading,
April 1977. (ERIC Document Reproduction Service No. ED 142 974;
37 p.)

Anderson, R. C., Spiro, R. J., and Anderson, M. C. Schemata as scaffold-
ing for the representation of information in connected discourse.
American Educational Research Journal, 1978, *15*(3), 433–440. (ERIC
No. EJ 189 658)

Anderson, R. C., Pichert, J. W., and Shirey, L. L. *Effects of the reader's schema at different points in time* (Technical Report No. 119). Champaign: University of Illinois, Center for the Study of Reading, April 1979. (ERIC Document Reproduction Service No. ED 169 523; 36p.)

Anderson, T. H. *Another look at the self-questioning study technique* (Reading Education Report No. 6). Champaign: University of Illinois, Center for the Study of Reading, September 1978.(a) (ERIC Document Reproduction Service No. ED 163 441; 19p.)

Anderson, T. H. *Study skills and learning strategies* (Technical Report No. 104). Champaign: University of Illinois, Center for the Study of Reading, September 1978.(b) (ERIC Document Reproduction Service No. ED 161 000; 41p.)

André, M. E. D. A., and Anderson, T. H. *The development and evaluation of a self-questioning study technique* (Technical Report No. 87). Champaign: University of Illinois, Center for the Study of Reading, June 1978. (ERIC Document Reproduction Service No. ED 157 037; 37p.)

Baker, L., and Brown, A. L. Metacognitive skills of reading. In P. D. Pearson (Ed.), *Handbook of reading research*. New York: Longman, in press.

Bartlett, F. C. *Remembering: A study in experimental and social psychology*. Cambridge: Cambridge University Press, 1932.

Bobrow, D. G., and Norman, D. A. Some principles of memory schemata. In D. G. Bobrow and A. M. Collins (Eds.), *Representation and understanding: Studies in cognitive science*. New York: Academic Press, 1975.

Brown, A. L. Learning how to learn from reading. In J. Langer and M. Smith-Burke (Eds.), *Reader meets author/bridging the gap: A psycholinguistic and sociolinguistic perspective*. Newark, Del.: International Reading Association, 1982.(ERIC Clearinghouse Accession No. CS 006 710)

Brown, A. L., Campione, J. C., and Day, J. D. Learning to learn: On training students to learn from texts. *Educational Researcher*, 1981, *10*, 14–21.

Cook-Gumperz, J., Gumperz, J., and Simons, H. *Language at school and at home: Theory, methods and preliminary findings*. Report to the National Institute of Education, 1979.

Gagné, E. D. Long-term retention of information following learning from prose. *Review of Educational Research*, 1978, *48*, 629–665. (ERIC No. EJ 200 561)

Garner, R., and Reis, R. Monitoring and resolving comprehension obstacles: An investigation of spontaneous lookbacks among upper-grade good and poor comprehenders. *Reading Research Quarterly*, 1981, *16*(4), 569–582. (ERIC No. EJ 248 382)

Goodman, K. S., and Goodman, Y. M. *Reading of American children whose language is a stable rural dialect of English or a language other than English*. Final report. (Project No. 3-0255, Contract No. NE-G-00-3-0087). Washington, D.C.: National Institute of Education, 1978. (ERIC Document Reproduction Service No. ED 173 754; 670p.)

Goodman, Y. M. Kid watching. *Journal of National Elementary Principals*, 1978, *57*(4), 41–45.

Harste, J. C., Burke, C. L., and Woodward, V. Children's language and world: Initial encounters with print. In J. Langer and M. Smith-Burke (Eds.), *Reader meets author/bridging the gap: A psycholinguistic and sociolinguistic perspective.* Newark, Del.: International Reading Association, 1982. (ERIC Clearinghouse Accession No. CS 006 710)

Hayes, D. A., and Tierney, R. J. *Increasing background knowledge through analogy: Its effects upon comprehension and learning* (Technical Report No. 186). Champaign: University of Illinois, Center for the Study of Reading, October 1980. (ERIC Document Reproduction Service No. 195 953; 81p.)

Langer, J. A. *An idiosyncratic model of affective and cognitive silent reading strategies.* 1980. (a) (ERIC Document Reproduction Service No. ED 174 939; 25p.)

Langer, J. A. Relation between levels of prior knowledge and the organization of recall. In M. L. Kamil and A. J. Moe (Eds.), *Perspectives in reading research and instruction* (Twenty-ninth Yearbook of the National Reading Conference). Washington, D.C.: National Reading Conference, 1980. (b)

Langer, J. A. From theory to practice: A pre-reading plan. *Journal of Reading,* 1981(a), *25*(2), 152–156.

Langer, J. A. Pre-reading plan: Facilitating text comprehension. In J. Chapman (Ed.), *The reader and the text.* London: Heinemann Books, 1981. (b)

Langer, J. A. Facilitating text processing: The elaboration of prior knowledge. In J. A. Langer and M. Smith-Burke (Eds.), *Reader meets author/bridging the gap: A psycholinguistic and sociolinguistic perspective.* Newark, Del.: International Reading Association, 1982. (ERIC Clearinghouse Accession No. CS 006 710)

Langer, J. A., and Nicolich, M. Prior knowledge and its effect on comprehension. *Journal of Reading Behavior,* 1981, *13*(4), 373–379.

Markman, E. M. Realizing that you don't understand: Elementary school children's awareness of inconsistencies. *Child Development,* 1979, *50*(3), 643–655. (ERIC No. EJ 212 942)

Paris, S., and Lindauer, B. The development of cognitive skills during childhood. In B. Wolman (Ed.), *Handbook of developmental psychology.* Englewood Cliffs, N.J.: Prentice-Hall, in press.

Pearson, P. D., Hansen, J., and Gordon, C. The effect of background knowledge on young children's comprehension of explicit and implicit information. *Journal of Reading Behavior,* 1979, *11*, 201–209.

Pearson, P. D., and Johnson, D. *Teaching reading comprehension.* New York: Macmillan, 1978.

Pichert, J. W., and Anderson, R. C. *Taking different perspectives on a story* (Technical Report No. 14). Champaign: University of Illinois, Center for the Study of Reading, 1976. (ERIC Document Reproduction Service No. ED 134 936; 30p.)

Polanyi, M. *The tacit dimension.* Garden City, N.Y.: Doubleday, 1966.

Reynolds, R. E., et al. *Cultural schemata and reading comprehension* (Technical Report No. 201). Champaign: University of Illinois, Center for the Study of Reading, April 1981. (ERIC Document Reproduction Service No. ED 201 991; 59p.)

Robinson, H. A. Facilitating successful reading strategies. Paper presented at International Reading Association, Houston, Texas, 1978.

Rosenblatt, L. *The reader, the text, the poem.* Carbondale: Southern Illinois University Press, 1978.

Rumelhart, D. E. Toward an interactive model of reading. In S. Dornic (Ed.), *Attention and performance* (Vol. 6). London: Academic Press, 1977.

Rumelhart, D. E., and Ortony, A. The representation of knowledge in memory. In R. C. Anderson, R. J. Spiro, and W. E. Montague (Eds.), *Schooling and the acquisition of knowledge.* Hillsdale, N.J.: Lawrence Erlbaum, 1977.

Spiro, R. J. Etiology of reading comprehension style. In M. Kamil and A. Moe (Eds.), *Perspectives in reading research and instruction* (Twenty-ninth Yearbook of the National Reading Conference). Washington, D.C.: National Reading Conference, 1980.

Steffensen, M. S., Jogdeo, C., and Anderson, R. C. *A cross-cultural perspective on reading comprehension* (Technical Report No. 97). Champaign: University of Illinois, Center for the Study of Reading, July 1978. (ERIC Document Reproduction Service No. ED 159 660; 41p.)

Tierney, R. J., and Cunningham, J. W. Research on teaching reading comprehension. In P. D. Pearson (Ed.), *Handbook on research in reading.* New York: Longman, in press.

4 Readers' Strategies

William D. Page
University of Connecticut

Theories of metacognition or metacomprehension, introduced to the reader by Langer in chapter 3, are in fact theories of the readers' strategies. Brown (1980) posed metacognition as "the deliberate conscious control of one's own cognitive actions" (p. 453). Brown identified reading strategies as instances of metacognition and described them as "any deliberate planful control of activities that give birth to comprehension" (p. 456). She listed clarification of purpose, identification of important parts of the message, focusing attention on "major content rather than trivia," monitoring comprehension, assessing progress toward goals, corrective behavior, and "recovering from disruptions and distractions" as reading strategies falling under the rubric of "metacognition." She identified some areas of metacognition difficulty for children: recognizing increased problem difficulty and "need for strategic intervention"; inferential reasoning to assess truth; predicting outcomes; predicting "task difficulty"; "time apportionment"; and monitoring degree of success. Brown concluded that the information concerning reading strategies is represented by a "scanty picture" that must be "filled in" with a "precise knowledge of component processes of metacomprehension skills" before "any attempts to construct training programs" are undertaken (p. 478).

In the struggle to organize extant research around some general principle, the theoretical areas of schema theory and context provide some help. Schema theory refers to the knowledge, background, and conceptual framework that a reader brings to a text. If we step back from the theory and the research, we can gain some perspective by considering what researchers actually do in examining reading. Other than theorizing, researchers mostly gather and analyze responses from readers. Page and Vacca (1979) pointed out, "The concepts of product and in-process indicators suggest a dimension of a corroborative framework that can be developed by searching for and creating ways of eliciting and organizing information from readers" (p. 59).

The dimension they referred to is a single principle that provides an inclusive continuum on which all readers' responses to print must fall. As suggested by Langer in chapter 3, all readers' responses are drawn prior to, during, or after the act of reading, and the treatments tested by researchers can be categorized similarly. Of course, many studies include responses or treatments focused on some combination of these benchmarks. In this chapter, the focus of the research—prior, during, or after—is arbitrarily assigned by the reviewer for the sole purpose of organization. Some research found in one category, admittedly, could be classified just as accurately in another.

Prior to Reading

Schema, the knowledge the reader has prior to reading, affects how the reader proceeds. In some sense, all schema-driven research—research concerned with what the reader knows before reading the text—could be classified in the prior-to-reading category, but instances of schema-driven research involve responses or treatments in all three categories. Clearly, the topic of advance organizers falls into the prior-to-reading category, along with some other research approaches.

Ausubel (1960) focused on the student's prior cognitive structure of what he or she attempts to learn. He theorized that bolstering that cognitive structure prior to reading can enhance learning from text. Ausubel (1968) set the scene for the notion of advance organizers when he stated that ". . . new ideas and information are learned and retained most efficiently when inconclusive and specifically relevant ideas are already available in the cognitive structure to serve a subsuming role or to furnish ideational anchorage" (p. 153). This statement echoes facets of apperception theory, namely, that ideas exist in the mind and that teaching is an effort to add new mental states to the growing store of extant ideas (Bigge, 1971). Perhaps because of their ancient heritage, Ausubel's ideas are the root of a large body of studies of advance organizers.

What do the studies on advance organizers reveal? When advance organizers are tested, the results are inconclusive and the definitions of advance organizers are vague (T. Anderson, 1980). Barnes and Clawson (1975) found twelve studies that supported

Ausubel's idea, but twenty that did not. This supports the conclusion that advance organizers work sometimes, but mostly they do not. Further, the type of advance organizer, the type of text, and the type of task, among other things, may be expected to have an effect. Further study is warranted, but the Barnes and Clawson review is not a warrant for widespread revision of teaching practice, nor of strong redirection of readers' strategies. More recent studies, such as those discussed below, may change this conclusion.

Crafton (1981) found that the schema or background knowledge of readers was affected by reading a passage about the same topic as the topic of the target passage. Readers who read the first passage and then the target passage comprehended better than those who only read the target passage. Although the finding is not a surprise, clearly reading about a topic is demonstrated to be a facilitative advance organizer for reading about a topic.

Alvermann (1980) found text that was randomly ordered or unorganized was recalled better by students exposed to graphic organizers than students not exposed to graphic organizers. In this context, a graphic organizer was a schematic representation chart, or diagram, of key vocabulary showing hierarchical and parallel relationships between concepts and details. Similar results were not obtained with text material that was organized according to superordinate and subordinate conceptual relationships and by comparisons and contrasts. Alvermann found that all tenth graders in her study recalled material better with a graphic organizer. She speculated that teachers should use organizers to help readers assimilate new information by relating the new information to the readers' extant information. She advised practitioners to be aware of the organization of texts and how readers are influenced by the organization of text. Gordon (1980) maintained, from her study, that comprehension is enhanced by providing students with a strategy for making use of schemata.

Raphael (1980) showed how metacognitive training in identifying text explicit and implicit questions facilitated performance in answering comprehension questions that were text explicit. In text explicit questions information required to answer the question is stated in the text and the text sentence is used as the structure for generating the question. In text implicit questions, the information required to answer the question is explicitly stated in the text, but the question is generated from a different sentence structure. Schema theory was cited as the explanation for her findings.

Advance organizers make commonsense as a way of helping readers to improve their strategies. The recent studies appear to be supportive of the theory, but the total picture still remains inconclusive.

During Reading

A number of studies focused on responses or treatment occurring during the reading process. Among them are a host of studies of miscues, oral reading responses that deviate from the text (Goodman, 1969). Another line of research focused on the visual perceptual span (McConkie and Raynor, 1974). A third approach focused on how readers treat more important aspects of text as compared with less important aspects of text, a topic related to early findings that readers remember more important ideas better than unimportant ones (Newman, 1939). The notion of environmental context or the conditions under which reading takes place was also shown to have effects on comprehension. Presented here are studies selected to provide the reader with the flavor of in-process research, ideas about how readers strategize as they read.

Underwood (1980) shed new light on the visual perceptual span finding that adults and children, both good and poor readers, acquire letter information from an area about two letters to the left and six letters to the right of the fixation point. Underwood used a form of the approach used by McConkie and Raynor which involves a computer technique coupled with a cathode ray tube to produce the display of print and a bite bar to maintain a forty-eight centimeter distance from the display. Underwood's findings conflicted with the general belief that skilled readers acquire information from a wider area of text than less skilled readers (Haber, 1978). Underwood found teaching students to read by phrases per fixation unwai.anted, but noted that eye movement studies must also begin to reflect theories suggesting that internal processing extends beyond the duration of a fixation and plays a part in guiding eye movements.

Although Underwood treated the internal processing idea as only a possibility, other researchers presented stronger positions. Reynolds (1979) found proficient readers spending more time on important portions of text when cued by questions as to which parts are more important—thus presenting evidence that fixations are guided. Memory plays a part. K. Goodman and Burke (1973) found 30 percent more miscues were related to the line below. Since the line above was previously processed, memory of the previously processed line coupled with the availability of the line above due to its close proximity indicated that internal processing is more than mere possibility. Underwood presented his subjects with print one line at a time, thus eliminating the possibility of looking at the lines above or below. Thus, Underwood's suggestion that readers do not process by phrases is questionable because phrases and other units can be held in memory, are available in the peripheral field of vision (K. Goodman and Burke), and can be processed while a longer fixation takes place on information deemed important by the reader (Reynolds). This does not discount the extremely important finding that the visual perceptual span identified by Underwood is constant (two letters to the left and six to the right) for good and poor readers and for adults and children. The finding understandably prompted Underwood to question the value of trying to teach or to encourage readers to expand their span of visual perception.

In contrasting older and younger readers, Dreher (1980) focused not on visual perceptual span as did Underwood, but rather on instantiation. Instantiation involves storing specific terms that are contextually appropriate when encountering general terms in sentences. For instance, suppose a reader encounters a general term such as "boys" in the sentence, "The boys played a good baseball game." Instantiation is said to occur when the reader responds to specific terms such as "baseball player," "ball player," or "player" in relation to the "boys" that are the referent for the terms. Dreher found that college students instantiate spontaneously while fifth and eighth graders instantiate when the specific term is provided for them, but not spontaneously. She suggested that, for readers at least through eighth grade, questions that exhibit retrieval cues corresponding to subject nouns in the text to which the questions refer may be more appropriate than some other types of questions. Dreher noted that her findings should be tested with connected discourse rather than, as she did it, with single sentences.

In some sense, control of the conditions under which reading takes place can be categorized as occurring during reading. For example, Diehl (1980) focused on conditions in employment situations in which reading takes place and examined adults' strategies in reading and writing with job-related materials. He found that extralinguistic cues from the job task itself aid the reader. Further, he noted that because subjects find job-related material is continually available to them, they need not *learn* it. Here is an interesting distinction between the real world application of information from text and many contrived circumstances in school. In the real world, individuals can usually look back at material as often as needed, while in schools individuals may be artificially deprived of their sources of information in order, supposedly, to test learning or memory. In some instances, school tasks should be reevaluated in terms of their similarities to, and unnecessary differences from, job-related reading and writing tasks. Diehl found workers able to read material in functional context that would be difficult or impossible for them to read in isolation.

Diehl also suggested that the literary demands of higher versus lower status occupations differ more in terms of the types of tasks than the difficulty of the material. A corporate executive is an example of a higher status occupation while various forms of unskilled labor are classified as lower status occupations. Higher and lower status occupations were classified according to the *Dictionary of Occupational Titles* (United States Employment Service, 1977) and occupational status rankings (Hodge, Siegel, and Rossi, 1966). Individuals in higher classified occupations tended to read to assess more than those in lower classified occupations who tended to focus on read-to-do and read-to-learn tasks.

Although Smith, Carey, and Harste explored the contexts of reading in depth in chapter 2, above, the effects of social context are mentioned here as central aspects of readers' strategies during reading. For example, Au (1980) maintained that the characteristics of social organization of a classroom affect reading achievement. Specifically, she stated that Hawaiian children who were used to following the rules of a "talk story" did better when the teacher understood the rules and maintained a balance of rights of speakers in teacher-pupil interactions in the classroom.

Huey (1908/1968) as far back as 1908 recognized context as influential in reading. Bartlett (1932) discussed context but his contemporaries seemed to have nearly ignored him, and only recently have psychologists revived some of his ideas. Some linguists have maintained context as a central theme: Malinowski (1923), Firth (1957a and 1957b), and Halliday (1970), for instance.

Sadoski (1981b) suggested that the R. Anderson et al. (1977) and Carey, Harste, and Smith (1981) finding that schema or background knowledge and context influence comprehension may be due to the "contrived ambiguity" of the text, which may have prevented readers from relying on cues ordinarily available in unambiguous text. Of course, Sadoski has a point, but since most language exhibits some degree of ambiguity, the R. Anderson et al. and Carey, Harste, Smith conclusions are tenable. Still, there are unanswered questions. Do the schema and context effects hold for highly unambiguous text? If not, to what extent does the text have to exhibit ambiguity before the effects are produced? Since it is technologically possible as well as feasible to answer these questions for both effects, we can probably expect studies in the area soon.

Clearly, what readers do while reading is a productive area of research if only to get better descriptions of the process itself. Better descriptions may lead to better models and new insights into the readers' strategies.

Following Reading

Studies in which responses or treatments may be loosely categorized as occurring after reading takes place are included here. In relation to reading comprehension, the category of "following reading" is probably the most researched category because most reading comprehension tests are traditionally administered after reading takes place. In this section some difficulties readers face in attempting to strategize about dealing with the extant tasks presented by traditional reading comprehension tests (Tuinman, 1979) are examined, and a study on levels of processing is probed so far as readers' strategies might influence comprehension. Additionally, several studies are discussed as examples of current outcomes of the schema theory thrust.

Tuinman (1973), Pyrczak (1975), Hanna and Oaster (1979), and Entin and Klare (1980) demonstrated that widely used standardized reading comprehension tests contain too many questions that can be answered without reading the passages to which the questions refer. One wonders what strategies readers can employ to cope with this difficulty other than worrying about the fact that their academic and, indeed, their resulting economic destinies are determined to some degree by tests that usually misassess reading comprehension.

Tuinman (1979) found another, related, serious flaw in the structure of comprehension testing: the folly of asking too many questions about very short passages. When this is done, the reader is forced to focus on details that quite appropriately would be overlooked in ordinary reading situations. As Tuinman noted, "The text is milked dry; the reader is forced to process it in a manner atypical of much natural reading" (p. 41). Again, we are in a quandary about what the reader can strategize to do, except perhaps to learn to read one way for tests and another way for real reading.

The difficulties with comprehension tests represent an area in which test constructors may be able to strategize, but readers, the test takers, have little room to strategize to overcome these difficulties. This is not the case in study techniques. Here readers can make choices and deliberately set up their own expectations. A number of studies provide insights into the readers' strategies in the area of studying text.

T. Anderson (1980) reanalyzed Arnold's (1942) data on comparing repetitive reading without writing, reading with underlining and writing notes in margins, reading and topical outlining, and reading and writing a brief summary. Comparisons were made on delayed testing scores with freshmen and sophomores with varying materials. T. Anderson concluded that repetitive reading works best, and that "outlining and precis writing are actually 'detrimental' to a baseline repetitive reading strategy" (p. 484). Related to rereading are findings in Crafton's study which showed that prior reading of a second text on the same topic facilitates comprehension with both fourth and eleventh graders. Crafton used a variety of comprehension techniques not hindered by the difficulties of item writing noted by Hanna and Oaster and by Tuinman (1979).

Wixson (1980) found that explicit or verbatim postreading questions inhibited children's integration of prior knowledge with information gained from text. An explicit or verbatim question is one in which the question and the answer to the question can be derived from the text and both the question and the answer are explicitly shown in relation to one another in a propositional network of the text. A propositional network is a representation of the structure of the text as shown by a description of the relationships among clauses, both surface and embedded. The impact of different types of postreading questions on comprehension performance was unmistakably demonstrated in this study; Wixson used schema theory to explain her findings. In contrast to her finding on verbatim or explicit questions, Wixson showed that implicit postreading questions facilitated learning of explicit information to a greater extent than unrelated postreading questions. An implicit question is one which calls for information not stated in the text explicitly (i.e., an inferential question).

Using Y. Goodman and Burke's (1972) miscue inventory with its retelling format Sadoski (1981a) found three hierarchical levels of processing in reading performance: (1) superficial processing,

(2) middle level processing, and (3) deep processing. Superficial processing is measured by the extent to which a reader can recall characters' names and characteristics from a story and is inversely related to the extent to which a reader can describe the theme. Middle level processing is measured by the extent to which a reader can recall events in the story, perform on a multiple-choice, passage-dependent question, comprehension test (Hanna and Oaster), and perform on a post oral-reading cloze test (Page, 1975). Deep processing is indicated by the Sadoski Index, the post oral-reading cloze test, and the extent to which a reader's retelling of the story reflects characteristics of the characters, the plot, and the theme. The Sadoski Index is an empirically tested combination of miscues that mathematically represents relationships of semantic acceptability and correction behavior to comprehension (Sadoski, Page, and Carey, 1981).

If Sadoski's findings hold up in future replication studies, then reading tasks can be classified as requiring predominantly superficial, middle, or deep level processing. The student could be made aware of the expectations entertained by teachers and testers in specific tasks with specific texts. Students may be able to strategize to meet teachers' expectations if teachers communicate those expectations.

Teachers should be concerned with the instructions given readers in various reading situations. For instance, when a reader is asked to read, he or she is seldom, in present practice, told whether the reading will be assessed in terms of how accurately a response conforms to the printed text, the degree of reconstruction of the author's message, or the degree of construction of knowledge about the author's message (Goodman and Page, 1979). It is reasonable to expect readers' strategies to differ if readers' are made aware of different expectations as part of the directions for accomplishing a reading task.

Furthermore, the nature or form of the postreading assessment should fit the type of—and purpose of—the reading assignment. T. Anderson (1980), in a summation of research on study techniques, concluded that adjunct questions, student-generated questions, elaboration techniques, and outlining techniques are used to exhibit effectiveness. Adjunct questions are those made available before, during, or after reading the text, and their effects are judged in terms of criterion test questions given after reading. R. Anderson and Biddle (1975) concluded that adjunct questions presented following reading produce better comprehension than questions presented before or during reading. Questions presented prior to reading help readers answer those same questions after reading, but do not help them answer different questions. Questions presented textually closer to the pertinent information produce better performance than those presented farther from the pertinent information. Questions requiring an overt response produce better performance than questions not requiring an overt response.

Paraphrasing, drawing implications, and sentence elaboration were shown by Weinstein (1975) to facilitate reading comprehension and recall. Barton (1930) demonstrated that outlining improved test performance for high school students studying history and geography. Paraphrasing and drawing or describing a verbal image were shown by Dansereau et al. (1974) to produce significantly better performance on objective tests. However, T. Anderson (1980) noted that elaboration, imagizing, paraphrasing, and outlining may be "overly time consuming and inefficient from the student's point of view" (p. 488).

Conclusion

The research suggests that reading a passage about a topic aids comprehension of another passage about the same topic. Graphic organizers or schematic diagrams of key vocabulary showing hierarchical or parallel relationships between concepts and details seems to aid comprehension of unorganized or poorly organized material.

The research also seems to point to the following specific teacher strategies:

1. Provide opportunities for readers to look back at material while they try to answer questions, just as they might in job situations outside of school.

2. Alert readers to cues they can get from the environmental context to help them understand what they are reading. For instance, in a literature class they can expect to read stories which have plots and characters, while in algebra class, sets and relations can be expected, not plots and characters.

3. Tell students what is expected of them. Are you, the teacher, expecting them to seek out the theme or main idea, or are you expecting them to note cause and effect relationships?

4. Because rereading a passage aids comprehension, provide opportunities for students to read important passages more than once.

5. Focus on helping students to understand what they read and help them to construct knowledge about a topic or concept. The research suggested that many students will not spontaneously store specific terms in memory just because they've been briefly introduced or encountered in text. For instance, if a story provides the sentence, "The heavily loaded vehicle careened around the corner," and in another part of a story the vehicle is shown to be a truck, mature readers will store and classify *vehicle* as *truck.* However, young and less able readers often require a prompt to do this or else they will not make the connection between "vehicle" and "truck." Either help to make the connection in such cases or choose text requiring fewer instances of this kind of performance.

Reading researchers have turned corners from preoccupation with decoding to recognizing comprehension as the purpose of reading, from focus on fragmented language to concerns about whole language, from believing in extant tests to questioning them, from treating reading in isolation to pursuing investigations into context, and from treating readers as passive to seeing them as active language users thinking their way through text. These ideas do not totally negate the knowledge of the former avenues, but rather they add dimensions to interpretation and reinterpretation of what is known about readers' strategies.

References

Alvermann, D. Effect of graphic organizers, textual organization, and reading comprehension level on recall of expository text (Doctoral dissertation, Syracuse University, New York, 1980). *Dissertation Abstracts International,* 1981, *41,* 3963A–3964A. (University Microfilms No. 8104509)

Anderson, R. C., and Biddle, W. B. On asking people questions about what they are reading. In G. Bower (Ed.), *Psychology of Learning and Motivation* (Vol. 9). New York: Academic Press, 1975.

Anderson, R., Reynolds, R., Schallert, D., and Goetz, E. Frameworks for comprehending discourse. *American Educational Research Journal,* 1977, *14*(4), 367–381. (ERIC No. EJ 184 138)

Anderson, T. Study strategies and adjunct aids. In R. Spiro, B. Bruce, and W. Brewer (Eds.), *Theoretical issues in reading comprehension.* Hillsdale, N.J.: Lawrence Erlbaum, 1980.

Arnold, H. F. The comparative effectiveness of certain study techniques in the field of history. *Journal of Educational Psychology,* 1942, *33*(5), 449–457.

Au, K. A test of the social organizational hypothesis: Relationships between participation structures and learning to read (Doctoral dissertation, University of Illinois, 1980). *Dissertation Abstracts International*, 1981, *41*, 4647A. (University Microfilms No. 8108441)

Ausubel, D. The use of advance organizers in the learning and retention of meaningful verbal material. *Journal of Educational Psychology*, 1960, *51*, 267–272.

Ausubel, D. *Educational psychology: A cognitive view*. New York: Holt, Rinehart and Winston, 1968.

Barnes, B. R., and Clawson, E. U. Do advance organizers facilitate learning? Recommendations for further research based on an analysis of 32 studies. *Review of Educational Research*, 1975, *45*(4), 637–659. (ERIC No. EJ 135 379)

Bartlett, F. C. *Remembering: A study in experimental and social psychology*. Cambridge: Cambridge University Press, 1932.

Barton, W. A. *Outlining as a study procedure*. New York: Columbia University, Bureau of Publications, 1930.

Bigge, M. *Learning theories for teachers*. New York: Harper and Row, 1971.

Brown, A. Metacognitive development and reading. In R. Spiro, B. Bruce, and W. Brewer (Eds.), *Theoretical issues in reading comprehension*. Hillsdale, N.J.: Lawrence Erlbaum, 1980.

Carey, R., Harste, J., and Smith, S. Contextual constraints and discourse processes: A replication study. *Reading Research Quarterly*, 1981, *16*(2), 201–212. (ERIC No. EJ 240 384)

Crafton, L. The reading process as a transactional experience (Doctoral dissertation, Indiana University, 1981). *Dissertation Abstracts International*, 1981, *42*, 154A–155A. (University Microfilms No. 8114938)

Dansereau, D. G., McDonald, B. A., Long, G. L., Actkinson, T. R., Ellis, A. M., Collins, K. W., Williams, S., and Evans, S. H. *The development and assessment of an effective learning strategy training program* (Final Technical Report No. 3). Fort Worth: Texas Christian University, 1974.

Diehl, W. Functional literacy as a variable construct: An examination of attitudes, behaviors, and strategies related to occupational literacy (Doctoral dissertation, Indiana University, 1980). *Dissertation Abstracts International*, 1980, *41*, 570A. (University Microfilms No. 8016683)

Dreher, M. The instantiation of general terms in children (Doctoral dissertation, University of California, 1980). *Dissertation Abstracts International*, 1980, *41*, 2528A. (University Microfilms No. 8027757)

Entin, E., and Klare, G. Components of answers to multiple-choice questions on a published reading comprehension test: An application of the Hanna-Oaster approach. *Reading Research Quarterly*, 1980, *15*(2), 228–236. (ERIC No. EJ 217 550)

Firth, J. R. *Papers in linguistics, 1934–1955*. London: Oxford University Press, 1957.(a)

Firth, J. R. Synopsis of linguistic theory, 1930–1935. In Philological Society, *Studies in Linguistic Analysis*. Oxford: Basil Blackwell, 1957.(b)

Goodman, K. S. Analysis of oral reading miscues: Applied psycholinguistics. *Reading Research Quarterly*, 1969, *5*(1), 9–30. (ERIC No. EJ 008 384)

Goodman, K. S., and Burke, C. L. *Theoretically based studies of patterns of miscues in oral reading performance. Final report* (U.S.O.E. Project No. OEG-0-9-320375-4269). Washington, D.C.: U.S. Department of Health, Education and Welfare, March 1973. (ERIC Document Reproduction Service No. ED 079 708; 459p.)

Goodman, K. S., and Page, W. D. *Reading comprehension programs: Theoretical bases of reading comprehension instruction in the middle grades. Revised final report* (Contract No. NIE-C-74-0140). Washington, D.C.: U.S. Department of Health, Education and Welfare, October 1978. (ERIC Document Reproduction Service No. ED 165 092; 264p.)

Goodman, Y., and Burke, C. *Reading miscue inventory*. New York: Macmillan, 1972.

Gordon, C. J. The effects of instruction in metacomprehension and inferencing on children's comprehension abilities (Doctoral dissertation, University of Minnesota, 1980). *Dissertation Abstracts International*, 1980, *41*, 1004A. (University Microfilms No. 8019528)

Haber, R. N. Visual perception. *Annual Review of Psychology*, 1978, *29*, 31–59.

Halliday, M. A. K. Language structure and language function. In John Lyons (Ed.), *New Horizons in Linguistics*. Harmondsworth, Middlesex, England: Penguin Books, 1970.

Hanna, G., and Oaster, T. Toward a unified theory of context dependence. *Reading Research Quarterly*, 1979, *14*(2), 226–243. (ERIC No. EJ 197 737)

Hodge, R. W., Siegel, P. M., and Rossi, P. H. Occupational prestige in the United States, 1925–1963. In R. Bendix and S. Lipset (Eds.), *In class, status, and power* (2nd ed.). New York: Free Press, 1968.

Huey, E. B. *The psychology and pedagogy of reading*. Cambridge: The MIT Press, 1968.

Malinowski, B. The problems of meaning in primitive languages. Supplement to C.K. Ogden and I.A. Richards, *The meaning of meaning*. London: Routledge and Kegan Paul, 1923.

McConkie, G., and Raynor, K. The span of effective stimulus during a fixation in reading. *Perception and Psychophysics*, 1974, *17*, 578–586.

Newman, E. Forgetting of meaning material during sleep and waking. *American Journal of Psychology*, 1939, *52*, 65–71.

Page, W. D. The post oral-reading cloze test: New link between oral-reading and comprehension. *Journal of Reading Behavior*, 1975, *7*(4), 383–389. (ERIC No. EJ 137 810)

Page, W. D., and Vacca, R. T. Overt indicators of reading comprehension: Product and process considerations. In J. Harste and R. Carey (Eds.), *New perspectives on comprehension* (Monograph in Language and Reading Studies No. 3). Bloomington: Indiana University Press, 1979.

Pryczak, F. A responsive note on measures of the passage dependence of reading comprehension test items. *Reading Research Quarterly*, 1975, *11*(1), 112–117. (ERIC No. EJ 129 274)

Raphael, T. The effect of metacognitive strategy awareness training on students' question answering behavior (Doctoral dissertation, University of Illinois, 1981). *Dissertation Abstracts International*, 1981, *42*, 544A. (University Microfilms No. 8114465)

Reynolds, R. E. The effect of attention on the learning and recall of important text elements (Doctoral dissertation, University of Illinois, 1979). *Dissertation Abstracts International*, 1980, *40*, 5380A. (University Microfilms No. 8009142)

Sadoski, M. The relationships between student retellings and selected comprehension measures [Doctoral dissertation, University of Connecticut, 1981.(a)]. *Dissertation Abstracts International*, 1981, *42*, 2628A. (University Microfilms No. 8125458)

Sadoski, M. Commentary: Right forest, wrong tree? A critique of Carey, Harste, and Smith's research. *Reading Research Quarterly*, 1981(b), *16*(4), 600–603.

Sadoski, M., Page, W. D., and Carey, R. F. Empirical testing of a new miscue sorting technique. *The New England Reading Association Journal*, 1981, *16*(3), 41–47.

Tuinman, J. Determining the passage dependency of comprehension questions in five major tests. *Reading Research Quarterly*, 1973, *9*(2), 206–223. (ERIC No. EJ 092 586)

Tuinman, J. Reading is recognition—When reading is not reasoning. In J. Harste and R. Carey (Eds.), *New perspectives on comprehension* (Monograph in Language and Reading Studies No. 3). Bloomington: Indiana University Press, 1979.

Underwood, N. R. Acquisition of visual information during reading: The perceptual span of children and adults (Doctoral dissertation, University of Illinois, 1980). *Dissertation Abstracts International*, 1981, *41*, 4663A. (University Microfilms No. 8108692)

United States Employment Service. *Dictionary of occupational titles* (4th ed.). U.S. Department of Labor, 1977.

Wixson, K. The effects of postreading questions on children's discourse comprehension and knowledge acquisition (Doctoral dissertation, Syracuse University, New York, 1980). *Dissertation Abstracts International*, 1981, *41*, 3512A–3513A. (University Microfilms No. 8104555)

Weinstein, C. E. Learning of elaboration strategies (Doctoral dissertation, University of Texas at Austin, 1975). *Dissertation Abstracts International*, 1975, *36*, 2725A–2726A. (University Microfilms No. 75-24, 981)

5 Instructional Strategies

Joseph L. Vaughan, Jr.
East Texas State University

The reader will find overlap between this chapter and the chapters that precede and follow it. Although each author has a different topic, the very nature of reading strategies demands such interaction. As in Page's chapter 4, the latter part of this chapter continues the structure of *before, during,* and *after* reading as a useful paradigm for categorizing strategies and helping teachers choose appropriate instructional strategies.

General Strategies

In the past five years, a flood of "how-to-do-it" textbooks have been published related to secondary school reading, and these texts, taken collectively, reflect a broad philosophical spectrum. Among the most widely recommended strategies are SQ3R (Survey, Question, Read, Recite, Review) and its innumerable modifications; directed reading-thinking activities (with several modifications); and uninterrupted sustained silent reading (also labeled in various novel ways). Teachers appear to have relied on these three strategies as much if not more than any others; yet, in spite of the vast number of research studies, empirical evidence supporting their effectiveness is sparse.

SQ3R apparently evolved from a note-taking strategy described by Robinson (1941; cf. Spencer, 1978) whereby a reader "is to read a section of his assignment . . . which develops a main point and then, without looking at the book, jot down the main point in his own words. He then reads the next section, takes notes, etc." (pp. 23–24). Robinson subsequently embellished upon and formalized this strategy (1946, 1961, 1970). Robinson (1946, 1970) cited several sources to support the value of an organized framework for study (e.g., Borass, 1938) as justification for SQ3R along with two studies

(Willmore, 1967; Wooster, 1958) that examined approaches to teaching SQ3R. Findings by Willmore and Wooster did not, however, bode well for SQ3R as it was found difficult to teach and other approaches to study (e.g., reading, reading and underlining) proved more effective, efficient, and appealing. Tierney, Readence, and Dishner (1980) suggested that the complexity of SQ3R might be its greatest problem since teachers have difficulty convincing "students of the value of such a procedure" (p. 88).

While SQ3R has the credibility of duration and is justifiable on the grounds of learning principles, it has not been subjected to careful empirical scrutiny (Johns and McNamara, 1980; Spencer, 1978; Wark, 1964). Two problems present obstacles for research with SQ3R. First, students are reluctant to modify their study habits; even Robinson (1970) noted the interference of students' "old study habits" in efforts to teach them to use SQ3R. Baker and Brown (1980) cited this factor in metacognition and study skills research as an instructional hazard; although students identify a new approach as being more effective or efficient, they continue to use "old study habits" even after learning new ones. A second potential problem with SQ3R research is also related to metacognition studies—the need for thorough instruction. Brown, Campione, and Day (1981) stressed the need for teachers to teach study strategies in-depth because they have found merely introducing a technique and directing students to use it insufficient. Modeling, guidance, and discussion are necessary for successful learning of new strategies.

As implied earlier, SQ3R does not seem to have been given the scrutiny one might have expected. Future inquiries relative to SQ3R would benefit from examination of the factors that may inhibit its effectiveness; however, until subsequent studies provide empirical support, SQ3R will remain an unsubstantiated tradition.

The directed reading-thinking activity (DRTA), developed by Stauffer (1969, 1975, 1980), was designed in accord with the principles of student-generated purposes and predictions for reading, students' resolution of those purposes and predictions, and subsequent justification of the resolution. The DRTA is a teacher-directed activity intended to increase readers' comprehension of narrative, descriptive, expository, and poetic text, and substantive empirical evidence supports its effectiveness (Stauffer, 1976, 1980) with *elementary level students.* Apparently, there are no studies that verify the success of DRTA with secondary level readers; however, enthusiastic support for its use with adolescents can be found among reading teachers and content-area teachers alike.

Uninterrupted sustained silent reading (USSR) emerged with the advent of widespread support for psycholinguistically-based reading instruction (in the late 1960s) along with rejuvenation of the idea that to become better readers, children must read. Accompanying this belief, free reading was recommended as an integral part of any reading program, and USSR (SSR to some) became a structured approach to free reading. In the face of philosophical controversy (e.g., "students need to spend more time developing their skills and free reading takes time away from skills practice"), several studies were conducted to determine the validity of claims for USSR (and free reading in general). The findings were mixed. Wilmot (1975) and Cline and Kretke (1980) reported significant gains in attitudes toward reading, an important finding given the high correlations between reading achievement and positive attitudes. In these studies, however, reading achievement scores did not reflect similar gains. Reasonable explanations were provided in each of these studies to explain the nonsignificant findings relative to achievement, including the insensitivity of standardized tests to general reading ability. Mikulecky and Wolf (1977a, 1977b) also reported no significant gains in either attitudes or achievement for students exposed to USSR over short periods of time (ten weeks); however, the duration of these studies was an obvious limitation. These findings did suggest that for USSR to be effective, extended exposure is needed; perhaps such an inference could have been stated more strongly had Mikulecky and Wolf continued their studies for longer periods to examine developmental shifts. Given that Sadoski (1980) and Salaman (1980) reported findings that corroborated the positive effects of USSR on adolescents' attitudes, it seems safe to conclude that USSR improves adolescents' attitudes toward reading but that no evidence exists to support claims that this strategy increases achievement or ability in reading. Perhaps researchers are overlooking a key variable—context—discussed further in the next section.

Instructional Context

Among the more prevalent limitations in secondary reading research is the tendency toward isolation of variables. Within the reading research literature and certainly within other chapters of this volume, increased attention has been given to the importance of instructional context (e.g., R. Anderson, et al., 1977; Carey, Harste, and S. Smith, 1981; Durkin, 1979; Rosenblatt, 1978). In a review of research on teaching reading comprehension, Tierney and Cunningham (1980) cited the failure of many researchers to identify the context in which instructional strategies were investigated and they identified this as a hindrance for generalized, or in some cases even specific, interpretations of results. Further, they emphasized the importance of knowing how classrooms function during reading instruction and the importance of determining what relationships exist between specific instructional strategies and the characteristics of the classrooms in which these strategies are used.

One study in particular, directed by Stallings (1979, 1980), was designed to address this matter directly. Through a series of sub studies, initiated in 1976 and still in progress, Stallings identified several variables within secondary reading classrooms which were highly correlated with improvement in adolescents' reading ability. Primary among these indices of success was frequent teacher-student interaction during instruction. Stallings found significantly greater overall improvement in reading proficiency in classrooms where teachers guided and directed students' reading as compared to classrooms where students were not engaged in interactive instruction. Of specific benefit were instances where teachers discussed selections with students and where teachers provided immediate feedback that was direct and explicit. Little improvement was found in classrooms where teachers spent most of their time apart from students (e.g., grading papers, writing reports) while students were completing work sheets or reading on their own.

These findings by Stallings seem to clarify the research related to SQ3R, DRTA, and USSR. The interactive strategy among these three is DRTA, and although the studies that support the effectiveness of DRTA have been conducted with elementary level readers, Stallings' findings support the hypothesis that similar studies with secondary level students will demonstrate equally conclusive results. Concurrently, investigations of three other frameworks for reading lessons that are also highly interactive in nature might also prove to be valuable strategies. These are the instructional framework (Herber, 1970, 1978), the bookthinking process (C. Smith, 1978), and the content reading lesson (Estes and Vaughan, 1978).

One might be tempted to place less credibility in SQ3R and USSR given the lack of supporting research and the absence of teacher-student interaction that characterizes these strategies. To do so, however, may be a mistake. Instead, increased attention should be given to the context of these strategies, both the context of their use and their inherent context. SQ3R and USSR have sound theoretical bases. Increased interaction between teacher and students could be incorporated into these strategies. For example, if USSR were used as part of a highly interactive classroom environment where guided activities (e.g., DRTA) were standard fare, USSR could become valuable "practice time" for students to increase proficiency with effective reading skills. The same issue of context applies to SQ3R; if it were taught in a highly interactive context where a teacher and students (individually or in small groups) discuss each part of the strategy after applying it and share reasons why it did or did not work, researchers might be able to identify its positive attributes and its less effective components.

The context within each of these strategies also deserves brief discussion. The prevailing theoretical perspective of reading is that the reader is an active agent who directs an interchange with a text (Estes, 1979; Goodman, 1979; Pearson and Kamil, 1978; Rosenblatt, 1978; Rumelhart, 1977). Consider then, this proposition: Adolescent readers who learn to use SQ3R actively in search of understandings of text will be in greater control of the process of reading. Further, during USSR sessions, students who realize the value of an active pursuit of meaning in text can use USSR occasions to practice active-oriented reading strategies. Metacognition researchers (e.g., Baker, 1979; Brown, Campione, and Day, 1981) have stated that successful, proficient readers are those who understand and control the interactive nature of reading. As researchers pursue validation of instructional strategies for adolescent readers, increased attention must be given to the context of their use and their potential for generating inter*action* between readers and text. Because a reader is exposed to SQ3R or USSR does not mean that strategies of reading are being used actively by the reader; thus, rather than discount these two activities, we need to explore them in far greater depth than we have to date.

Prereading Strategies

Among the more widely accepted and applied tenets of reading instruction is this: Prior knowledge is a significant determiner of what a reader will understand and remember from text. It is no surprise that effective teachers initiate reading lessons by seeking to heighten readers' awareness of relevant prior knowledge and that the prereading components of SQ3R and DRTA are among the most attractive features of these two strategies. The additional strategies which follow, designed as prereading activities, are often recommended to teachers.

Among the prereading strategies for which empirical findings are positive, one trait seems dominant; it is, again, the interaction between teachers and students. For example, Manzo's reciprocal questioning (ReQuest) technique (1969, 1970) engages a teacher and students in a series of questioning sessions following their reading each of the first several sentences of a selection. By heightening students' awareness of and interest in a selection, ReQuest stimulates an initial interaction between readers and text and establishes a foundation that readers can use as they continue to read the selection independently. Although research findings exist for ReQuest only with narrative selections, teachers' verification of its effectiveness with various forms of text abounds; empirical evidence of ReQuest's flexible effectiveness would seem desirable.

Langer's (1981, 1982) prereading plan (PReP) elicits readers' prior knowledge of key elements of a topic through word association tasks and subsequently leads the students to explore the depth and breadth of their awareness. PReP also includes a metacognitive dimension: the teacher asks students to identify how they happen to know what they know. Langer provides substantial empirical support for PReP, notably with expository text.

The structured overview (Herber, 1978; Vacca, 1981) is another widely recommended prereading strategy; however, support for its use in the context of prereading is limited at best. Interestingly, researchers seem convinced of its potential effectiveness but seem equally frustrated by the absence of positive findings. Moore and Readence (1980) and A. Smith (1978) provided insights into the problem with structured overviews as a prereading strategy. Smith remarked that "successful utilization of (structured) overview(s) may hinge on student participation in construction" (p. 78). In an historical review of this strategy, its originator, Barron (1979) cited student involvement as the primary determiner of its effectiveness and he clarified some of the procedures for its use. Brandt (1978) and Alvermann (1980) confirmed the importance of student involvement. Brandt's findings also suggested that organizational structure of text may be a confounding variable and that teachers who use structured overviews as a prereading strategy should sensitize students to text structure while preteaching concepts in relation to one another. From Alvermann's conclusions, one might be advised to focus discussion on top level, primary concepts rather than on secondary concepts during structured overview activities. In sum, the waters surrounding structured overview as a prereading strategy are murky; however, when factors such as student participation, text structure, and where to focus conceptual discussion are examined more thoroughly, researchers may resolve the confusion.

The strategies included in this section are primarily recommended for use with expository text; yet secondary reading teachers often express consternation, even frustration, over the difficulty that students seem to have comprehending fiction, especially short stories. Graves, Palmer, and Furniss (1976) and Graves (1981) described and validated a previewing strategy that facilitates adolescents' comprehension of difficult short stories. Although similar to Ausubel's (1960, 1978) advance organizer, Graves' previewing techniques differ from advance organizers "in that they provide specific information about a selection in addition to information written at higher levels of abstraction" (p. 39). Given the clearly supported value of these previews, teachers are encouraged to familiarize themselves with this strategy. (For a thorough discussion of this technique, see Graves and Cooke, 1980.)

Integrally related to prereading strategies is the issue of preteaching vocabulary. While it is widely acknowledged that vocabulary knowledge and reading comprehension are highly correlated (R. Anderson and Freebody, 1979; Davis, 1971), studies of efforts to improve comprehension by preteaching vocabulary have generally resulted in nonsignificant findings (e.g., Jenkins, Pany, and Schreck, 1978). In such studies, however, the instructional focus has been on the introduction of "new" or "difficult" words in isolation and/or in sentence context accompanied by discussion of definitions.

Estes and Vaughan (in press) and Johnson and Pearson (1978) suggested a modification whereby teachers focus discussion on concepts, initially in terms familiar to students, prior to presentation of the words themselves. Evans (1981) and Vaughan and Castle (1981) found that students comprehend more and retain meanings of new words better when the preteaching of vocabulary centers on a discussion of concepts in familiar contexts. Swaby (1977) and Graves and Bender (1980) consistently validated a procedure whereby new words are introduced in a paragraph that is rich in its elaboration of the meaning of that word and students then choose an appropriate synonym for the word itself. These approaches verify the usefulness of contextualizing vocabulary instruction by introducing new terms in a meaningful context. Thus, it seems, rather than initiating preteaching vocabulary activities with the new words themselves, teachers are likely to find better results if they reveal new terms *after* discussion or reveal the new terms in a context that clearly elaborates the concepts associated with the new terms.

Related to this conclusion, Barrett and Graves (1981) found that the teaching of content-area vocabulary in reading classes can substantially increase adolescents' reading ability and vocabulary proficiency when that vocabulary is taught through semantic categories that extend across content-area boundaries. This suggests that when students perceive vocabulary terms and their meanings in a context that is broader than a specific instance, it is more meaningful and more easily remembered. Thus vocabulary instruction research seems to indicate that a focus on concepts and meanings in familiar contexts is more profitable than a focus on words, especially in isolation.

Extensive reviews of research by Gaus (1978) and Hayes (1978) revealed no evidence to support the contention that adolescents generally benefit from instruction in word elements, or word analysis strategies such as phonics, syllabication, and structural analysis. One exception seemed to be prefixes. Students who learn to recognize prefixes and their meanings in words they already know seem to be able to use their knowledge of those prefixes with specific and constant meanings as a generative tool when they encounter new words containing those prefixes (Graves and Hammond, 1980; Nichol, 1980). While Ames (1966), Dulin (1968), and Quealy (1969) indicated that context clues are aids to adolescents' understanding unfamiliar words and that adolescents sometimes use context as a clue to meaning identification, there appears to be no empirical evidence to suggest that instruction in the use of specific context clues per se results in either improved ability to use such clues or an overall improved reading ability among adolescents.

Strategies during Reading

Like their counterparts at other levels, secondary reading teachers are often actively involved during their students' reading. They usually try to guide, direct, and otherwise facilitate students' comprehension. Stallings' (1979, 1980) research tended to support the value of such involvement during reading; however, the nature of the involvement is varied, and the empirical support for it seems mixed. For example, except for tentative, correlational, and perhaps over-generalized findings by Stallings, no evidence has been found to support the use of oral reading with adolescents to increase their comprehension or reading ability. Other types of activities, however, deserve consideration.

Herber (1970, 1978) advocated the use of study guides to increase readers' comprehension of given selections and, over a period of time, to increase adolescents' reading ability through experience with such guides. In some circumstances, study guides have proven effective as facilitators of passage-comprehension, especially when used with small-group, teacher-directed discussions (e.g., Estes, 1973; Vacca, 1977). Here again the role of teacher-student interaction is apparently a major factor. As with many other areas of secondary reading research, study guides require further investigation; subsequent studies are also likely to identify the context and the variables related to their greatest effectiveness.

Many sources can be identified that advocate the use of questioning as an aid to students' comprehension. In fact, Durkin (1979) reported that, to her dismay, much of what is purported to be reading comprehension instruction is actually questioning (testing) students about what they have read; hence, much of comprehension instruction is actually little more than comprehension testing. Guszak (1967) reported similar findings and noted that with rare exception teachers ask very detailed, literal questions with little regard for whether students actually understand the gist of what they have read. Extensive research has been conducted on the effects of questions (e.g., type, placement) on comprehension, and thorough reviews are available elsewhere (e.g., R. Anderson and Biddle, 1975; Rickards and Denner, 1978). While the findings consistently favor the use of questions inserted in text (adjunct questions) over prereading questions or postreading questions, only one study could be found to verify this with adolescent readers. Graves and Clark (1981) reported that the comprehension of low-achieving adolescent readers was significantly increased (relative to literal level questions—other question types were not examined) when these readers answered adjunct questions that were imbedded in the text immediately following the segments in which their answers were found. It seems that adjunct questions stimulate an interaction with text for readers who may not otherwise stop to reflect upon what they have read. Perhaps adolescents do benefit generally from the use of adjunct questions, as do college students, but that conclusion requires further scrutiny with varied types of text and nonliteral questions.

Postreading Strategies

The value of postreading review and reflection as an aid to memory is a widely recognized learning principle, and teachers who perceive reading as a learning process often encourage students to reinforce their understanding through follow-up activities. Several such strategies are considered here.

Postreading questioning is a frequently applied strategy to reinforce comprehension. After reviewing this technique, Tierney and Cunningham (1980) concluded that

> it is likely that teachers can facilitate learning by asking application type or inference questions based on such text derived information, assuming such facilitation is measured by a text which asks the same questions and assuming little time elapses between postquestioning and testing. (p. 37)

Continuing, however, these reviewers noted that very few researchers examined relationships among text-type (e.g., narrative, descriptive, expository) and postreading questioning strategies. Stallings (1979) found interactive discussion of questions to be positively correlated with adolescents' improvement in reading, but how this was related to or confounded by pertinent feedback is not yet clear. Apparently, more investigations are needed across all grade levels on this issue.

Although Manzo's (1975) guided reading procedure (GRP) is useful *during* reading, it primarily involves postreading activities and is, therefore, included here. When engaged in a GRP, students first "read to remember everything." Following the reading, students tell the teacher all they can remember as the teacher records the recall on a chalkboard. The teacher then guides the students in an outlining activity to model the process of organizing and associating concepts. While little research exists to either support or reject its effectiveness, Bean and Pardi (1979) confirmed the suspicions of some authorities that this strategy, as described, has greater effects when used in conjunction with prereading activities than when used alone.

Teacher questioning and GRP are representative activities that are intended to facilitate postreading recall, but to some they have the disadvantage of being teacher-dependent activities. As the reader knows from the emphasis in earlier chapters, increased attention is being given by reading researchers to student *inde-*

pendence in comprehension, reflection, and synthesis; specific instruction in the use of student-directed learning and study strategies seems to be more desirable than teacher-dependent activities.

Primary among student-directed and applied strategies is the graphic postorganizer. This activity is a reader-generated, structured overview. Either during reading or following reading, students arrange concepts graphically and relate concepts by drawing lines between those concepts that are somehow closely associated. In some sense, the graphic postorganizer functions like an outline, but many students seem to prefer the more vivid display and freer form offered by a graphic postorganizer. Barron and Stone (1974) and Moore and Readence (1980) clearly verified the effectiveness of student-generated graphic postorganizers as an activity that increases adolescents' reading comprehension.

Semantic mapping as advocated by Pearson and Johnson (1978) and Armbruster and T. Anderson (1980) is very similar to graphic postorganizers and what others, like Dansereau (1978), call networking. Semantic mapping requires that as concepts are graphically depicted, the specific relationship between concepts (e.g., temporal, causal) be delineated and incorporated into the graphic depiction. While semantic mapping has been effective with college students (Armbruster and T. Anderson, 1980), it has yet to be empirically verified with adolescents. Teachers would seem best advised at this time to rely on graphic postorganizers more than semantic mapping when working with adolescents, while keeping a watchful eye for verification of semantic mapping activities as refinements in protocols and procedures are made and field-tested.

Eanet (1978) reported that another postreading activity, REAP, significantly improved adolescents' comprehension. REAP is an acronym for read-encode-annotate-ponder. After reading a selection, students generate a written retelling. They then annotate their retelling to synthesize their understanding. REAP requires that students become adept at constructing various types of annotations and its value for a student is dependent upon the student's skill as an annotator and the ease with which a text lends itself to annotation. When students recognize these constraints, REAP appears to be an effective strategy for postreading synthesis.

Conclusion

It seems clear that research on instructional reading strategies in secondary schools is sparse at best. Graves and Clark (1981) pointed out the need for careful research focused on strategies used with secondary students:

> the vast majority of strategies currently being recommended to [secondary level] teachers lacks rigorous empirical validation. Moreover, . . . some of the practices which both common sense and reading authorities strongly suggest will work frequently do not work. (p. 8)

Graves and Clark added the logical and important concept for future researchers that strategies "advocated for secondary students [should] be tested with that population rather than being tested with college students and then used with secondary students" (p. 13).

References

Alvermann, D. E. Effects of graphic organizers, textual organization, and reading comprehension level on recall of expository prose (Doctoral dissertation, Syracuse University, 1980). *Dissertation Abstracts International*, 1981, *41*, 3963A–3964A. (University Microfilms No. 8104509)

Ames, W. S. The development of a classification scheme of contextual aids. *Reading Research Quarterly*, 1966, *2*, 57–82.

Anderson, R. C., and Biddle, W. B. On asking people questions about what they are reading. In G. H. Bower (Ed.), *The psychology of learning and motivation* (Vol. 9). New York: Academic Press, 1975.

Anderson, R. C., and Freebody, P. *Vocabulary knowledge* (Technical Report No. 136). Champaign: University of Illinois, Center for the Study of Reading, August 1979. (ERIC Document Reproduction Service No. ED 177 480; 71p.)

Anderson, R. C., Reynolds, R. E., Schallert, D. L., and Goetz, E. T. Frameworks for comprehending discourse. *American Educational Research Journal*, 1977, *14*, 367–381. (ERIC No. EJ 184 138)

Armbruster, B. B., and Anderson, T. H. *The effect of mapping on the free recall of expository text* (Technical Report No. 160). Champaign: University of Illinois, Center for the Study of Reading, February 1980 (ERIC Document Reproduction Service No. ED 182 735; 49p.)

Ausubel, D. P. The use of advance organizers in the learning and retention of meaningful verbal material. *Journal of Educational Psychology*, 1960, *51*, 267–272.

Ausubel, D. P. In defense of advance organizers: A reply to the critics. *Review of Educational Research*, 1978, *48*, 251–257. (ERIC No. EJ 189 544)

Baker, L. *Do I understand or do I not understand: That is the question* (Reading Education Report No. 10). Champaign: University of Illinois, Center for the Study of Reading, July 1979. (ERIC Document Reproduction Service No. ED 174 948; 27p.)

Baker, L., and Brown, A. L. *Metacognitive skills and reading* (Technical Report No. 188). Champaign: University of Illinois, Center for the Study of Reading, November 1980. (ERIC Document Reproduction Service No. ED 195 932; 74p.)

Barrett, M. T., and Graves, M. F. A vocabulary program for junior high school remedial readers. *Journal of Reading*, 1981, *25*, 146–150. (ERIC No. EJ 253 661)

Barron, R. F. Research for the classroom teacher: Recent developments on the structured overview as an advance organizer. In H. L. Herber and J. D. Riley (Eds.), *Research in reading in the content areas: The fourth report*. Syracuse, N.Y.: Syracuse University, Reading and Language Arts Center, 1979.

Barron, R. F., and Stone, V. F. The effect of student-constructed graphic post organizers upon learning vocabulary relationships. In P. L. Nacke (Ed.), *Interaction: Research and practice in college-adult reading* (Twenty-third Yearbook of the National Reading Conference). Clemson, S.C.: National Reading Conference, 1974.

Bean, T. W., and Pardi, R. A. A field test of a guided reading strategy. *Journal of Reading*, 1979, *23*, 144–147. (ERIC No. EJ 214 059)

Borass, H. A. A comparative study of the brief, the précis, and the essay with respect to speed of reading and ease of learning. *Journal of Educational Psychology*, 1938, *29*, 231–236.

Brandt, D. M. Prior knowledge of the author's schema and the comprehension of prose. Unpublished doctoral dissertation, Arizona State University, 1978. *Dissertation Abstracts International*, 1979, *39*, 5605A–5606A. (University Microfilms No. 79-11123)

Brown, A. L., Campione, J. C., and Day, J. D. Learning to learn: On training students to learn from text. *Educational Researcher*, 1981, *10*, 14–21. (ERIC No. EJ 241 605)

Carey, R. F., Harste, J. C., and Smith, S. L. Contextual constraints and discourse processes: A replication study. *Reading Research Quarterly*, 1981, *16*, 201–212. (ERIC No. EJ 240 384)

Cline, R., and Kretke, G. An evaluation of long-term SSR in the junior high school. *Journal of Reading*, 1980, *23*, 503–506. (ERIC No. EJ 222 578)

Dansereau, D. F. The development of a learning strategies curriculum. In H. F. O'Neil, Jr. (Ed.), *Learning Strategies*. New York: Academic Press, 1978.

Davis, F. Psychometric research in reading comprehension. In F. Davis (Ed.), *Literature of research in reading with emphasis upon models*. Brunswick, N.J.: Rutgers University Press, 1971.

Dulin, K. L. The role of contextual clues in the acquisition of specific reading vocabulary by mature readers (Doctoral dissertation, University of Washington, 1968). *Dissertation Abstracts International*, 1969, *29*, 2112A. (University Microfilms No. 69-01166)

Durkin, D. What classroom observations reveal about reading comprehension instruction. *Reading Research Quarterly*, 1979, *14*, 481–533. (ERIC No. EJ 206 147)

Eanet, M. G. An investigation of the REAP reading/study procedure: Its rationale and efficiency. In P. D. Pearson and J. Hansen (Eds.), *Reading discipline inquiry in process and practice* (Twenty-seventh Yearbook of the National Reading Conference). Clemson, S.C.: National Reading Conference, 1978.

Estes, T. H. Guiding reading in social studies. In H. L. Herber and R. F. Barron (Eds.), *Research in reading in the content areas: Second year report.* Syracuse, N.Y.: Syracuse University, Reading and Language Arts Center, 1973.

Estes, T. H. Congruence on philosophy and pedagogy of reading. In J. L. Vaughan and P. L. Anders (Eds.), *Research on reading in secondary schools: A semi-annual report* (Monograph No. 4). Tucson: University of Arizona, 1979. (ERIC Document Reproduction Service No. ED 191 004; 82p.)

Estes, T. H., and Vaughan, J. L. *Reading and learning in the content classroom.* Boston: Allyn and Bacon, 1978.

Estes, T. H., and Vaughan, J. L. *Reading and learning in the content classroom* (2nd ed.). Boston: Allyn and Bacon, in press.

Evans, B. *Effects of pre-teaching key vocabulary and the proposition type of story on retention.* Paper presented at Secondary Reading Research Symposium, National Reading Conference, Dallas, 1981.

Gaus, P. J. Word analysis in context: Facts and superstitions. In J. L. Vaughan and P. J. Gaus (Eds.), *Research on reading in secondary schools: A semi-annual report* (Monograph No. 1). Tucson: University of Arizona, 1978. (ERIC Document Reproduction Service No. ED 177 509; 56p.)

Goodman, K. S. The know-more and the know-nothing movements in reading: A personal response. *Language Arts,* 1979, *56,* 657-663. (ERIC No. EJ 209 259)

Graves, M. F. *Previewing difficult short stories.* Paper in preparation, 1981. (Available from the author, College of Education, University of Minnesota, Minneapolis, MN 55455)

Graves, M. F., and Bender, S. D. Preteaching vocabulary to secondary students: A classroom experiment. *Minnesota English Journal,* 1980, *10,* 27-34.

Graves, M. F., and Clark, D. L. The effect of adjunct questions on high school low achievers' reading comprehension. *Reading Improvement,* 1981, *18,* 8-13.

Graves, M. F., and Cooke, C. L. Effects of previewing difficult short stories for high school students. In P. L. Anders (Ed.), *Research on reading in secondary schools: A semi-annual report* (Monograph No. 6). Tucson: University of Arizona, 1980. (ERIC Document Reproduction Service No. ED 203 286; 99p.)

Graves, M. F., and Hammond, H. K. A validated procedure for teaching prefixes and its effect on students' ability to assign meaning to novel words. In M. L. Kamil and A. J. Moe (Eds.), *Perspectives on reading research and instruction* (Twenty-ninth Yearbook of the National Reading Conference). Washington, D.C.: National Reading Conference, 1980.

Graves, M. F., Palmer, R. J., and Furniss, D. W. *Structuring reading activities for English classes.* Urbana, Ill.: National Council of Teachers of English, 1976. (ERIC Document Reproduction Service No. ED 128 784; 36p.)

Guszak, F. J. Teacher questioning and reading. *The Reading Teacher*, 1967, *21*, 227–234.

Hayes, D. Teaching extracontextual word analysis in the secondary grades: A review of the research literature. In J. L. Vaughan and P. J. Gaus (Eds.), *Research on reading in secondary schools: A semi-annual report* (Monograph No. 1). Tucson: University of Arizona, 1978. (ERIC Document Reproduction Service. No. ED 177 509; 56p.)

Herber, H. L. *Teaching reading in the content areas.* Englewood Cliffs, N.J.: Prentice-Hall, 1970.

Herber, H. L. *Teaching reading in the content areas* (2nd ed.). Englewood Cliffs, N.J.: Prentice-Hall, 1978.

Jenkins, J. R., Pany, D., and Schreck, J. *Vocabulary and reading comprehension: Instructional effects* (Technical Report No. 100). Champaign: University of Illinois, Center for the Study of Reading, August 1978. (ERIC Document Reproduction Service No. ED 160 999; 50p.)

Johns, J. L., and McNamara, L. P. The SQ3R study technique: A forgotten research target. *Journal of Reading*, 1980, *23*, 705–708. (ERIC No. EJ 227 607)

Johnson, D. D., and Pearson, P. D. *Teaching reading vocabulary.* New York: Holt, Rinehart and Winston, 1978.

Langer, J. A. From theory to practice: A prereading plan. *Journal of Reading*, 1981, *25*, 152–156. (ERIC No. EJ 253 662)

Langer, J. A. Facilitating text processing: The elaboration of prior knowledge. In J.A. Langer and M. Smith-Burke (Eds.), *Reader meets author/bridging the gap: A psycholinguistic and sociolinguistic perspective.* Newark, Del.: International Reading Association, 1982. (ERIC Clearinghouse Accession No. CS 006 710)

Manzo, A. V. The ReQuest procedure. *Journal of Reading*, 1969, *13*, 123–126. (ERIC No. EJ 011 534)

Manzo, A. V. Reading and questioning: The ReQuest procedure. *Reading Improvement*, 1970, *7*, 80–83. (ERIC No. EJ 031 491)

Manzo, A. V. Guided reading procedure. *Journal of Reading*, 1975, *18*, 287–291. (ERIC No. EJ 110 648)

Mikulecky, L., and Wolf, A. The effect of uninterrupted sustained silent reading and of reading games on changes in secondary students' reading attitudes. In P. E. Pearson (Ed.), *Reading: Theory, research and practice* (Twenty-sixth Yearbook of the National Reading Conference). Clemson, S.C.: National Reading Conference, 1977.(a)

Mikulecky, L., and Wolf, A. *Effects of uninterrupted silent reading and of reading skills instruction on changes in secondary students' reading attitudes and achievement.* Paper presented at the National Reading Conference, New Orleans, December 1977.(b)

Moore, D. W., and Readence, J. E. A meta-analysis of the effect of graphic organizers on learning from text. In M. L. Kamil and A. J.

Moe (Eds.), *Perspectives on reading research and instruction* (Twenty-ninth Yearbook of the National Reading Conference). Washington, D.C.: National Reading Conference, 1980.

Nichol, J. A. *Effect of prefix instruction on students' vocabulary size.* Unpublished master's thesis, University of Minnesota, 1980.

Pearson, P. D., and Johnson, D. D. *Teaching reading comprehension.* New York: Holt, Rinehart and Winston, 1978.

Pearson, P. D., and Kamil, M. L. *Basic processes and instructional practices in teaching reading* (Reading Education Report No. 7). Champaign: University of Illinois, Center for the Study of Reading, December 1978. (ERIC Document Reproduction Service No. ED 165 118; 29p.)

Quealy, R. J. Senior high school students use of contextual aids in reading. *Reading Research Quarterly*, 1969, *4*, 514–553. (ERIC No. EJ 008 380)

Rickards, J. P., and Denner, P. R. Inserted questions as aids to reading text. *Instructional Science*, 1978, *7*, 313–346.

Robinson, F. P. *Diagnostic and remedial techniques for effective study.* New York: Harper and Bros., 1941.

Robinson, F. P. *Effective study.* New York: Harper and Bros., 1946.

Robinson, F. P. *Effective study.* (3rd ed.). New York: Harper and Row, 1961.

Robinson, F. P. *Effective study* (4th ed.). New York: Harper and Row, 1970.

Rosenblatt, L. M. *The reader, the text, the poem.* Carbondale: Southern Illinois University Press, 1978.

Rumelhart, D. E. Toward an interactive model of reading. In S. Dornic (Ed.), *Attention and performance* (Vol. 6). Hillsdale, N.J.: Lawrence Erlbaum, 1977.

Sadoski, M. C. An attitudinal survey for sustained silent reading programs. *Journal of Reading*, 1980, *25*, 721–726. (ERIC No. EJ 227 610)

Salaman, S. K. The effectiveness of sustained silent reading at the secondary level. In P. L. Anders (Ed.), *Research on reading in secondary schools: A semi-annual report* (Monograph No. 6). Tucson: University of Arizona, 1980. (ERIC Document Reproduction Service No. ED 203 286; 99p.)

Smith, A. L. The structured overview: A prereading strategy. In J. L. Vaughan and P. J. Gaus (Eds.), *Research on reading in secondary schools: A semi-annual report* (Monograph No. 2). Tucson: University of Arizona, 1978. (ERIC Document Reproduction Service No. ED 177 510; 87p.)

Smith, C. B. *Teaching reading in secondary school content subjects.* New York: Holt, Rinehart and Winston, 1978.

Spencer, F. SQ3R: Several queries regarding relevant research. In J. L. Vaughan and P. J. Gaus (Eds.), *Research on reading in secondary schools: A semi-annual report* (Monograph No. 2). Tucson: University of Arizona, 1978. (ERIC Document Reproduction Service No. ED 177 510; 87p.)

Stallings, J. A. How to change the process of teaching reading in secondary schools. *Educational Horizons*, 1979, *57*, 196–201. (ERIC No. EJ 219 056)

Stallings, J. A. *The process of teaching basic reading skills in secondary schools.* Report submitted to National Institute of Education, December 1980. (ERIC Document Reproduction Service Nos. ED 210 669, 186p.; ED 210 670, 279p.; ED 210 671, 30p.)

Stauffer, R. G. *Teaching reading as a thinking process.* New York: Harper and Row, 1969.

Stauffer, R. G. *Directing the reading thinking process.* New York: Harper and Row, 1975.

Stauffer, R. G. *Action research in language-experience approach instructional procedures.* Newark: University of Delaware, 1976.

Stauffer, R. G. *The language-experience approach to the teaching of reading* (2nd ed.). New York: Harper and Row, 1980.

Swaby, B. E. R. The effects of advance organizers and vocabulary instruction on the reading comprehension of sixth grade students (Doctoral dissertation, University of Minnesota, 1977). *Dissertation Abstracts International*, 1978, *39*, 115A. (University Microfilms No. 7809754)

Tierney, R. J., and Cunningham, J. W. *Research on teaching reading comprehension* (Technical Report No. 187). Champaign: University of Illinois, Center for the Study of Reading, November 1980. (ERIC Document Reproduction Service No. ED 195 946; 125p.)

Tierney, R. J., Readence, J. E., and Dishner, E. K. *Reading strategies and practices.* Boston: Allyn and Bacon, 1980.

Vacca, R. T. An investigation of a functional reading strategy in seventh grade social studies. In H. L. Herber and R. T. Vacca (Eds.), *Research in reading in the content areas: The third report.* Syracuse, N.Y.: Syracuse University, Reading and Language Arts Center, 1977.

Vacca, R. T. *Content area reading.* Boston: Little, Brown, 1981.

Vaughan, J. L. Research and reading in secondary schools. In J. L. Vaughan and P. J. Gaus (Eds.), *Research on reading in secondary schools: A semi-annual report* (Monograph No. 2). Tucson: University of Arizona, 1978. (ERIC Document Reproduction Service No. ED 177 510; 87p.)

Vaughan, J. L., and Castle, G. *Focusing on concepts as a means of preteaching vocabulary and its effects on comprehension across several conceptual levels.* Paper presented at Secondary Reading Research Symposium, National Reading Conference, Dallas, 1981.

Wark, D. M. Survey SQ3R: System or superstition. *Third and fourth annual yearbook, North Central Reading Association.* Minneapolis: University of Minnesota, 1964.

Willmore, D. J. A comparison of four methods of studying a college textbook (Doctoral dissertation, University of Minnesota, 1967). *Dissertation Abstracts International*, 1967, *27*, 2413A–2414A. (University Microfilms No. 6700888)

Wilmot, M. An investigation of the effect upon the reading performance
    and attitude toward reading of elementary grade students, of includ-
    ing in the reading program a period of sustained, silent reading
    (Doctoral dissertation, University of Colorado, 1975). *Dissertation
    Abstracts International*, 1976, *36*, 5029A-5030A. (University Micro-
    films No. 76-03968)

Wooster, G. F. Teaching the SQ3R method of study: An investigation of
    the instructonal approach (Doctoral dissertation, The Ohio State
    University, 1953). *Dissertation Abstracts International*, 1958-59, *19*,
    2067A-2068A. (University Microfilms No. 58-00777)

6 The Nature and Structure of Text

Thomas H. Estes
University of Virginia

The answer to the clever question forming the title of Wanner's (1973) article, "Do we understand sentences from the outside-in or from the inside-out?" is "Yes." What's inside the reader (knowledge, beliefs, attitudes, etc.) interacts with what's outside the reader (the printed words, illustrations, figures, etc.) in infinitely complicated ways. What readers understand *is* meaning, and meaning

> will emerge from a network of relationships among the things symbolized *as the reader senses them.* . . . The selection and organization of responses to some degree hinge on the assumptions, the expectations, or sense of possible structures, that he brings out of the stream of his life. Thus built into the raw material of the literary process itself is the particular world of the reader. (Rosenblatt, 1978, p. 11)

Rosenblatt took a phenomenological view of text, a view which posits text as neither a simple reality (words on a page) nor an ideal entity (ideas of a reader) but an active interaction. This is the first thing to understand about the nature of text; it implies that the structure of text inheres in this interaction—the text *as the reader realizes it.*

One insight of the last few years concerning the relationship between textual properties and comprehension is that the "grammar" of narration seems to correspond to "rules" of thought and action familiar to most children by school age. Children enter school familiar with courses of human events; they know that events and responses comprise episodes which lead to plans, actions, and consequences. These "rules," tacitly and naturally understood, are congruent with the way simple stories are typically structured, so even very young readers approach text with "assumptions, expectations, and a sense of possible structures":

> Once upon a time (the setting, long ago), there was a king who wished his daughter to marry the bravest suitor in the land (an event, wishing something). He declared a day of feasts and contests (a response, involving a plan, actions, and eventual consequences).

Researchers responsible for recognizing this congruence include Rumelhart (1975; 1977), Meyer (1975), and Frederickson (1975). However, as Calfee and Curley (1982) pointed out, most work to date on the issue of text structure and comprehension has been limited to the understanding of brief, simple narrative and exposition. The applicability of this line of research in attempts to understand more complicated text encountered by older students remains problematical. In part, the reason for this is that the "grammars" of these texts, the rules governing their structure, are much more difficult to specify than those of simpler texts. Whatever they are (if, indeed, they even exist as such), these rules are undoubtedly not like the modes of thought familiar to unsophisticated readers.

Olson (1977) elaborated this last point in some detail, taking a rather pessimistic view of the effects of allowing the explicit prose of textbooks to dictate the kinds of thinking necessary to acquire an education. Olson went so far as to say,

> The means has become the end. The acquisition of knowledge has become nothing other than the construction of a particular view of reality appropriate to the requirements of explicit logical text. (p. 86)

In other words, textbooks represent a particular mode of communication which determines a kind of view of reality. Specifically, that view is "divorced from practical action" and "represented in terms of linguistic symbols" (p. 65). Olson concluded that

> to take explicit written prose (of textbooks, for example) as the model of language, knowledge, and intelligence has narrowed the conception of all three, down grading the more general (and inherently familiar) functions of ordinary language and common sense knowledge. (p. 75)

Be that as it may, there is no denying the importance of meeting the "requirements of explicit logical text" if a student is to succeed in school. To do so will require more than an intuited familiarity with the structure of simple stories.

Most attempts to describe the typical structures of exposition have unfortunately oversimplified matters to the verge of ridiculousness. As Calfee and Curley (1982) noted, there is no generally agreed-upon taxonomy of prose structures. Thus, practitioners and researchers have tended to go in numerous directions leading nowhere in particular. For example, it now seems naive to talk about contrast, comparison, cause/effect, and so on, as if they were unifying patterns which might differentiate texts and which might be taught to readers. [I don't mean to indict anyone but myself here—see Estes and Vaughan (1978) in which we talk about study guides focused on patterns of organization.] We need now to abandon the attempt to find simple descriptions of what are essentially and necessarily very complex matters—the structures of texts. There is another way to look at the problem: by asking not what the structure is, but how well text is structured; by asking not whether students can see the structure in text, but whether they can realize structures for texts.

The Reader and the Text

It is in the nature of text that its organization is in the mind of the reader as much as on the page. Within limits governed by the text, readers organize what they read, or should do so, in the very process of comprehending it. Texts vary in their susceptibility to comprehension so far as they lend themselves to "realization" by readers. The structure of a text is something readers perceive; this perception is governed simultaneously by characteristics of readers and features of text.

The best way to see how and why the structure of text is a perceived property is to assume the perspective of schema theory (discussed in chapter 4, above). Schema is the currently most popular metaphor for the acquisition and use of knowledge. It has limitless implications for how the "structure" of an individual's knowledge might interact with the "structure" of a text to result in understanding.

It seems useful to combine notions of schema theory with perceptual theory, especially as advanced by Neisser (1976). During the process of reading, the schemata of the reader direct the reader to sample the text with the effect of modifying the schemata. This happens in whatever time intervals reading occurs, depending on what text segments interest the reader. At the level of letters, for example, the reader sees portions from which to infer wholes, and at the level of word, phrase, sentence, paragraph, chapter, section, and whole work, the experience is similar. Reading as sampling is not a new idea [see Goodman (1967), the now widely read article on reading as a psycholinguistic guessing game]. But what determines what is sampled? In major part, it is the reader's schema: what the reader knows or believes, the reader's attitude toward it, and the reader's general and specific inclinations. And what is sampled? Clearly, what is sampled is the structure of the unit: of the letter (from "r" it is easy to infer "p"); of the word (from "read" it is easy to predict "read"); of the sentence (from "Once up . . ." it is easy to predict "Once upon a time"). In stories, experienced readers know settings will be described, problems will arise, solutions will be attempted (two or three will fail), and a resolution will be found. Their explorations of stories will sample enough of the text to enable them to fill in the rest. The bigger the unit the reader can deal with, the more efficient the reading; where the reader is able to use most of his or her energy at the level of what Kintsch (1974) calls macrostructure, reading will be most successful and satisfying. This means that the text whose structure is most apprehensible or realizable is the one which readers have the best chance of understanding.

Structures of Expository Prose

We almost universally use stories to teach people to read because their structures are easily perceived, their scripts are easy to follow. Problems often arise, though, when young readers encounter textbooks. The schemata of the young reader seem insufficient to provide the necessary direction for the reading. In one part, the young reader may lack the necessary background of knowledge, attitude, and inclination for the topic. But, in another part, the young reader may find the text difficult to predict at a structural level. The structure of textbooks is often difficult to perceive and realize especially if the reader is fairly unsophisticated about a given topic. Ironically, it is this lack of sophistication which leads to the assignment of the reading in the first place.

Anderson, Armbruster, and Kantor (1980) and Armbruster and Anderson (in press) examined the structure of samples of expository prose from textbooks of various subject areas at various grade levels. They chose the rhetorical desiderata of structure, coherence, unity, and appropriateness as the basis of their analyses. Their main assumption was that to understand is to perceive a relationship between what is known and what is being learned. Their main conclusions were that textbooks tend to be "organized" around misleading titles and subtitles, that they obscure their main ideas, omit crucial information, lack coherence, contain contradictory information, and are logically inconsistent and ambiguous. If these researchers were not overstating their case, it is a wonder that students *ever* understand their textbooks. When they do, it is seemingly *in spite of* the structure of what they are reading.

Anderson, Armbruster, and Kantor were, however, asking only half the question of text structure. It is significant that they remind us to question not what the structure is but how well text is structured. Furthermore, we can ask how features of text interact with characteristics of readers to result in a better or worse realization of text. In a research project at the University of Virginia, we have begun to take that step.

To quantify the perceived structure of text (the text which readers realize), we used four interrelated measures. [These have been described elsewhere (cf. Estes and Shebilske, 1980), but they are summarized here in order to present some additional activities and results.] One, we asked readers to divide text selections into idea units, to tell us where they thought each idea began and ended, and we analyzed these markings to determine normative units of text. [See Rotondo (1980) for a detailed description of our procedures.] Two, we asked readers to rate the importance of these units with respect to what they saw as the author's main points. From this, we derived an importance rating for each normative unit. Third, we asked readers to rate the familiarity of each unit. Fourth, we asked readers to read the text passages and to record immediately everything they could recall from their reading. Sometimes different groups performed these tasks for us, and other times the same readers performed two or more of the tasks. The result was a picture of several texts as readers perceive them; and we now have methods for deriving similar pictures for other texts. In sum, we have defined structure as something readers perceive or don't perceive in text in terms of the ideas a text contains, the relative importance and familiarity of those ideas, and the likelihood of the recall of those ideas after reading the text.

Two of our interesting findings were that the best predictor of recall is familiarity with an idea (that's not news), but there is only a moderate relationship between an idea's importance and the likelihood of its recall (that's bad news). We asked ourselves, therefore, how it could be that readers might on the one hand see an idea as important and fail to recall that idea following a reading of the text. The correlation we found in this case was consistently just under +0.40 which didn't seem high enough.

When we looked closely, we could see that there were several highly important idea units which were recalled by only a small portion of our readers and there were several meaning units of relatively low importance which were recalled by a disconcertingly high proportion of readers. When these problematic units were reviewed aside from the rest of the text, a curious (but now we find, rather widespread) pattern of characteristics emerged. Important but poorly recalled ideas were often extremely dense, containing much information in few words. For example, consider the density of this sentence: "A species is a population of individuals that are more or less alike and that interbreed and produce fertile offspring under natural conditions." Also, important principles were often never explicitly stated or were not given sufficient emphasis. Some examples were inconsistent or unrepresentative of the principles stated. The striking similarity among unimportant but frequently recalled ideas was the absurd or vivid examples they contained. Consider this passage:

> Alaska brown bears and polar bears ... in the Washington Zoo have successfully mated and produced vigorous, fertile offspring. However, in the wild no such cross has ever been discovered. The reason? Brown bears live in forests, eating berries, small animals, and fish they catch in streams. Polar bears live on snowfields and ice floes, catching seals for food. Thus brown bears and polar bears rarely, if ever, see each other—except in zoos.

And what do readers recall of that? Mainly that polar bears live on ice floes, catching seals for food but brown bears live in forests, eating berries. Very few of our readers recalled the notion of geographic isolation as a contributing factor in the maintenance of species differentiation.

Wetmore (1980) described characteristics of a textbook she analyzed and reported results of a study to see what might be done to the text to correct the anomalies in it. The problem with this text, and with many other textbooks, is that it is not particularly well structured to facilitate the reader-text interaction necessary to comprehension. When Wetmore restructured this text, she was able dramatically to affect its potential understandability. She tried deliberately not to create a new text, which of course is the temptation, but to take the conservative route of just trying to make clearer what the text might potentially mean. The gist of each idea was unchanged and the order of the meaning units was kept the same. These were the principles of rewrite that Wetmore formulated:

1. Write unimportant ideas as briefly as possible, avoiding the use of vivid examples
2. Tighten the relationship between examples and important ideas
3. Turn negative statements of important principles into positive ones
4. Enumerate important points
5. Attach semantic labels to important concepts
6. Underline technical terms
7. Indicate straw-men

The result of this rewriting was an increase in total number of ideas recalled, in number of important ideas recalled, and in the correlation between the importance of an idea and the likelihood of its recall.

Reder and Anderson (1980) conducted a similar study in which they constructed summaries of passages to convey the main points and eliminate peripheral detail. They found that summaries produced better understanding than did the passage in its original form. But if Wetmore (1981) is right, such radical restructuring of text may not be necessary or appropriate. Her findings indicated that rewriting is superior to summarizing as a means of making the ideas of text more apprehensible.

If it is true, as schema theory, perceptual theory, and phenomenology suggest, that understanding is a result of an interaction between the structure of thinking and the structure of what is to be understood, then to make understanding more likely, one must modify one or the other or both of these structures. The work of Ausubel and others, like Bruner, in the 1960s was concerned with modifying the structure of thinking. The results were promising; the clear implication was that where higher order (today we would say macrostructural) propositions in the thinking of an individual could be established or clarified, learning could be enhanced (Ausubel, 1968). But to date there seems to have prevailed a common assumption that texts, often the vehicle for what is to be understood, are as well constructed as they might reasonably be expected to be. This is open to question.

Our preliminary analysis of several textbooks in addition to the one studied by Wetmore leads us toward confirmation of our worst suspicions: stories tend to be well structured and apprehensible, though this is not to say all stories are easy to understand. The opening pages of *The Sound and the Fury*, Faulkner's masterpiece, are difficult to follow. However, a writer like Faulkner is consistent, not contradictory; he is coherent despite complication, and the structure of his writing is masterfully crafted. Textbooks, by contrast, are far from being masterpieces of literary quality. Why shouldn't we hold textbook authors responsible for at least the rudiments of rhetorical quality?

Guidelines for Readability

To combine the elements of our perceived structure analysis with basic rhetorical desiderata similar to those used by Anderson, Armbruster, and Kantor (1980), we formulated the following guidelines. We hope that as we refine our procedures we will be creating a new perspective on readability which is able to take into account the nature and structure of text.

Try this procedure on a textbook selection of 3,000 words or less, to keep things manageable. The goal is to determine how many ideas readers see in the text, what those ideas are, what the relative perceived importance of the ideas is, how familiar the ideas are, and how well the ideas are structured as text. The result will be a shared perspective between teacher and students regarding the "demands of explicit logical text."

To begin, ask students to read through the selection one time. Following this, instruct students to place lightly-penciled slash marks in the selection wherever they think one idea ends and another begins. Don't try to define what an idea is—that's what you're asking the readers to do. (It is possible to do this and, following steps by yourself, use your own perceptions in the analyses. This works well if you don't assume what you see will be what students would see necessarily. Differences between your own and the perceptions of students are part of the problem which text poses for students.)

Determining how many ideas are in the text and what those ideas are is a two-step procedure. There is, of course, no way to know how many ideas a text has; the question itself really doesn't make sense if you think the answer depends on individual reader's perceptions. The best way we've found around this problem is to compute the average number of ideas readers have seen and to use that as a working figure. Have students count how many slash marks they used and add one to count for the end of the last idea unit. Average all the numbers the students arrive at.

To determine which are "the" ideas (and we use quotes to suggest that this count too reduces individual perceptions to something admittedly consensual but manageable), count by a show of hands the number of students who chose each possible break between ideas. Virtually any space between words is a possible break between ideas, though of course a relatively small number of those will be chosen. You'll find this count easiest to take with an overhead projector and a transparency copy of the text. Simply insert the number of students opting for the choice at each point in the text seen as a break between ideas. Then, as the last step in determining "the" ideas, count the most frequently chosen break as one, the next most frequently chosen as two, and so on through the break which equals the average number of breaks chosen. Incidentally, there will be some points in text where only a word or two separates slash marks. It will probably be reasonable to count these as a single mark. For instance, it really makes little difference whether a mark occurs before or after a conjunction or some other cohesive element.

Now students can re-mark their own text in accord with the composite picture the group obtained, erasing their previous marks. What they and you will now see is how the students generally saw the reading selection, how they "read" it. With this picture before them, you can now ask students to do two things which will tell you and them much about the comprehensibility of the text selection.

First, have the students rate each idea unit on a scale of one to seven with regard to how important they think it is to the author's message and intent, where seven means the idea is very important and one means it is very unimportant. Then each student can pick out the five or so most important ideas and the five or so least important ideas. The number will depend on how long the selection is and how many ideas the students have seen. The discussion about why some ideas are important and others relatively less so will tell you much about the comprehensibility of the text.

Second, have the students again rate each idea unit on a scale of one to seven, this time with regard to whether they think the idea is familiar or unfamiliar, where a rating of one means the idea is very familiar and a rating of seven means the idea is very unfamiliar. Text which is comprehensible usually contains mostly familiar material; what is new is the way the ideas are interrelated. In contrast, text which is incomprehensible will usually contain too much new, or unfamiliar, material. It will require more effort to comprehend than most readers are able or willing to bring to bear. When students count up how many ideas have a familiarity rating of six or seven and how many have a rating of one or two, they will have a good estimate not only of how comprehensible the text is but also of how much effort and help will be required to understand it. This should be interesting to both you and them, and one of the best things about it is you will have come to some important insights together.

Conclusion

The text does play a role in its own comprehensibility and as a complement to the perceived structure analysis just completed, it is useful to examine the text with respect to desirable rhetorical features. Diverging somewhat from Anderson, Armbruster, and Kantor (1980), we analyzed texts on the basis of classic compositional qualities (Brooks and Warren, 1949/1979): namely, unity, coherence, and emphasis. Looking at textbooks section by section, and idea unit by idea unit, we asked three questions. (1) Do the ideas all obviously relate to the subject of the selection? This is the question of unity. Often we find that two or three issues will be raised in a section or that a section may be unified in its own contents but not clearly related to the topic of the chapter of which it is a part. (2) Are the ideas organized to give *continuous development* to the subject? This is the question of coherence. Often ideas will arise in text which are quite irrelevant and disconcerting. The effect is to get the reader off the subject. (Remember those brown bears eating berries.) (3) Does the text emphasize what it should, given the topic? Emphasis is achieved by flat direct statement; by position, in that things mentioned first or last are usually interpreted to be important; and by proportion, in that most important ideas should get the most press, so to speak. This is perhaps the worst problem with textbooks, particularly those written in an inductive style where what things are about is never made clear. Often main ideas are buried in irrelevancy or left to inference.

Textbooks might, it would seem, try to say what they mean. It is, after all, in the nature of exposition to do so. Unfortunately, they don't always do so for the people who are assigned to read them.

References

Anderson, T. H., Armbruster, B. B., and Kantor, R. N. *How clearly written are children's textbooks? Or, of bladderworts and alfa* (Reading Education Report No. 15). Champaign: University of Illinois, Center for the Study of Reading, August 1980. (ERIC Document Reproduction Service No. ED 192 275; 63p.)

Armbruster, B. B., and Anderson, T. H. *Problems/solution explanation in history textbooks, or So what if Governor Stanford missed the spike and hit the rail?* In press.

Ausubel, D. P. *Educational psychology: A cognitive view.* New York: Holt, Rinehart and Winston, 1968.

Brooks, C., and Warren, R. P. *Modern Rhetoric.* New York: Harcourt Brace Jovanovich, 1949/1979.

Calfee, R., and Curley, R. Structures of prose in the content areas. In J. Flood (Ed.), *Understanding reading comprehension.* Book in preparation, 1982.

Estes, T. H., and Shebilske, W. L. Comprehension: Of what the reader sees of what the author says. In M. L. Kamil and A. J. Moe (Eds.), *Perspectives on reading research and instruction* (Twenty-ninth Yearbook of the National Reading Conference). Washington, D.C.: National Reading Conference, 1980.

Estes, T. H., and Vaughan, J. L. *Reading and learning in the content classroom.* Boston: Allyn and Bacon, 1978.

Fredericksen, C. H. Representing logical and semantic structures of knowledge acquired from discourse. *Cognitive Psychology,* 1975, *1,* 371–458.

Goodman, K. S. Reading: A psycholinguistic guessing game. *Journal of the Reading Specialist,* 1967, *4,* 126–135.

Kintsch, W. *The representation of meaning in memory.* Hillsdale, N.J.: Lawrence Erlbaum, 1974.

Meyer, B. J. F. *The organization of prose and its effect on memory.* Amsterdam: North-Holland, 1975.

Neisser, U. *Cognition and reality.* San Francisco: W. H. Freeman, 1976.

Olson, D. R. The languages of instruction: On the literate bias of schooling. In R. C. Anderson, R. J. Spiro, and W. E. Montague (Eds.), *Schooling and the acquisition of knowledge.* Hillsdale, N.J.: Lawrence Erlbaum, 1977.

Reder, L. M., and Anderson, J. R. A comparison of texts and their summaries: Memorial consequences. *Journal of Verbal Learning and Verbal Behavior,* 1980, *19,* 121–134.

Rosenblatt, L. *The reader, the text, the poem.* Carbondale: Southern Illinois University Press, 1978.

Rotondo, J. A. *Clustering analysis of subjective partitions of text.* Unpublished manuscript, 1980. (Available from Thomas H. Estes, School of Education, University of Virginia, Charlottesville, VA 22903)

Rumelhart, D. E. Notes on a schema for stories. In D. Bobrown and A. Collins (Eds.), *Representation and understanding: Studies in cognitive science.* New York: Academic Press, 1975.

Rumelhart, D. E. Understanding and summarizing brief stories. In D. LaBerge and S. J. Samuels (Eds.), *Basic processes in reading: Perception and comprehension.* Hillsdale, N.J.: Lawrence Erlbaum, 1977.

Rumelhart, D. E. Schemata: The building blocks of cognition. In R. J. Spiro, B. C. Bruce, and W. F. Brewer (Eds.), *Theoretical issues in reading comprehension.* Hillsdale, N.J.: Lawrence Erlbaum, 1980.

Wanner, E. Do we understand sentences from the outside-in or from the inside-out? In E. Haugen and M. Bloomfield (Eds.), *Language as a human problem.* New York: W. W. Norton, 1973. (Also in *Daedalus,* 1973, *102,* 164.)

Wetmore, M. E. *Improving the comprehensibility of text.* Paper presented at the meeting of the National Reading Conference, San Diego, December 1980.

Wetmore, M. E. *Restructuring text to improve comprehensibility.* Manuscript submitted for publication, 1981. (Available from M. E. Wetmore, Reading Center, School of Education, University of Virginia, Charlottesville, VA 22903)

7 Learning from Text

Robert J. Tierney
Harvard University

Earlier chapters have provided the reader with a picture of the settings for reading, the characteristics of readers, the reading process, some instructional strategies, and the nature and structure of text. In this chapter advantage is taken of all the previous information as a backdrop for its essence: helping students to self-regulate their learning as they attempt to learn from text independently.

The critical question for teachers is: Can students be taught or be made aware of knowledge and strategies which will transfer to their reading of passages when they are reading or studying on their own—without the presence or assistance of the teacher? Based upon what we know about learning and the current state of teaching, we should not assume either that transfer is happening or that it will just happen. The research of Brown, Campione, and Day (1981) suggests that a great deal of thought and effort needs to go into what and how instruction must proceed if it is to have such an impact. The research of Schallert and Tierney (1982) indicated that there is very little effective independent learning from text occurring in most secondary subject matter classrooms. An analysis of secondary students' reading behaviors and text-based difficulties (Tierney, LaZansky, and Schallert, 1982; Schallert and Tierney, 1982) indicated that students are having difficulty with text beyond what might be adjusted simply by text engineering, readability mandates, or modifying instruction. The solution to the problem—deciding what should be taught and how—is not simple.

The development of self-monitoring abilities is fundamental. As Brown, Campione, and Day (1981) suggested:

> What we are advocating is an avoidance of blind training techniques and a serious attempt at informed, self-control

training, that is, to provide novice learners with the information necessary for them to design effective plans of their own.
The essential aim of training is to make the trainee more
aware of the active nature of learning and the importance
of employing problem-solving trouble-shooting routines to enhance understanding. If learners can be made aware of (1)
basic strategies for reading and remembering, (2) simple rules
of text construction, (3) differing demands of a variety of tests
to which their information may be put, and (4) the importance
of activating any background knowledge which they may have,
they cannot help but become more effective learners. Such
self-awareness is a prerequisite for self-regulation, the ability
to orchestrate, monitor and check one's own cognitive activities.
(p. 20)

What has yet to be made clear is (1) what this knowledge and these
strategies might be, and (2) how this knowledge and these strategies might be presented to students.

What Reading Strategies Might Be Developed?

It is helpful for developing strategies to meet the needs of secondary students to regard reading comprehension as akin to model-
building. In this light, the reader driven by hypotheses works to
develop an interpretation of the information represented by the
text. The model-building involves initiating and sustaining simultaneously a variety of behaviors including: activating and refining
predictions, maintaining and varying focus, interrelating ideas,
self-questioning, attending to important information, dismissing
irrelevant information, following topical development, recognizing
relationships, evaluating understandings, considering the worth of
ideas, deciding what is new information, sensing mood and tone,
sometimes visualizing, sometimes adding information, redefining,
analogizing, editing, and reshuffling ideas. With respect to self
regulation, it entails knowing and being able to implement strategies for dealing with text, including any difficulties which are
incurred. Taken together these behaviors relate to maintaining a
flexible balance between reader-based and text-based processing
en route to developing an interpretation which is (1) plausible, in
terms of what the reader knows and the information represented
within the text itself; and (2) complete, interrelated and coherent.

In many ways, the task of reading comprehension is analogous
to a listener's task during a conversation or lecture. In conversation
a listener forms a model of what the speaker is trying to say
consistent with what the listener perceives the speaker's intentions

to be. In reading text, a comprehender tries to form a model of
what the author is trying to do. For purposes of self-regulation, a
mature reader supervises, monitors, and directs the behaviors for
so doing.

But do secondary students have such strategies and, if they do
not, will students develop them naturally over time if left to their
own devices? Several recent studies suggest that many secondary
students either lack these abilities and awarenesses or fail to utilize
them. In a recent study (Tierney and Raphael, 1981; Raphael and
Tierney, 1981), fifth grade students frequently floundered when
confronted with inconsiderate text situations (inconsistencies inserted within texts), especially with passages dealing with unfamiliar versus familiar topics and text written without dialog. Unless
informed that the text was inconsiderate, students seemed to assume that the text they were reading was faultless and proceeded
to comprehend the text as if the text was autonomous. To further
investigate this finding, Tierney, LaZansky, and Schallert (1982)
completed an extensive survey of the text difficulties and study
habits of secondary students enrolled in social studies and biology
classes in Illinois and Texas. Although the data were limited by
the self-report nature of the survey, subsequent analyses and observations conducted in conjunction with this survey provided the
following picture.

First, students responded to the general probe: Which of the
following study strategies do you use? The strategies students
reported that they used in order of frequency were: memorize
portions of the chapter (91% reported they did so sometimes, often,
or always); complete textbook questions/activities (82%); discuss
chapter with others (82%); take notes (77%); ask teacher to explain
(76%); read the chapter through once (74%); self-question (72%); ask
other students to explain (65%); summarize the chapter (64%);
evaluate extent of prior knowledge (62%); reread chapter several
times (60%); underline (56%); construct an outline (56%); review
headings (56%); read chapter summary (55%); read chapter aloud
(47%); read other sources (25.5%).

A second probe to which the students responded was: When you
study a chapter in your textbook, how difficult is it for you to . . .?
In order of frequency, the study behaviors with which they incurred most difficulty were attempts to do the following: remember what was read a week later (83%); concentrate while reading
(74%); identify relationships between ideas (63%); know how well
information read will be remembers (63%); summarize the chapter (61%); prepare for exam or quiz (61%); remember what was

read a day later (59%); know how well information read is understood (59%); identify important ideas (57%); understand difficult vocabulary (57%); construct an outline (54%); self-question while reading (51%); recall something to relate to what is being read (51%); complete textbook questions/activities (49%); complete teacher questions/activities (45%); change reading rate to suit purpose (41%); understand diagrams, graphs, etc. (31%); take notes (31%).

What emerges from the first set of data is a picture of students who read with a single disposition (to memorize) for a single purpose (completing class assignments) and who typically restrict themselves to a single reading of a single textbook. From the second set of data one gets the sense that students have a great deal of difficulty accomplishing what they set out to do as well as knowing whether or not they have achieved what they pursued. Their difficulties seem likely compounded by the apparent mismatches across what they do (i.e., read a single text only once), what they are taught or given as tasks (i.e., questions to answer, practice in a restricted array of study techniques) and what they need (i.e., self-regulatory abilities to cope with a variety of needs).

Students seem to lack the strategies needed to cope with their pursuits in subject matter classrooms. Certainly the text being used may contribute to these problems, but their attitude of reverence to these texts together with the restricted repertoire of strategies available to them seem to be their major stumbling blocks. It is as if students lack both the awareness and abilities by which to self-regulate their own pursuits. With this in mind the logical question to ask is: Can these self-regulating abilities be developed? Several recent studies bear on this issue.

Gordon, (1980) looked into the effects of inference training upon the responses of forty-two fifth graders. Specifically, Gordon compared the effects of two intervention strategies directed at improving the readers' ability to engage prior knowledge and utilize text cues. One treatment focused on building prior knowledge for instructional selections along with an awareness of text structures. The second treatment focused on providing students with strategies for inferring. A control group received a "language-related" curriculum. In general, the results Gordon obtained favored the inference strategy group, especially on the transfer tasks—that is, the delayed posttests. As Gordon rationalized, this treatment group "had the advantage through the use of a metacognitive strategy which showed them when and how to draw on relevant schemata" (p. 220).

Day (1980) studied the effectiveness of summarization training with and without explicit cuing. Specifically, college students were given either: (a) encouragement to summarize and capture main ideas; (b) instructions for modelling certain rules; (c) instructions for modelling certain rules and encouragement; or (d) instructions for modelling certain rules and rules for using these rules. Across pre- and posttest measures, Day found that providing students with rules for summarizing influenced the students' abilities to summarize, detect main ideas, and delete trivial information, but the influence of this training varied with the sophistication of the students. In other words, although all students profited from the training conditions, less sophisticated students (students with writing problems) needed more explicit training (i.e., training in the rules and their application). As Brown, Campione, and Day (1981) reported:

> Training results in greater use of the rules, and improvement is effected with less explicit instruction with more advanced students. For those students with more severe learning problems, training results in less improvement and more explicit training is needed before we can get any effect of training. (p. 16)

Palincsar (1981) worked with four seventh-grade students on their questioning ability. During the study each student experienced two interventions, corrective feedback and modelling. The corrective feedback was given to students' responses on questions following reading. The modelling occurred in conjunction with the making of predictions and the initiation of a reciprocal questioning technique between student and teacher. Analyses of comprehension measures suggested that while both corrective feedback and strategy training had a positive effect, the modelling accompanying questioning training had more carry over to other class work.

Other studies by Bartlett (1978), Dansereau, Holley, and Collins (1980), and Geva (1980) provided data supporting the value of strategies directed at text-based processes. Bartlett, for example, examined the effects of teaching ninth graders to recognize commonly found rhetorical structures on their ability to identify and use these structures in their own recall protocols and on the amount of information they could remember. The instruction focused on how to identify and use four commonly found top-level structures (patterns of organization) in classroom text. Special aids for identifying the top-level structure were faded out over the week of instruction, while the passages studied became increasingly more complex and students became more and more self-regulatory. Students in the training group and control group read and recalled passages prior to training, one day after the training program, and three weeks after the completion of the program. The instruction resulted in significantly increased use and identification of the top-level structure as well as almost a doubling in the amount of information recalled by the training group on the posttest measures.

Guidelines for an Instructional Agenda

In response to the question, "Can students be taught knowledge or strategies which will transfer to their independent reading?" the findings from all these studies suggest it can be done, provided a great deal of care and thought go into the instruction to be operationalized. It is this issue of operationalization which suggests five guidelines for developing instructional agenda to these ends. They relate to the notions of relevance, explicitness, student as informant, self-regulation, and application. Relevance refers to the extent to which any skill or strategy is legitimate to teach. Explicitness pertains to the *how*, *when*, and *why* of strategy utilization. Student as informant relates to inducing students to offer and explore their own generalizations for coping with texts. Self-regulation refers to the self-orchestration, monitoring, and assessment of one's own behavior and outcomes. Application refers to the provision of opportunities for the extension of these abilities and strategies to "real-world" situations.

Relevance

At issue in the presentation of any skill or strategy is: To what extent is the skill or strategy worth teaching? In particular, in what situations and in what ways might said skill or strategy be beneficial? Consider the situation when students are being directed to deal with the patterns represented by texts. For example, based upon structural analyses of stories and informative texts, suppose some educators offered procedures for teaching students to recognize the patterns associated with text (e.g., compare-contrast, problem-solution, definition, etc.). The question to be considered is: What is the relevance or legitimacy of teaching such a strategy? To address this issue fully the answers to additional questions need to be considered. First, do students need the strategy? If we examine the research on student responses to complex expository text we find that the ability of students to cope with such texts may be related to their inability to discern text patterns. But this inability varies across texts, purposes for reading, and from one reader to the next. Indeed, teaching certain students this strategy may be redundant given the reader's familiarity with the topic of the text being addressed, the purpose for reading, and other factors.

Even assuming the legitimacy of planning to teach the strategy, the methods for so doing must be carefully conceived. It is easy to forget that the mastery of the strategy should not displace reading for meaning. Teaching the prototypical patterns of different texts would seem inappropriate unless such instruction occurs in conjunction with helping students acquire meaning from texts. Consider the example below. There is no reference to the notion that determining the patterns of texts will help a student comprehend better. The activities bear little relationship to helping students understand the texts. It is as if the mastery of the strategy is "out of context"—the task of finding the text pattern has displaced the purpose for which it is taught.

Teaching Text Patterns

In each of the passages underline the main idea. Then circle a, b, c, or d (the top-level organization of the writer).

1. Martha was worried about her health. The doctor had told Martha that her system was overtaxed. As a result she tried to rest more and to eat at regular times. She knew her life-style had to change.
   a. description c. problem-solution
   b. before—as a result d. favored view vs. opposite view

2. Pollution is a problem for our rivers. Polluted rivers are eyesores. They are also health hazards. One solution is to stop the dumping of industrial waste.
   a. description c. problem-solution
   b. before—as a result d. favored view vs. opposite view

3. Our class reunion was held last year. We saw many old friends there. The business of the meeting was kept to a minimum. We spent most of our time socializing.
   a. description c. problem-solution
   b. before—as a result d. favored view vs. opposite view

4. Despite the argument that smoking is harmful many claim it is not so. Certainly, smoking has been related to lung cancer, high blood pressure, and loss of appetite. But, for some people smoking may relieve tension.
   a. description c. problem-solution
   b. before—as a result d. favored view vs. opposite view

In general such activities assume a rote-learning quality unless there is a provision for both students and teachers to discuss the specific relevance of any skill or strategy. That is, in conjunction with applying a strategy across a number of texts read for different purposes students need to consider when a strategy is worth enlisting and when it isn't. It may involve examining the worth of the strategy from a cost/benefit ratio perspective. That is, do the benefits outweigh the efforts necessary to achieve the goals. Students often discount the worth of study procedures, such as outlining and mapping, when such tasks require more effort than they are persuaded their tasks demand. Sometimes making explicit the *when, how,* and *why* of strategy utilization serves this function.

Explicitness

The notion of explicitness is tied to the notion that students should be informed with respect to the *why, when, where,* and *how* to use specific strategies. Several of the past research studies and some additional examples give some guidance as to how to be explicit. Day's (1980) students were placed in situations where they expected to summarize texts and were given explicit rules by which they might do so. For example, students were given various colored pencils and shown how to delete redundant information in red, delete trivial information in blue, write in superordinates (major propositions or topics) for any lists, underline topic sentences if provided, and write a topic sentence if needed.

In situations where a self-questioning behavior is being developed, students can be given models of questions as well as information describing the intent of the question. For example, teachers might use a think-aloud strategy to accompany the questions. That is, they might state that they wish the reader to consider how an event (e.g., Stockman's resignation as budget director) relates to a previous event (e.g., a fall on Wall Street) and then ask the question, "How do you think the fall on Wall Street influenced Stockman?" Or, consider the following example for teaching main idea. It offers an explicit explanation as to why and how students might proceed.

Teaching Main Idea

Teacher says: The passage below deals with the topic of lions. Let's read the passage and find out if it does.
Pupils and teacher read the passage.
The teacher explains the passage is about lions. It tells how fierce the lions are. The reason I think this is so is because: (1)

I noticed that the first sentence tells how lions attack other animals. (2) The second sentence tells about how angry lions are.

Remember finding the main idea involves deciding what a passage is all about. This involves finding the facts and deciding what they tell about.

The teacher directs the student to the next paragraph. The teacher says: The passage tells more about lions. The teacher and students read and indicate the facts they are given about lions. The teacher says: We are given a number of facts; I believe the main idea is not about how the lions fly; the facts do not tell about where lions live (note discrimination activity). Instead I believe the facts tell about what lions eat. The facts tell about the different foods lions eat.

Remember the main idea tells what a text is all about. In the next example, I want you to find the main idea yourself. Remember determining the main idea involves finding the facts and deciding what they are about. Choose whether the main idea is:

> how lions sleep
> where lions live
> how lions move

Before we check your answer, decide how well you did the following:

Did you find the facts?

Did you decide what these facts were about?

Does your choice of a main idea fit into the facts you found?

Are there any facts which don't?

If so, you should choose another. Now let's check your answer.

While teacher modelling has proven useful for research purposes, the use of teacher models should not be considered more effective than the use of a discovery approach. Indeed, discovery learning may be, for a number of reasons, better in some ways than a modelling approach. Consider the use of discovery procedures for purposes of having students explore how to summarize. By comparing different summaries of a text students can suggest alternative approaches to summarizing. With some additional direction, they can assess the applicability of alternative guidelines across a variety of different texts. Without much effort, situations can be created or capitalized upon as they occur. These situations can vary from discussing notetaking, determining the main idea, relating what is being read to your own experience, to initiating alternative heuristics (who? what? when? where? why? vs. what is the author trying to get you to think?) to determining how to cope with difficult text.

Student as Informant

Using the student as his or her own informant is based upon the notion that effective learning—at least learning which endures—is induced rather than given. Integral to making learning explicit are situations within which students explore strategies for themselves. Consider the situation when a teacher intends to develop text-coping abilities, such as dealing with an unknown word or an ambiguous idea, or learning techniques such as summarizing. Instead of being given rules for so doing, students should develop their own guidelines. That is, rather than a teaching procedure which provides students with an explicit explanation, students should be given opportunities to explore their own generalizations. Apart from the normal advantages a discovery approach affords, if students become their own informants then they are more apt to learn how to access that strategy as well as use the strategy spontaneously. If strategies can be induced rather than taught directly, students will acquire them more readily, and access them more frequently with greater flexibility across a greater variety of situations, including transfer situations.

There are other problems which the student-as-informant notion circumvents. First, if we use a student as his or her own informant, the problems of presenting students appropriate rules or exceptions to rules is alleviated. Also, by having students describe strategies in their own words, teachers are no longer burdened by the difficulties which arise due to an inappropriate choice of words for purposes of describing such rules.

A procedure often integral to the notion of the student as informant is the use of analogy for purposes of exploring self-regulatory abilities. On the simplest level, this might entail having the student consider the worth of what is being done in a familiar text with what might be done in an unfamiliar text situation. It might entail having students compare a concrete situation (e.g., how a detective determines the relevance of clues) with the text situation (e.g., how a reader determines the relevance of details). With respect to certain self-regulating abilities, it might entail having the students compare how they monitor themselves during other activities (e.g., horseriding, skateboarding, gymnastics, etc.) with how they might monitor their reading experiences. The notion of analogizing is built upon the tenet that what the student does in one situation can and should be related to other situations. Certainly there exists the possibility that the analogy may "breakdown" and result in mislearnings. For this reason, it might be important to have the students explore how their reading experience differs from the situation to which it is being compared. All things considered, analogies are likely to provide a vehicle by which complex strategies for use with text can be developed more effectively at the same time as students maintain a sense of ownership of their learning.

Self-Regulation

The fourth guideline relates to the notion of independence in learning. Throughout this discussion, it has been assumed that the task of teaching is to provide students the support and guidance by which they can become self-directing and self-teaching. This entails moving students beyond situations where they depend upon the teacher or an adjunct (e.g., teacher-inserted questions) to self-initiation and student-generated questions.

Unless students are guided to develop self-regulatory abilities, it is questionable whether they will develop these abilities efficiently and effectively. In Day's (1980) study, while the various training regimens had an effect, the treatment group which received awareness training on top of cognitive training exhibited the most significant long-term gains. In Bartlett's (1978) study, the use of detailed explanations of the benefits of the strategy along with checklists (as in the following example) provided the vehicle by which both the explicit explanation and self-regulation of the strategy could be supported.

Checklist for Teaching Text Patterns

1. Did you pick out the organization as *problem-solution*?
   If so, _____ great!
   If not, _____ did you ask the two questions before reading?
   or,
   _____ did you find the main idea? ("The problem is . . . sugar and starch?")
   _____ did you find how this main idea was organized? (one part about a *problem*, another part about a *solution*)
2. Did you write the name of the top-level organization at the top of the recall page?
   If so, _____ so far, so good!
   If not, _____ mmmmm!
3. Did you write down the main idea as the first sentence?
   If so, _____ keep it up!
   If not, _____ oh no!

4. Did you have *two* parts in arranging your sentences?
   If so, _____ not far to go now!
   If not, _____ tut tut!

5. Were the *two* parts: one for the problem, one for the solution?
   If so, _____ I bet you remembered a lot!
   If not, _____ Oh cripes!

6. Did you check?
   If so, _____ double halo!
   If not, _____ don't be overconfident!

Beyond the use of checklists for purposes of facilitating self-regulation, the displacement of teacher support with student initiative should not be overlooked. This might entail beginning a main idea lesson with a think-aloud illustration provided by a teacher (such as the exercise, Teaching Main Idea, above) which, in turn, is gradually displaced by main idea examples students discuss with and without teacher support. For purposes of developing self-questioning behavior displacement may involve a reciprocal questioning procedure wherein the amount of teacher support provided will vary with the teacher's intuitions of the needs of the students *en route* to independence. The teacher's task is to provide not only the opportunity for students to work independently, but also sufficient guidance, input, and feedback by which to develop self-regulatory abilities to accompany their efforts.

Application

The acid test of these and other guidelines relates to application. Can the students initiate, self-regulate, and appraise what to do and how to proceed in transfer situations without teacher support? Will the students' expertise transfer to nonschool related situations? Will the students be able to self-regulate for themselves?

If students are never given situations which stimulate the transfer tasks to which they are expected to put these skills, strategies, and awarenesses, it is doubtful that a student's ability to learn from text will have much transfer value. Providing students additional activities and practice of the same type will equip students to do little more than that same type of activity. In contrast, providing students opportunities to discuss and try out strategies in various situations affords transfer possibilities. If, for example, a teacher is preparing a student to cope with a science textbook, the student needs to have direct experience developing and applying strategies in conjunction with using this method. Ideally, students should be guided to induce and test strategies throughout an instructional sequence. This includes initially as well as during and after any sequence of lessons. Integral to helping somebody who is learning to cope with new tasks is the provision of experiences applying such strategies.

Conclusion

The principles of application, self-regulation, student as informant, explicitness, and relevance when considered concurrently are intended to bridge the void between teaching and learning. Certainly there are other teaching objectives essential to successful schooling, but few seem to be as highlighted by recent research efforts as these five. In essence, these guidelines should suggest that the type of support students need goes beyond what presently exists and what might be reasonably provided by any single textbook.

If the goal is to help students learn from text, there is need for major changes in our expectations for students and instructional support, regardless of the changes or improvements to text. With these notions in mind, our task as educators requires a careful consideration of what we are trying to do as well as how we are planning to accomplish these goals. With respect to what we might teach, we need to reconsider the behaviors students engage in during reading. With respect to how we teach, the notions of relevance, explicitness, student as informant, self-regulation, and application suggest an era of teaching which reflects a commitment to the possibility of learning.

References

Bartlett, B. J. Top-level structure as an organizational strategy for recall of classroom text (Doctoral dissertation, Arizona State University, 1978). *Dissertation Abstracts International*, 1979, *39*, 6641A. (University Microfilms No. 79-11113)

Brown, A., Campione, J., and Day, J. Learning to learn: On training students to learn from texts. *Educational Researcher*, 1981, *10*(2), 14-25.

Dansereau, D. F., Holley, C. D., and Collins, K. W. *Effects of learning strategy training on text processing.* Paper presented at the annual meeting of the American Education Research Association, Boston, April 1980.

Day, J. D. Teaching summarization skills: A comparison of training methods. Unpublished doctoral dissertation, University of Illinois, 1980.

Geva, E. Meta-textual notions and reading comprehension (Doctoral dissertation, University of Toronto, 1980). *Dissertation Abstracts International*, 1981, *42*, 1057A.

Gordon, C. J. The effects of instruction on metacomprehension and inferencing on children's comprehension abilities (Doctoral dissertation,
   University of Minnesota, 1980). *Dissertation Abstracts International,*
   1980, *41*, 1004A. (University Microfilms No. 8019528)

Palincsar, A. *Directed feedback and strategy training to improve the comprehension of poor readers.* Unpublished manuscript, University of
   Illinois, 1981.

Raphael, T., and Tierney, R. J. *The influence of topic familiarity and the
   author-reader relationship on the detection of inconsistent information.*
   Paper presented at the National Reading Conference, San Diego, 1981.

Schallert, D., and Tierney, R. J. *Learning from expository text: The
   interaction of text structure with reader characteristics.* Report prepared
   in conjunction with research grant from the National Institute of
   Education, 1982.

Tierney, R. J., LaZansky, J., and Schallert, D. *Secondary students' use of
   social studies and biology text.* Report prepared in conjunction with
   research grant from the National Institute of Education, 1982.

Tierney, R. J., and Raphael, T. *Factors controlling the inferences of fifth
   graders: An extended examination of the author-reader relationship
   during discourse processing.* Paper presented at the annual meeting
   of the American Educational Research Association, Los Angeles,
   April 1981.

8 Assessment: Responses to Literature

S. Lee Galda
University of Georgia

This chapter and the next one by Johnston and Pearson divide between them two interrelated aspects of assessment of reading. In this chapter we concentrate on poetry and imaginative literature and in the next we focus on responses to exposition. Rosenblatt (1968) helped us to make the distinction through the following discussion:

> This "way" of a poem or any literary work of art is what differentiates it from ordinary reading. In other kinds of reading, we are simply concerned with the information of ideas that will be left with us once the reading has ended, as, for example, when we are reading a text that gives us directions about how to do something. In reading the poem, we not only bring about the "happening" by responding to the verbal symbols that make up the text, but also our attention is focused on the qualities of the very happening that we are bringing to pass. We are directly involved, we are participants, active participants, in the "happening." We are aware of what the symbols call forth in us. They point to sensations, objects, images, ideas. These we must pattern out of the material that we bring to the work from our past knowledge of life and language. And these in addition call up in us associated states of feeling and mood.
>
> The text is the guide and control in all this, of course. We must pay attention to the order of the words, their sound, their rhythm and recurrence. Our attention oscillates between the texture of the sound and rhythm of the words, and all that these evoke in us. We vibrate to the chiming of sound, sense, and associations. Our attention must be focused on this electric charge set up between the text and us. The verbal symbols stir much more in us than is relevant to the text; we must crystallize out and organize those elements that do justice to the particular words in their particular places.
>
> This live circuit between the reader and the text is the literary experience. Literature is, first of all, this sensing,

> feeling, thinking, this ordering and organizing of image, idea,
> and emotion in relation to a text. The texture and structure of
> the reader's experience in relation to the text becomes for him
> the poem, the story, or the play. As teachers of literature, our
> task is to foster this particular "way of happening," this mode
> of perceptive and personal response to words, this self-aware-
> ness in relation to a text. (p. 341)

Such an active and idiosyncratic view of reading a literary text makes pronouncements about *one* correct interpretation rather impossible. "One text is potentially capable of several different realizations, and no reading can ever exhaust the full potential, for each individual reader will fill in the gaps in his own way, thereby excluding the various other possibilities" (Iser, 1972, p. 285). If this is the case, then there is no one "correct" reading for a particular text but merely readings which are more or less complete so far as they encompass the information presented explicitly in the text and make use of the "gaps" in that text to create a personal mean- ing. However, that meaning can and should be anchored to the text, and should also be explainable by reference to aspects of the text which stimulated and regulated the creation of that meaning.

Since an interactionist theory of reading a literary text renders obsolete the traditional focus on particular interpretations espoused by various critical schools, the problems of assessment of responses to literature become complex. The question of how we assess degree of involvement and reactions as well as comprehension arises. Other problems spring from the nature of response. Chief among them is the fact that the only responses we can assess are overt verbal responses, what students tell us and each other about the books they read. These responses "may indicate very little of the inner response" (Harding, 1968). Written responses, in particu- lar, may inhibit many students because of poor writing ability and/or because once something is written down it seems final; it is much less ephemeral than an oral response. When teachers encour- age students to express their own ideas rather than what they think the teacher/critic would like to hear, the more likely will the students' responses be honest. [For ideas encouraging honest re- sponses, see Bleich (1975) and Purves (1972).]

With so many potential problems, can and should responses to literature be assessed? The answer is *yes*, if by assessment we mean consideration and analysis of individual responses rather than comparison with an arbitrary standard. It is only after we understand, analyze, and appreciate students' responses that we may be able to help them expand and extend their responses. Hence, the remainder of this chapter focuses on methods of obtaining, describing, and analyzing responses; what research employing these approaches has told us about responses; and the implications for actual classroom practice.

Ways of Analyzing Responses

Purves (1968) developed a way of describing the content of written responses to literature. His system of five categories of response to literary works became the basis for many studies of response. The first category, engagement-involvement, encompasses statements about "the ways in which [the responder] has experienced the work or its various aspects" (p. 6). Perception statements, the second category, are those which speak of the literary work as an object separate from the response to that object. The third major category, interpretation, consists of attempts "to find meaning in the work, to generalize about it, to draw inferences from it, to find analogues to it in the universe that the [responder] inhabits" (p. 7). Interpretive statements could be of either form or content. The fourth category, evaluation, could be based on either subjective or objective criteria. The fifth category is miscellaneous. Each of the four main categories can be then broken down into subcategories and then elements, which results in a fairly precise but unwieldy tool. This system was unwieldy in large scale research and certainly for classroom use as Purves and his colleagues discovered: it was time consuming and yielded more data than needed for comparisons.

There is a modification of Purves' system which makes it useful for the classroom teacher. Purves and Beach (1972) suggested an amended analytic system and this was used by Odell and Cooper (1976). The system is comprised of the four original main categories, each with at least two subcategories that reflect a synthesis of elements found important by a number of researchers and theoreticians (Frye, 1957; Purves, 1968; Squire, 1964, among others). The amended categories, as presented by Odell and Cooper (1976), are as follows:

Modified Purves Categories

Personal Statement
1. about the reader, an "autobiographical digression"
2. about the work, expressing a personal engagement with it

Descriptive Statement
3. narrational, retelling part of the work
4. descriptive of aspects of the work: language, characters, setting, etc.

Interpretive Statement
5. of parts of the work
6. of the whole work

Evaluative Statement
7. about the evocativeness of the work [emotional appeal]
8. about the construction of the work
9. about the meaningfulness of the work [significance/ applicability to life] (pp. 205–206)

This system, when applied to written responses scored by independent clauses, adequately describes the content of written responses to literature. Analysis with this system of only nine categories yields relatively quick scoring. Further, this, like the original, more complex system, reveals what is focused on in a response, what is ignored in a response, and the patterns present across responses (Odell and Cooper, 1976). The data which this kind of analysis yields tell us a great deal about a reader's written response.

However, the content analysis of written responses only provides information about the content; it tells us nothing about the process of formulating the response. Odell and Cooper (1976) drew on the rhetorical theory of Young, Becker, and Pike (1970) to discover the intellectual strategies operating when responding to a literary text. They examined written responses by independent clause for evidence of focus, contrast, classification, references to change, time sequence, logical sequence, and physical context. They argued that examining the use of these strategies gives insight into the processes used to formulate written responses. Again, however, the complexity of this additional analysis makes it of doubtful value as a tool for classroom teachers.

Another way of describing responses using the Purves system is to do so holistically. Holistic analysis involves classifying the response as a whole rather than clause by clause. The response is read or heard and the category which best describes the gist of the response is assigned to it. Purves (1968) suggested this as a possible methodology but felt that the analysis would yield too gross a picture of response. Other researchers have found holistic analyses quite adequate. The National Assessment of Educational Progress (NAEP) in Writing, Reading, and Literature (see chapter 1, above), a federally funded survey begun in 1969, used the holistic scoring method because detailed scoring was too time consuming and yielded data unnecessarily precise for the purpose of the study (Mellon, 1975). When Cooper and Michalak (1981) compared individual analyses of statements using the amended categories, holistic essay analysis, and the Response Preference Measure (discussed below), they concluded that "in future literary response studies we should retain *essay analysis* as the most valid measure for determining an individual's preferred mode of response" (p. 164). These studies provided evidence that holistic scoring using the modified Purves system, which is much less time consuming than independent clause scoring, yields an equally or more accurate picture of response. Ease of implementation and accuracy make holistic analysis a useful classroom tool.

Another way of analyzing response is to measure the response preferences of readers. The Response Preference Measure (RPM) asks students to choose which questions or statements they would like to address in responding to a story. The questions or statements which comprise the RPM reflect the major Purves categories. Using an RPM would enable teachers to determine general patterns in the response preferences of their classes and of individual students.

The methods for analysis were developed for describing written responses. Oral responses can be classified using the modified Purves categories, although this presents problems if the responses occur in the context of a discussion. For example, one person's responses could be classified as interpretive statements when viewed individually but when examined within the context of the whole discussion that person's responses might have a clearly evaluative intent. It was because of situations like this that Galda (1980) found holistic scoring of oral responses yielded a clearer picture of the responses than did scoring with the modified Purves system by independent clause.

Patterns of Response to Literature

There have been several studies of responses to literature which use one or more of the aforementioned methods of analysis. These studies yield information about individual responders as well as about general patterns of response.

One question which has been investigated is whether individuals have a preferred mode of response which holds across texts. Cooper (1969) used an RPM and found that individuals have a preferred mode of response regardless of text. This finding was corroborated by Mertz (1972) and Michalak (1976). However, the results of the International Educational Achievement (IEA) study* revealed a "tendency of different stories to elicit different response" (Purves, 1981, p. 14). Individual consistency, especially in American fourteen year olds, was tempered by variation across stories. However, a cross-national development of consistency between the ages of fourteen and eighteen was noted. A separate study, the First National Assessment of Educational Progress in Writing, Reading, and Literature, had similar findings. The results of this study indicated that responses became more consistent with age. The number of interpretive responses increased dramatically between the thirteen-year-old and seventeen-year-old groups. This increase was noted in scored written responses. It is, however, difficult to "tell whether the interpretive response mode constitutes the true preference of the seventeens, or merely the category they have been conditioned to choose" (Mellon, 1975).

Perhaps the most striking finding of the IEA study was the differences in response preferences across countries. Within the Response Preference Measure framework students in the United States chose questions focusing on content and impersonal response as opposed to, for example, New Zealand students, who chose questions focusing on form and personal responses. These results suggested that response preferences depend on both the text and the nationally defined cultural environment, especially as it is embodied in the school. Further, since teachers' preferences and students' preferences were positively correlated, it seems that teachers can and do teach their students how to respond to literature. The data from the first NAEP corroborated this finding. It is interesting to note that American students seemed to fall into three groups by the end of high school, each group with a slightly different thrust to its preferences, but all three concerned with moral questions. If Purves' (1981) conclusions are valid, this concern with morality might spring from the books adolescents read, since many deal with questions of personal morality. Another source of this emphasis on morality may be a concern for personal morality operating in both the home and the school, where books are often

---

*This study began in the mid 1960s and was completed by the mid 1970s. Several countries participated in the study which examined achievement in six areas: reading, literature, science, civic education, English as a foreign language, and French as a foreign language (Purves, 1981). Some results of the reading and literature studies are discussed here.

talked about in light of what we can "learn" from the moral stance in the story. It would seem, then, that a "thematic and moralistic pattern of response is learned" (p. 103).

Other general patterns were evident in the NAEP data. Now that the third National Assessment has been completed, we are aware that our students, by age seventeen, seemed able to express their responses, especially personal reactions, but unable to explain those responses by referring to the text or to their personal feelings and opinions. Overall, students were less able to make adequate interpretations and support them than they were in 1970–71.

> Though most [students] have learned to make simple inferences about such things as a character's behavior and motivation, for example, and can express their own judgments of a work as "good" or "bad," they generally did not return to the passage to explain the interpretations they made. (NAEP, 1981)

It seems that students have learned to describe the emotions a text arouses in them, but cannot analyze the text in terms of mood, character, or theme. Further, they focus on the content of a passage rather than the form (NAEP, 1981). Finally, different passages evoked different kinds of responses, with difficult passages promoting the most inadequate responses.

These data substantiated findings from other studies. In short: (1) students can respond to text but cannot express reasons for that response; (2) students focus on content when they respond to literature; (3) comprehension directly affects response; (4) different pieces of literature promote different kinds of responses.

Factors Influencing Responses to Literature

Comprehension of and personal involvement with a text affect responses. There is "a pattern of response that shifts with comprehension as if the better one understands a text, the further one is able to consider it" (Purves, 1981, p. 99). Liking a literary text is also involved in comprehension and has similar effects on response preferences (Purves, 1978, 1981). Readers who like a text "tend to be concerned with the nature of their involvement with it and with the organization and relation of form to content. They appear to wonder about what has happened to them and about aesthetic aspects of the selection" (Purves, 1978, p. 294). Readers who don't like a text tend to want to place the text in a distancing context such as "generic, historical, or personal" and to avoid emotional questions (Purves, 1978, p. 295). Students who dislike a text seem to be unable to "get into" the text. The question of whether comprehension creates involvement or involvement heightens comprehension and the strength of the interaction between them is as yet unanswered (Purves, 1978).

Squire (1964) examined the ways in which the responses of ninth and tenth grade students developed during the reading of four different stories. He divided the stories into six segments and taped the response of each student after each segment was completed. Using categories similar to the Purves (1968) system, Squire found a pattern which indicated that his readers approached the texts from a "literary judgment" stance which as the story progressed gave way to an increasing number of self-involvement responses. The results of his study were similar to those of others in subsequent studies (Cooper, 1969; Mellon, 1975; Purves, 1981): interpretation is the dominant form of response for American high school students. His finding that responses change as the story unfolds was validated by Angelotti (1972), who also concluded that the ability to understand literature was a major determinant of the form of response, a finding subsequently validated in the IEA study (Purves, 1981). Clearly, then, it is important that our students understand what they read both for basic reading comprehension and as a foundation for response.

Petrosky (1975) isolated five factors important to the responses of the five adolescent readers in his study: stage-specific cognitive operations, identity theme (way of looking at the world), past experience, reader expectations, and reading ability. [Reading ability, past experience, and reader expectations were reported as important variables in other studies (Angelotti, 1972; Purves, 1981).] Petrosky found cognitive operations to be yet another factor influencing response. Galda (1980) also observed the influence of cognitive development on responses. She found that students who were at a concrete operational level were limited in their responses, especially to realistic fiction. These students were "reality-bound," that is, they understood the fictional text only as it related to their concept of reality. Since cognitive development influences responses, any assessment of a student's responses to a literary text should be tempered by an understanding of that student's cognitive development.

Responses in the Classroom

Before we begin to teach literature, much less assess responses, we should have a clear idea of our goals and criteria. If pleasure is the only goal perhaps we should simply let our students read whatever they want to read and tell us whether or not they liked it. However, if our goals go beyond pleasure to include reading for understanding, both emotional and intellectual, and the ability to vary responses according to the demands of the text and the task, then some criteria can and should be set. This brings us to a problem. Is there a "perfect" response, or even a perfect response pattern? And if we attempt to assess responses, against what do we judge them?

The idea that responses should vary according to text also enters into this problem. Historically, we have assumed that differences in texts call for differences in the focus of responses. However, if the IEA data are accurate, our teaching has failed to reflect that assumption, since students seem to learn a predominately moralistic interpretive response stance. We have also assumed that the ability to be flexible in response is a desirable state, that the academically superior student is a flexible responder. Again, the IEA data seemed to challenge this assumption. In that sample the higher achieving students chose fewer different kinds of responses than did the lower achieving students. These results, however, must be understood in the context of choice of *preferences* rather than *abilities* and probably also in light of the powerful influence teachers have. Since we seem to teach our students to respond in a certain way, that is, to make moralistic interpretations, should we be surprised that the academically superior students, who presumably learn what we teach them, prefer to respond in limited ways?

A criterion, then, against which to measure our assessment of responses might be *flexibility*. Perhaps we need to expand what we assess from "response" to "responses," looking at any one student's pattern of responses across texts and time. Could we say that a "good" (albeit not perfect) response is a flexible one which encompasses the interaction of textual demands and a reader's experiences (which include learned response styles), abilities, and predilections? A "good" response would then vary across texts and readers. Assessment would have to consider both the choices the reader makes and the options the texts allow.

A second criterion against which to measure our assessment of responses might be the amount of support or documentation provided by the student. At present our students do not do this well (NAEP, 1981). Mellon (1975) suggested that it "is not so much *which* interpretation students put forward as *how* they support the positions they choose by critical readings of the text in question" (p. 88). Even though, for a specific text an overall interpretive response might be more appropriate than an engagement response, either must be assessed according to the support given for the response. Does the responder freely express his or her views but also return to the text for documentation?

The evidence that students learn response patterns (Purves, 1981) and that students do not adequately explain their responses (NAEP, 1981) can have a direct impact on teaching. First, we must help our students read with some degree of involvement and understanding. Second, we should structure our written assignments or oral discussions to encourage a variety of kinds of responses. Third, we should encourage our students to think about their responses, stimulating them to elaborate on their opinions and reactions with specific references to the text.

We must also keep in mind the demands of the tasks. For example, oral discussion is one method we might employ. If so, we must consider the differences between individual and group oral situations. Beach (1972) found that the opportunity to respond to a poem in a free, oral, individual response situation resulted in engagement-involvement responses; subsequent group discussions consisted of more interpretive responses and fewer digressions than did the discussions of those who had not the opportunity to respond previously. Cullinan, Galda, and Tolman (1981) also found a difference between individual and group oral responses, especially in the responses of young adolescent boys, although Galda (1980) found no substantive differences between the individual and group responses of young adolescent girls. It seems likely, however, that the presence and opinions of others does influence response (Holland, 1975) just as the opportunity to respond individually influences group responses (Beach, 1972). Our students need the opportunity to engage in both kinds of oral responses. A group situation may make responders more guarded about what they say, but it also provides "food for thought" in the exchange of ideas among peers.

Keeping this in mind, a teacher can listen to what students say about a text, and then use the amended Purves categories to analyze what is being said. The teacher might want to listen with the following questions in mind: Are the students expressing a positive or negative involvement with the text? Do they make personal statements about themselves? Do they describe the text by retelling bits of it or in terms of literary aspects? Do they attempt interpretation and, if so, of parts of the text or the text as a whole? Do they evaluate? Is the evaluation based on what the text has evoked, how it is constructed, or how meaningful it is?

Analysis of this type will necessarily be holistic and can be done for the group as a whole or individual students in a group. The idea is not to attempt to classify each utterance but to be able to get a sense of the gist, a global picture of the discussion. Group oral response analysis should be supplemented with analyses of individual oral responses, either audiotaped or given in individual reading conferences.

Once the general patterns have emerged, questions to encourage flexibility and documentation might be used to guide discussions. Questions such as those used in the National Assessment could be used to elicit different kinds of responses according to the demands of the story and needs of the students. These questions/directions consisted of: "(1) Tell me what you most want to say about the story or poem. (2) What did you especially notice in the story or poem? (3) Tell me what you think about the story" (Mellon, 1975, p. 88). The three questions were designed to elicit responses in the four Purves categories, engagement-involvement, interpretation, perception, and evaluation, respectively. Other questions specific to a particular text should be added. These should also be designed to encourage specific kinds of responses. Of course, the question, "What in the text makes you think that?" or a variant, should be asked repeatedly.

Written response assignments have constraints different from those of oral response assignments. That mode of discourse affects response was illustrated by Beach's (1972) finding that the mode helped determine the kinds of response. He found that free oral response conditions resulted in primarily engagement-involvement responses, while free written assignment conditions resulted in primarily interpretive responses.

As alluded to earlier, writing ability also influences the quality and quantity of response and perhaps the kind of response. We must hold in mind the particular constraints of written response. We need to remember that students' written responses are affected by the relative rhetorical ability underlying the response (Mellon, 1975). A fair assessment of a student's written response to litera-ture would have to be tempered by a consideration of that student's writing ability. A short and superficial or an inappropriate re-sponse may be as much or more the result of a lack of fluency in writing as a lack of understanding or involvement in reading.

Obviously, students who have difficulty writing shouldn't be asked to respond to literature only through writing. This would result in both an unfair assessment and a situation which stifles student responses. That, in turn, leads to unpleasant encounters with literature—something we all try to avoid. Rather, these students should be encouraged to respond in other ways, through other media. Although the area of the "creative" or artistic response has not been discussed here, multi-media responses to literature have grown in popularity and have been used with success with students at a variety of ability levels. Some of these kinds of responses may be more appropriate for less able students than are written responses. Oral responses are also a viable alternative to writing.

Aside from problems with the responses of nonfluent writers, teachers must be aware of other characteristics of written responses. First of all, the assignment must be considered. If an assignment is specific, then assessment is relatively easy: Does the paper cover what needed to be covered? However, if the assignment is to "respond" to a literary text, the content of that response should be free to vary according to the preference of the responder.

This highlights another complication in the response assessment process. When measures such as the RPM are used, the results indicate preferences, not abilities. So, to a certain extent, do the products of free written responses. The appearance of one kind of response "does not substantiate the respondent's inability to make" other kinds of responses. "It merely indicates the kind of response one preferred to make initially on that particular occasion" (Mellon, 1975, p. 97). Just because a student consistently writes descriptive responses does not necessarily mean that that student cannot make evaluative responses. The type of response students write may be the result of their perception of what the teacher wants and what they have been taught.

If we want our students to respond flexibly and with documentation, we need to structure our assignments accordingly. One way to do so is to give assignments to respond in a specific way and support that response. For example, the assignment might be to evaluate the effectiveness of the message conveyed by a particular book and to support that evaluation with examples from the book. Assignments like this might be preceded (as a preorganizer) by an oral discussion focused on the same topic. Assignments will vary, of course, according to the needs of the students and the demands of the texts.

Conclusion

There are three major points to consider. First, if the kinds of responses we hear or read are different from what we expect, we need to remember the importance of the reader in the creation of a response and not penalize our students for their preferred way of responding. We do, however, need to teach them to respond in a variety of ways so that they will have access to various kinds of responses and can learn to critically distinguish effective modes of response in relation to the text as well as to their own reactions. Secondly, we can look for the rationale behind our students' responses, and teach them to look as well. What was it about the text that evoked a particular response? How did the text and reader interact to produce a certain response? This will result in more flexible and knowledgeable responders and also better readers, readers conscious of the process as well as the product.

Finally, and perhaps most importantly, before any response is assessed we need to consider the degree of involvement and understanding of our students. Clearly this is a teaching problem as well as an assessment problem. Indeed, much of what we have learned about responses to literature tells us that our teaching practices and the kinds of responses our students make are inextricably bound. As we consider how we should assess our students' responses to literature we must also consider how we assess our teaching of literature.

References

Angelotti, M. L. A comparison of elements in the written free response of eighth graders to a junior novel and an adult novel (Doctoral dissertation, The Florida State University, 1972). *Dissertation Abstracts International*, 1972, *33*, 2603A. (University Microfilms No. 72-32, 754)

Beach, R. W. The literary response process of college students while reading and discussing three poems (Doctoral dissertation, University of Illinois, 1972). *Dissertation Abstracts International*, 1973, *34*, 656A. (University Microfilms No. 73-17, 112)

Bleich, D. *Readings and feelings: An introduction to subjective criticism.* Urbana, Ill.: National Council of Teachers of English, 1975. (ERIC Document Reproduction Service No. ED 103 832; 118p.)

Cooper, C. Preferred modes of literary response: The characteristics of high school juniors in relation to the consistency of their reactions to three dissimilar short stories (Doctoral dissertation, University of California, Berkeley, 1969). *Dissertation Abstracts International*, 1970, *31*, 1680A-1681A. (University Microfilms No. 70-17, 535)

Cooper, C., and Michalak, D. A note on determining response styles in research on response to literature. *Research in the Teaching of English*, 1981, *15*, 163-169. (ERIC No. EJ 245 616)

Cullinan, B., Galda, L., and Tolman, K. *Developmental factors in children's responses to literature.* Unpublished manuscript, New York University, 1981.

Frye, N. *Anatomy of criticism.* Princeton: Princeton University Press, 1957.

Galda, S. L. Three children reading stories: Response to literature in preadolescents (Doctoral dissertation, New York University, 1980). *Dissertation Abstracts International,* 1980, *41,* 2438A-2439A. (University Microfilms No. 8027440)

Harding, D. W. Response to literature: The report of the study group. In J. R. Squire (Ed.), *Response to literature: Papers relating to the Anglo-American seminar on the teaching of English* (Dartmouth College, New Hampshire, 1966). The Dartmouth Seminar Papers. Champaign, Ill.: National Council of Teachers of English, 1968. (ERIC Document Reproduction Service No. ED 026 350; 85p.)

Holland, N. N. *Five readers reading.* New Haven: Yale University Press, 1975.

Iser, W. The reading process: A phenomenological approach. *New Literary History,* 1972, *3,* 279-300.

Mellon, J. C. *National assessment and the teaching of English: Results of the first national assessment of educational progress in writing, reading, and literature—Implications for teaching and measurement in the English language arts.* Urbana, Ill.: National Council of Teachers of English, 1975. (ERIC Document Reproduction Service No. ED 112 427; 133p.)

Mertz, M. Responses to literature among adolescents, English teachers and college students: A comparative study (Doctoral dissertation, University of Minnesota, 1972). *Dissertation Abstracts International,* 1973, *33,* 6066A. (University Microfilms No. 73-10693)

Michalak, D. The effect of instruction in literature on high school students' preferred way of responding to literature (Doctoral dissertation, State University of New York at Buffalo, 1976). *Dissertation Abstracts International,* 1977, *37,* 4829A. (University Microfilms No. 77-03566)

Reading, thinking, and writing: Results from the 1979-80 National Assessment of Reading and Literature (Report No. 11-L-01). Denver, Colo.: National Assessment of Educational Progress, 1981. (ERIC Document Reproduction Service No. ED 209 641; 82p.)

Odell, L., and Cooper, C. Describing responses to works of fiction. *Research in the Teaching of English,* 1976, *10,* 203-225. (ERIC No. EJ 151 216)

Petrosky, A. R. Individual and group responses of 14 and 15 year olds to short stories, novels, poems, and thematic apperception tests: Case studies based on Piagetian genetic epistemology and Freudian psychoanalytic psychology (Doctoral dissertation, State University of New York at Buffalo, 1975). *Dissertation Abstracts International,* 1975, *36,* 852A. (University Microfilms No. 75-16, 956)

Purves, A. C. (Ed.). *How porcupines make love.* Lexington, Mass.: Ginn/Xerox, 1972.

Purves, A. C. Using the IEA data bank for research in reading and response to literature. *Research in the Teaching of English,* 1978, *12,* 289-296. (ERIC No. EJ 195 927)

Purves, A. C. *Reading and literature: American achievement in international perspective.* Urbana, Ill.: National Council of Teachers of English, 1981. (ERIC Document Reproduction Service No. ED 199 741; 251p.)

Purves, A. C., and Beach, R. W. *Literature and the reader: Research in response to literature, reading interests, and the teaching of literature.* Urbana, Ill.: National Council of Teachers of English, 1972. (ERIC Document Reproduction Service No. ED 068 973; 215p.)

Purves, A. C., with Rippere, V. *Elements of writing about a literary work: A study of response to literature.* Champaign, Ill.: National Council of Teachers of English, 1968. (ERIC Document Reproduction Service No. ED 018 431; 102p.)

Rosenblatt, L. M. A way of happening. *Educational Record,* 1968, *49*(3), 339-346.

Squire, J. R. *The responses of adolescents while reading four short stories.* Champaign, Ill.: National Council of Teachers of English, 1964. (ERIC Document Reproduction Service No. ED 022 756; 76p.)

Young, R. E., Becker, A. L., and Pike, K. L. *Rhetoric: Discovery and change.* New York: Harcourt, Brace, and World, 1970.

9 Assessment: Responses to Exposition

Peter Johnston
State University of New York at Albany

P. David Pearson
University of Illinois at Urbana-Champaign

When teachers obtain the results of children's reading tests, they usually simply get one or two numbers. What do these numbers mean? What kinds of underlying skills, knowledge, and behavior in each student helped to produce the numbers? We ask this question because we are committed to the notion that no one should ever give a test (standardized or teacher-made) unless he or she intends to use the data to make a decision about an individual or a group. This is not a chapter about how to gauge differences in percentiles, standard scores, grade norm scores, and stanines; the test manuals and texts in educational psychology will tell you more than we could hope to. Our real goal is to promote better and more-informed instructional decisions.

In this chapter, we point out what various areas of research have to say about assessment of reading comprehension. We first describe what we now know about current assessment practices. Subsequently, we make some research-based suggestions for improvements and new directions. Please note that while we have focused our remarks on assessing the reading of exposition (especially on the sort of content one would find in science or social studies classes), we feel that much of what we report is also applicable to the literary materials Galda considered in chapter 8.

What information do we really get from reading comprehension assessment? The answer to this question is not immediately obvious since the information obtained differs across individuals and tests. But whatever the information, it is highly correlated with vocabulary test scores (e.g., Coleman, 1971) and with measures of intelligence (e.g., Tuinman, 1979). Reading comprehension tests seem to be measuring something like general ability. Of course, some of this relationship between reading comprehension and intelligence is only to be expected, but how much of it is a fact of life and how much of it merely reflects our approach to measurement? In order to answer this, let us first briefly consider what reading comprehension involves in light of our interest in assessment.

Reading comprehension is a complex behavior in which a reader uses various strategies, consciously and unconsciously, to build a model of the meaning of the text—a model that the reader assumes the writer intended when he or she wrote it. The reader constructs this model using both direct cues from the message in the text *and* prior knowledge to generate hypotheses which are tested by applying various logical and pragmatic reasoning strategies. Much of the model must be inferred, since no text is ever fully explicit. Writers always omit from their presentation precisely that information they think readers will be able to fill in (i.e., infer) on their own. In fact, as readers, we would get awfully bored by text that was wholly explicit; carried to the nth degree, fully explicit text would even define the meaning of *all* the terms used in the text. Nonetheless, serious mismatches in comprehension can occur when the information the author assumes the reader will fill in is not the same as that which the reader possesses (or assumes the author wanted filled in).

Factors Which Influence Reading Comprehension

In this rather abbreviated definition, we have introduced several factors which influence reading comprehension and which are discussed more fully elsewhere in this book: (1) prior knowledge, (2) textual cue systems, and (3) reasoning strategies. However, these three are not the only influences on reading comprehension. Reading must occur in a context, which is interpreted by readers with different characteristics. Thus, further aspects also discussed in this chapter include, (4) situational context, (5) reader's purpose, and (6) test-taking skills.

Prior Knowledge

It is clear that the reader's prior knowledge plays a big part in the comprehension process. In fact, prior knowledge influences the process at all levels: at the decoding-word recognition level by delimiting the set of words that could possibly appear in a sentence slot; at the short-term memory level by determining the amount which can be stored in working memory; at the inference stage by determining which inferences, if any, should be made; and at the storage level by determining which information will be stored, in what form it will be stored, and whether or not it will be retrieved. Consequently, there should be a strong relationship between prior knowledge and reading comprehension, and this is indeed the case. Johnston and Pearson (1982) demonstrated that a brief measure of prior knowledge can account for a large proportion of reading comprehension score variance, even after reading ability has been taken into account.

Amount and/or nature of prior knowledge relates directly to the question of what we get from our measurement of reading comprehension. Prior knowledge differences cause various forms of test bias. Racial bias is the most publicized of these biases, but there are others. In fact, tests will be biased against any individual or group who has either a deficit or a difference in their prior knowledge about the topic addressed in a particular text.

In order to avoid or diminish the problems relating to differing prior knowledge requisites in tests, test constructors have attempted to devise tests of reading comprehension which are independent of prior knowledge. Two approaches to this problem have emerged to date. Both approaches are evident in the current tests of reading comprehension.

The first method of accommodating the prospect of student variation in relevant prior knowledge might be labeled a "shotgun" approach. Test constructors use a number of relatively brief passages, each about a different topic. This strategy is apparently based on the idea that a wide spread of topics will allow all readers to strike at least some passages for which they have reasonable prior knowledge, and that, overall, each student gets an equitable spread of familiar texts. The net effect of such a strategy is to ensure that readers with stronger general knowledge will be better prepared for a test of reading comprehension. These same students will also be the ones who score more highly on tests of intelligence since general knowledge is a large part of IQ, at least as it is currently measured.

The second method of accommodation is to eliminate all test items that are not shown to be "passage dependent." These items are ones which students with extensive prior knowledge could have answered before they read the passage. Unfortunately, as demonstrated by Johnston and Pearson, this does not remove the problem, since the effects of prior knowledge are evident in all test item types, even those which are not appreciably passage independent.

There is a third approach, still in its infancy, that shows promise as a way of taking prior knowledge into account. Since it is discussed more fully below, we only mention it here. Rather then eliminate prior knowledge as a potentially biasing factor, Johnston (1981) suggested that we measure it. Then, he argued, we would be in a position to make differential judgments about a student's comprehension based upon what we knew about his or her background knowledge for a particular body of content.

Text Characteristics

Many aspects of the text itself influence the likelihood that, and extent to which, a reader will comprehend it, and most of these are not recorded by readability formulae. For example, it has been demonstrated that comprehension is influenced by a number of text characteristics: the concreteness and imageability of the text (Paivio, 1971); density of the information—number of ideas per unit, like a sentence (Kintsch and Keenan, 1973); density of new information (Aiken, Thomas, and Shennum, 1975); and the density of arguments in propositions—a proposition is akin to a clause and an argument is akin to a modifier (Kintsch et al., 1975). Furthermore, the structure of the text also influences a reader's comprehension of it (Thorndyke, 1977; Meyer, 1975; Meyer, Brandt, and Bluth, 1981). This structural aspect is especially important, since the predominant types of organizational structures will differ across content areas, and they will all differ from the largely narrative text with which the students were taught to read in their elementary reading courses (Pearson et al., in preparation).

The importance of these research findings becomes apparent when we consider how the texts in tests of reading comprehension compare with those which students are normally required to read. The material in tests is generally shorter and more information-laden (Tuinman, 1979), with less obvious structure. This means that currently the texts which are used in assessing reading comprehension do not reflect normal reading materials well at all, either in length or structure.

Reasoning Strategies

The past decade has witnessed an abundant body of research on strategies that readers use to understand, organize, and retrieve information from text in order to demonstrate that they have understood it. Additionally, research has focused on readers' awareness and monitoring of these strategies. Still other research has attempted to help (especially) poorer students learn to use and monitor kinds of strategies that better students seem to use spontaneously. It is difficult to summarize this large body of research in a short space; however, we highlight a few pertinent findings, recognizing that we are oversimplifying many issues.

First, as might seem obvious from common sense, better readers use more appropriate strategies more efficiently. They are more sensitive to what is important in text (e.g., Brown and Smiley, 1977) and they use their sensitivity to importance in order to organize their recall of text. Second, they are more sensitive to the patterns of text organization provided by the author and tend to use author organization to structure their more elaborate recalls (Meyer, Brandt, and Bluth, 1981). Third, they are better at predicting strategies they should use in order to produce answers to questions asked of them. Furthermore they tend to change these strategies in accordance with the task demands of the questions and the information available in the text; poor readers tend to apply the same strategies, however inappropriate, to all types of probes (Raphael, Winograd, and Pearson, 1980).

It is worth noting that each of these strategies, as well as students' ability to monitor their use of such strategies, is amenable to instruction. Students can be trained to create better summaries of important ideas in a text (Day, 1980), they can be trained to recognize and use author organization to enhance recall of information (Bartlett, 1978), and they can be trained to differentiate their use of text and/or prior knowledge in accordance with questions that require different strategies (Raphael, 1980). The question-answering work is probably most relevant for assessment since most formal and informal tests rely on questions to determine content learning. Pearson (1982) summarizes these teaching strategies in more detail. (See below for a technique that teachers can add to their tests in order to make judgments about the appropriateness of student strategies.)

The Assessment Task

Consider the difference between tasks involved in everyday classroom reading comprehension, especially in the content areas, and in our assessment procedures. The "real world" tasks usually involve remembering and applying new information. Having read the text, the student must discuss or compose in the absence of the text. This task requires study skills and the integration of new information with old information for storage. Tests of reading comprehension, on the other hand, test readers' skills at finding requested information in the text. These two situations provide different outcomes (Johnston, 1981), and the problem is very probably compounded by the fact that reading comprehension tests usually contain texts which are considerably shorter than those used in the classroom.

There is a further aspect of the task which can produce important differences in the numbers which reading comprehension tests give us. The questions which are asked in order to assess reading comprehension are not all created equal. Unfortunately it is not simply the case that some are harder than others (Johnston, 1981). Some are harder than others in some situations and easier than others in other situations. Take for example questions constructed from information which is clearly stated in one or more sentences in the text. If such questions test information which is not central to the text, then students will have little trouble answering them if they have ready access to the text while answering, but lots of trouble if they do not have the text available. However, if the information tested is very central to the text, the text access while answering questions will make little difference to performance. Nevertheless, having the text available tends to bias them toward using it, even when it is not appropriate to do so. On the positive side, we should mention that Raphael and Pearson (1982) found that students can be trained to overcome such a bias.

Situational Context

The context or setting in which reading takes place (discussed in chapter 2, above) also has a powerful influence on the outcomes of the reading. Harste, Burke, and Woodward (1982) showed that when children retell stories to teachers, their recall is generally not the same as when they must retell them for other students *who have not read the text.* In this latter instance, children's recalls are much more complete than when they know that the listener has already read the text. Spiro (1977) also showed that under certain circumstances, such as those in a psychological study (similar to a testing situation), readers tend to keep the new information separate from their prior knowledge rather than try to integrate it as they do in normal reading. Apparently a testing expectation leads to different sorts of processing and storage than does a more "natural" expectation about why one is reading.

The point of these studies is that teachers can never assume that testing performance is typical performance, largely because test tasks are never truly representative of real reading tasks. Also, teachers can expect variation in a given student's performance depending upon when, where, and how the assessment occurs.

The Reader's Purpose

The issue of reader purpose is very important when it comes to the interpretation of test scores. A major threat to the validity of test scores is the fact that many readers, realizing that the material to be read for a test will probably never have to be dealt with again, make no attempt to integrate it with what they already know (Spiro, 1977). This means that what we have a measure of is not exactly what we had intended to measure; while we may want to measure knowledge integration, we end up measuring short term regurgitation.

As a second example of the effects of reader purpose, Pichert (1979) found that when readers read a text about a house with the intent of finding out what a prospective homebuyer needs to know, they learn and remember different text information than they do if they are reading to learn how to best burglarize the place. Similarly, if the reader's purpose is to read in order to answer multiple-choice questions, the reader reads with a different strategy than if he or she was reading in order to write an essay about the passage (Wilson, 1982). Another study emphasizing the importance of purpose (Reynolds, 1979) demonstrated that students who are repeatedly asked one type of question at regular intervals as they proceed through a long text start paying more attention in subsequent text segments to information of the sort they are being quizzed about.

On Taking Reading Comprehension Tests

Test taking, in general, is a learned skill. Millman, Bishop, and Ebel (1965) provided an examination of the skills required for taking tests in general. As education and assessment currently stand, students could flunk a test of reading comprehension not because they were inept at reading comprehension, but because they were inept at taking tests. Unfortunately, the score we receive from a standardized test does not show which factor—comprehension ability or test-taking ability—has been responsible for the score. More specifically, if readers score well, we can be reasonably sure that they will have little difficulty with reading (and schoolwork in general); however, if they score low, we cannot predict with certainty that they will do poorly in schoolwork generally or in a given class in particular. We can make the assertion about high scores because high scores tell us that students possess reading ability, test-taking ability, and at least reasonable intelligence. However, low scores tell us little about their cause. Mere test-taking ability alone, for example, may have caused a low score, regardless of reading ability or intelligence. High scores imply the integration of several factors; low scores imply only that at least a single factor was missing.

Reader personality characteristics can also influence students' performance on reading comprehension tests. One such characteristic is their anxiety level. This factor interacts with various contextual influences sometimes in complex ways. For example, the time limits which are imposed in standardized tests are a strongly negative influence on test performance of anxious children. This effect will also be influenced by students' perceptions of the function of the test and its impact upon their lives (Wigfield, 1981).

Thus, the test itself and the test situation influence students' scores on our tests, but in a given student's score, we cannot tell how much of the score is due to these factors and how much is due to what we wanted to measure.

Using Research to Better Assess Reading Comprehension

While research has pointed out problems with our assessment of reading comprehension, at the same time it has indicated some remedies to the problems and some new directions for us to develop. In this section we examine these two implications of the research discussed in the previous section.

Assessing Prior Knowledge

The nature and effects of methods of dealing with the influence of prior knowledge were examined above. Johnston (1981) suggested a different approach. This approach is to cease treating prior knowledge as a nuisance variable and instead try to measure it. This would give us a valuable context within which to interpret students' reading comprehension performance. Such an approach would have these added advantages:

1. One could see whether or not failure could be attributed simply to the fact that the reader had insufficient prior knowledge to allow adequate comprehension.
2. One could identify students whose failure was due not to a lack of prior knowledge, but to a failure to *use* it.

3. Since reading unfamiliar material often requires a different set of strategies from those required to read familiar material, one could assess the availability and use of such strategies.

We *could* get this type of information by modifying our reading comprehension tests and possibly our vocabulary tests. For example, we might have vocabulary tests which are specific to the passages in our comprehension tests. Such modifications could be advantageous not only on standardized tests, but also on the kinds of informal tests given in content-area classes and in reading laboratories. We already know that prequestioning functions to orient the readers to the topic and encourages them to actively engage their prior knowledge in their reading (e.g., Hansen, 1981). However, there is a second less recognized function of pretests, particularly ones that focus on existing knowledge about a topic and the key vocabulary relevant to the text to be read, namely, to inform the teacher about the extent of the students' prior knowledge. With this information the teacher can evaluate the students' subsequent mastery of the context. Suppose student A scores well on the prior knowledge assessment and student B scores poorly. Then suppose they both score poorly on an end of the unit content mastery test. Student A probably needs some work on comprehension skills or maybe even some lower level reading skills; student B, on the other hand, probably needs concept development work on the specific topic of the unit.

Assessing Textual Characteristics

Problems with the prior knowledge factor have forced test designers to acknowledge the fact that the texts used in reading comprehension tests have not been representative of the normal texts. With current tests, all we can do is remember to take scores with a grain of salt, knowing that the texts are not representative. However, by taking the Johnston approach to the prior knowledge problem, test constructors would no longer be bound to using many short texts. Instead, they could use a few substantial texts, with more structure built into them, thus producing a more valid task.

Interestingly, studies have indicated that readers differ in their ability to *use* the structure in text to help them comprehend (e.g., Meyer, Brandt, and Bluth, 1981; Gordon, 1980). This is a serious problem for a secondary school student and even more serious a problem at the college level. However, it does seem eminently remediable, so perhaps we can begin to assess directly whether or

not a reader benefits from text structure by evaluating performance on texts which exhibit different structures (including, of
course, those with no apparent structure).

The common types of structure which occur in content-area
texts could be taught by content teachers since knowledge of such
structures assists readers in their comprehending of the text [see
Bartlett (1978) for a demonstration of the beneficial effects of such
instruction]. If structures are taught, then such knowledge becomes
a target for assessment—we need to know whether or not our
instruction has worked. Use of structure leads directly to the issue
of reader purpose, since that can determine how the reader uses
the text structure.

Assessing Reasoning Strategies

Raphael (1980) worked out a relatively simple way to assess the
kinds of questioning-answering strategies students use to generate
and/or select answers to questions. A more elaborate description of
the process can be found in other sources (Raphael, 1980; Raphael
and Pearson, 1982; or Raphael, 1982); however, we detail its
essential features here.

The process assumes that there are three basic approaches a
student can use to generate an answer to a question (Pearson and
Johnson, 1978). Upon getting a question, a student can search the
text in order to find the sentence from which the question was
generated and then select an answer from *that particular sentence.*
Pearson and Johnson called this a text-explicit (TE) strategy; when
Raphael used the approach with junior high students, she used the
mnemonic, "RIGHT THERE," to capture the notion that the answer
was "right there where the question came from." Second, a student
can find the sentence the question came from, but select an answer
from another part of the text, recognizing (hopefully) that there is
a logical relationship between question and answer. Pearson and
Johnson called this strategy text-implicit (TI); Raphael labelled it
"THINK AND SEARCH," in order to capture the notion that you
have to both search the text and think about how the two ideas can
be integrated. Third, a student can recognize that while the question is motivated by the text, the answer must come from his or
her prior knowledge. Pearson and Johnson called this script-
implicit (SI, where script = prior knowledge); Raphael coined "ON
YOUR OWN," to capture the notion that the answer came from

the student's own knowledge base. In the simplified example below, the three types of strategies are illustrated.

> Matthew broke both of Susan's rackets the night before the tennis match. He was afraid she would beat him.
> 1. RIGHT THERE
>   Q: When did Matthew break both of Susan's rackets?
>   R: The night before the tennis match.
> 2. THINK AND SEARCH
>   Q: Why did Matthew break both of Susan's rackets?
>   R: He was afraid she would beat him.
> 3. ON YOUR OWN
>   Q: Why was Matthew afraid Susan would beat him?
>   R: He knew she was a better player.

It takes about fifteen to thirty minutes to teach students this little scheme. Then they can attempt to apply it to the test-question answers they either generate or select. They can simply code which of the three strategies they thought they had used. It takes only a few seconds per response for students who have been oriented to the scheme to add this additional coding.

The information gained can be used in three ways. First, a teacher can make differential judgments about response quality for items on which students did or did not use the strategy most obviously invited by the question and the information available. Second, teachers can evaluate the degree to which students are able to monitor their own strategies—how often the students actually use the strategies they say they use. Third, teachers can use the data diagnostically to form groups composed of students who need more training on how to allocate their available resources (text and prior knowledge) appropriately. Raphael (1982) outlined both formal and informal instructional procedures.

Assessing Reader Purpose

Reading for a specific purpose becomes increasingly important in secondary school. Some readers are possibly less able to adjust their reading strategies to suit their purposes than are others. This is another aspect of mature reading comprehension which we must begin to evaluate in secondary school.

Sometimes, reader purpose is at odds with writer purpose. The writer might intend to persuade, and the reader might intend to gather facts. In such cases the readers must know how to override the structure of the text and to impose their own structure. There is a great need for research on how to teach and how to assess this ability.

Assessing Test Taking

Since part of a student's test score will be determined by test-taking ability rather than reading comprehension ability, we must either find out the extent of its influence for each individual (as suggested for prior knowledge) or try to minimize its effects. Measuring each individual's test-taking ability would be very difficult indeed, so the alternative is to minimize its effects. This can be done, in part, by teaching all students to be test wise. Millman, Bishop, and Ebel (1965) provided the necessary strategies, and showed that instruction in these strategies can be effective. From secondary school onwards (if not before) test-taking skill is a survival skill in all subjects, so the suggested instructional investment would be readily justified in the curriculum.

The fact that more anxious students perform less well on tests may require alternatives in testing practice and in instruction. At least some of this negative pressure can be removed in this way:

1. Increase the time allowed to complete the test.
2. Use instructions which reduce fear of failure by reducing evaluative pressure. For example, reassure students that missing some problems is expected because some are hard (since older students take the test too). This suggestion is probably not entirely adequate for reducing fear of failure since it is often so deeply engrained. A more systematic attempt would require teaching the student throughout school what tests are for (to assist in instructional decisions) and how best to perform on them.
3. One could administer tests both with and without time limits, and take the best of the two.
4. One could also build into testing programs indices of test anxiety level. All it requires is a few attitudinal response items included before and/or after the body of assessment items. Teachers could temper their judgments about content knowledge in light of such anxiety data.

Conclusion

This chapter makes four main points. First, there are several important limitations on the interpretation of current reading comprehension test scores. If nothing else, the reader has been warned of the frailties of the information obtained from tests. Forewarned, we trust, is forearmed.

Second, certain aspects of reading comprehension which are especially relevant to secondary schools, and which have been neglected in our assessments include readers' use of the various text structures provided by authors, their abilities to overcome such built-in structures, and their use of various strategies to remember information and answer questions. These are important aspects of reading which we should begin to assess, at least informally.

Third, biasing factors must be taken into account when reading comprehension is being assessed. In the past, we have dealt with prior knowledge differences by trying to provide enough different topics that we can ignore such reader differences. Since such differences are important for our interpretation of a reader's comprehension ability, we suggest that a better alternative is to actually measure the differences. This approach is also suggested for differences in anxiety level which would otherwise color our interpretation of scores.

Fourth, we should make explicit to the student the demands and strategies involved in our assessments. This means teaching students not only how to comprehend, but also how to demonstrate in a test situation that they have comprehended. We should also honestly inform students of the purpose of the test and teach them how to deal with that purpose and its implications for them. We should also teach them how to vary their strategies for answering questions. Perhaps students will learn that assessment serves a valuable function, and possibly they will even find it profitable to self-assess. Indeed, perhaps we should directly inculcate such ideas, even teaching beneficial procedures such as those suggested by the work of Day (1980), Bartlett (1978), or Raphael (1980). Consider the advantages of students shouldering the burden of their own assessment. How much more profitably teachers could spend their time—instructing rather than assessing.

References

Aiken, E. G., Thomas, G. S., and Schennum, W. A. Memory for a lecture: Effects of notes, lecture rate and informational density. *Journal of Educational Psychology*, 1975, *67*, 439–444.

Bartlett, B. J. Top-level structure as an organizational strategy for recall of classroom text (Doctoral dissertation, Arizona State University, 1978). *Dissertation Abstracts International*, 1979, *39*, 6641A. (University Microfilms No. 79-11113)

Brown, A. L., and Smiley, S. S. Rating the importance of structural units of prose passages: A problem of metacognitive development. *Child Development*, 1977, *48*, 1–8. (ERIC No. EJ 162 644)

Coleman, E. B. Developing a technology of written instruction: Some determinants of the complexity of prose. In E. Rothkopf and P. Johnson (Eds.), *Verbal learning research and the technology of written instruction*. New York: Columbia University Teachers College Press, 1971.

Day, J. D. Training summarization skills: A comparison of teaching methods. Unpublished doctoral dissertation, University of Illinois, 1980.

Gordon, C. J. The effects of instruction in metacomprehension and inferencing on children's comprehension abilities (Doctoral dissertation, University of Minnesota, 1980). *Dissertation Abstracts International*, 1980, *41*, 1004A. (University Microfilms No. 8019528)

Hansen, J. The effects of inferencing training and practice on young children's reading comprehension. *Reading Research Quarterly*, 1981, *16*, 391–417. (ERIC No. EJ 245 663)

Harste, J., Burke, C., and Woodward, V. Children's language and world: Initial encounters with print. In J. Langer and M. Smith-Burke (Eds.), *Reader meets author/bridging the gap: A psycholinguistic and sociolinguistic perspective*. Newark, Del.: International Reading Association, 1982. (ERIC Clearinghouse Accession No. CS 006 710)

Johnston, P. Prior knowledge and reading comprehension test bias (Doctoral dissertation, University of Illinois, 1981). *Disseration Abstracts International*, 1982, *42*, 3856A. (University Microfilms No. 8203497)

Johnston, P., and Pearson, P. D. *Prior knowledge, connectivity, and the assessment of reading comprehension* (Technical Report No. 245). Champaign: University of Illinois, Center for the Study of Reading, June 1982.

Kintsch, W., and Keenan, J. Reading rate and retention as a function of the number of propositions on the base structure of sentences. *Cognitive Psychology*, 1973, *5*, 257–274.

Kintsch, W., Kozminsky, E., Streby, W. J., McKoon, G., and Keenan, J. M. Comprehension and recall of text as a function of content variables. *Journal of Verbal Learning and Verbal Behavior*, 1975, *14*, 196–214. (ERIC No. EJ 119 504)

Meyer, B. J. F. *The organization of prose and its effect on memory*. The Hague: Moulton, 1975.

Meyer, B. J. F., Brandt, D. M., and Bluth, G. J. Use of top-level structure in test: Key for reading comprehension of ninth-grade students. *Reading Research Quarterly*, 1981, *16*, 72–103. (ERIC No. EJ 234 112)

Millman, J., Bishop, C. H., and Ebel, R. An analysis of test-wiseness. *Educational and Psychological Measurement*, 1965, *25*, 707–726.

Paivio, A. *Imagery and verbal processes*. New York: Holt, 1971.

Pearson, P. D. *A context for instructional research on reading comprehension* (Technical Report No. 230). Champaign: University of Illinois, Center for the Study of Reading, 1982.

Pearson, P. D., and Johnson, D. D. *Teaching reading comprehension.* New York: Holt, Rinehart and Winston, 1978.

Pearson, P. D., Gallagher, M., Goudvis, A., and Johnston, P. *Analysis of text flow patterns in children's exposition.* Book in preparation, 1982.

Pichert, J. W. *Sensitivity to what is important in prose* (Technical Report No. 149). Champaign: University of Illinois, Center for the Study of Reading, November 1979. (ERIC Document Reproduction Service No. ED 179 946; 64p.)

Raphael, T. E. The effects of metacognitive strategy awareness training on students' question answering behavior (Doctoral dissertation. University of Illinois, 1981). *Dissertation Abstracts International*, 1981, *42*, 544A. (University Microfilms No. 8114465)

Raphael, T. E. *Improving question answering performance through instruction* (Reading Education Report No. 32). Champaign: University of Illinois, Center for the Study of Reading, 1982.

Raphael, T. E., and Pearson, P. D. *The effects of metacognitive training on children's question-answering behavior* (Technical Report No. 238). Champaign: University of Illinois, Center for the Study of Reading, 1982.

Raphael, T. E., Winograd, P., and Pearson, P. D. Strategies children use in answering questions. In M. L. Kamil and A. J. Moe (Eds.), *Perspectives on reading research and instruction* (Twenty-ninth Yearbook of the National Reading Conference). Washington, D.C.: National Reading Conference, 1980.

Reynolds, R. E. The effect of attention on the learning and recall of important text elements (Doctoral dissertation, University of Illinois, 1979). *Dissertation Abstracts International*, 1980, *40*, 5380A. (University Microfilms No. 8009333)

Spiro, R. J. Remembering information from text: The "state of schema" approach. In R. C. Anderson, R. J. Spiro, and W. E. Montague (Eds.), *Schooling and the acquisition of knowledge.* Hillsdale, N.J.: Lawrence Erlbaum, 1977.

Thorndyke, P. W. Cognitive structures in comprehension and memory of narrative discourse. *Cognitive Psychology*, 1977, *9*, 77–110.

Tuinman, J. Reading is recognition—When reading is not reasoning. In J. C. Harste and R. F. Carey (Eds.), *New perspectives on comprehension* (Monograph in Language and Reading Studies No. 3). Bloomington: Indiana University Press, 1979.

Wigfield, A. *Teaching test-taking skills and developing positive test motivation in the classroom.* Paper presented at the annual meeting of the American Education Research Association, Los Angeles, 1981.

Wilson, P. T. The effects of test expectancy on inspectional behavior and on the selection of retrieval cues during studying. Unpublished doctoral dissertation, University of Virginia, 1982.

10 Organization and Management of Programs

Joan Nelson
State University of New York at Binghamton

Harold L. Herber
Syracuse University

Research directly related to the organization and management of secondary school reading programs is scarce. More research is reported on the use of particular instructional strategies or materials within secondary reading programs than on the organization and management of the programs themselves. Nonetheless, it is possible to draw productive inferences for the operation of secondary reading programs from related research on the needs of secondary school students, on the nature of reading comprehension, on the efficacy of instructional strategies, and on the salient features of successful school reading programs.

This chapter contains the following: (1) a general description of current reading programs in secondary schools; (2) a review of the questionable educational assumptions on which these programs appear to be based; (3) a presentation of the research evidence and authoritative opinion related to these assumptions; and (4) a discussion of the implications to be drawn from all of the above for the organization and management of secondary school reading programs.

Current Programs

In spite of a growing concern for the improvement of reading instruction, the organization and management of secondary reading programs has changed relatively little over the past two decades. The predominant mode of organization is the creation of special reading classes for limited groups of students. Usually, these take the form of small remedial classes for students who appear to be severely deficient in reading performance and/or larger corrective classes for students who are performing a year or two below their expected levels of achievement. For the most part, these classes provide instruction to increase students' proficiency in the identical basic reading skills taught in the elementary schools. Occasionally, developmental classes are offered for students who are performing at or above their expected achievement levels; these are intended to refine students' present skills and to develop more advanced study skills. Local resources and perceived needs dictate the number of classes and the balance among these three types in any given secondary school. Only rarely does one find reading programs that include a sustained commitment to providing reading instruction for all students in every class where reading is needed to be successful. Even then, it is likely to be a supplement to the special classes.

This predominance of remedial and corrective reading classes exists in spite of advice and admonitions to the contrary, extending back to early in this century. Recommendations for providing reading instruction to all students through the content of the various courses and for reducing the reading classes organized for special groups appear with increasing intensity and frequency in a progressive review of the literature (Artley, 1944; Gates, 1960; Herber, 1970, 1978; Karlin, 1977; Robinson, 1975, 1978; Vacca, 1981; and a host of others). However, these recommendations have either been ignored or dealt with mostly in lip service by decision makers in secondary schools. The reasons for the gap between textbook principles and classroom practice seem to be based on pragmatics, tradition, faulty assumptions, and the inertia that results from not knowing how to make the necessary changes.

Pragmatics and Tradition

The pragmatics of conforming to criteria for categorical aid from state and federal funds have dictated the nature of secondary school reading programs more than have research and enlightened commentary. This was especially true during the 1960s and 1970s. Most aid for secondary school reading programs was directed to special groups and required "pull-out programs" that created special reading classes for eligible students. The availability of funds enabled the hiring of reading specialists trained to function in traditional remedial reading programs stressing a deficit skills-recycling model. Naturally, they set up reading laboratories and remedial and corrective reading classes, which multiplied and flourished because supporting funds were provided. Too often such classes were created not because of students' assessed needs but because funds were increasingly available. School districts suddenly found large numbers of deficient readers among their secondary school student population, "requiring" the districts to set up the special classes and, of course, to draw funds from the categorical aid. Financial support was not given to programs that emphasized reading instruction for all students in content areas. Thus, such programs were rarely created or instituted. None of this is surprising if one understands the pragmatics involved in operating a school.

When placed in a stressful position that requires a productive response, one instinctively resorts to what is familiar. Reading personnel faced with what appears to be a large number of students needing reading instruction will resort to what is familiar. In the main, what is familiar is the reading instruction that is appropriate either for the elementary grades or for the reading clinic. Students' learning needs are perceived in light of the teachers' instructional strengths. The program is dictated by that relationship. The teachers' instructional strengths are sources of security because they are familiar. Thus the traditional forms of remedial and corrective reading practice were transferred from the elementary school to the secondary school without serious consideration of the kind of reading instruction that is needed by secondary students in their efforts to apply the skills they possess to the more difficult and sophisticated reading tasks required of them in content-area textbooks.

It should be noted here that we are not against secondary remedial and corrective reading classes for students who really need them. What we object to is recycling larger and larger numbers of students through basic reading skills because of a misinterpretation of the difficulties that students encounter in reading their content-area textbooks and because remedial and corrective instruction is the only game in town.

Questionable Assumptions

The existence of remedial and corrective reading classes as the predominant response to secondary school reading needs seems to be based on several questionable assumptions. These inherent assumptions are discussed below in the light of research and authoritative opinion.

Assumption one: Elementary school reading instruction is adequate and sufficient to meet the more sophisticated and challenging reading tasks of the secondary school curriculum. Many students experience learning problems as they move from the relatively protected environment of self-contained classrooms in intermediate grades to the less solicitous, more demanding environment of junior and senior high school. These learning problems are frequently observed in students' reading performance. As students make the transition from elementary to secondary schools, they leave behind them carefully controlled reading materials and are confronted with a variety of resources, embodying new and increasingly sophisticated concepts, couched in complicated language, and saturated with unfamiliar terminology.

School personnel sometimes misinterpret this phenomenon. Believing that the reading instruction provided in elementary grades should be sufficient for a lifetime, they may leap to the conclusion that students are lacking in basic skills when they experience difficulty in reading their content-area textbooks. Lower achieving students, particularly, are viewed as lacking in the basic reading skills when they stumble over unfamiliar words in their content-area texts, when they have difficulty formulating sophisticated concepts out of a multiplicity of information, or when they are unable to infer ideas not explicitly stated in the text. What is lacking is not students' basic skills but a recognitoin by educators that

> the transition from reading materials containing common words and familiar concepts to content-area textbooks containing uncommon vocabulary and unfamiliar concepts involves a change in the reading process from recognition of known words to acquisition of new words, from reconstruction of meaning out of experience to creative construction of new meanings and new experience. (Nelson and Herber, 1981)

What is being observed by educators and experienced by these students is not necessarily the result of poor instruction or flawed learning, but a manifestation of the need for a continuation of instruction in reading. Even as students once had to "learn to read" they must now "learn to read to learn" (Herber, 1981).

The instruction needed for students to "learn to read to learn" is different from what they received in elementary grades. Unfortunately, the traditional response to students with this perceived need is to assume they did not acquire what was taught in the elementary program and to recycle them through the same instruction—over and over again, if deemed necessary—in remedial and corrective reading classes. But this is only one result of misjudging the sufficiency of elementary reading instruction for the demands of secondary school education.

Many students of average achievement and above do *not* manifest reading problems when responding to their content-area texts. When given assignments, they can reproduce the information from the text without apparent difficulty. This is taken as evidence for the adequacy of their reading skills and, consequently, they receive no further instruction in reading. They are not taught the more sophisticated aspects of comprehension: developing concepts by drawing inferences from the text; synthesizing newly-acquired, content-specific knowledge with previously-held world knowledge. Some students of average achievement and above "learn to read to learn" on their own, more by chance than by design, and they perform well in their courses. Many do not, and limp along on the minimal skills they were able to adapt in their transition from elementary to secondary schools.

Though there is ample evidence that students are learning the basic decoding and comprehension skills (Farr, Tuinman, and Rowls, 1975; Farr, Fay, and Negley, 1978; Farr and Blomenberg, 1979; Micklos, 1980), the data from the National Assessment for Educational Progress (NAEP, 1981) reviewed in chapter 1, above, suggest a need for concern regarding the performance of secondary school students. These findings have several implications for secondary school reading programs. While elementary school students have made significant gains on all measures, secondary school students have not. Further, the data indicating a significant decline in secondary school students' ability to draw inferences from what they read raise serious questions about the organization and management of secondary reading programs and the assumption that elementary reading skills are sufficient for secondary needs. It seems a paradox that in content-area classes, where the need for higher level inferential reading-reasoning skill is constant, teachers generally are not prepared to teach the skill as part of their curriculum; and in corrective reading classes, trained reading teachers recycle students through skills that apparently are not those in which students are generally deficient. In short, secondary school reading programs rarely provide instruction in the skills most needed for successful performance in secondary schools. The NAEP results should not be surprising to anyone. Students cannot be held responsible for what schools do not teach.

The assumption of the sufficiency of elementary instruction to meet secondary school reading needs is clearly inappropriate. Only a small percentage of secondary school students need to be recycled through elementary reading skills. Indeed, there is evidence that these measures have been helpful for students experiencing severe difficulties in reading (Spache, 1976); however, what most secondary students need is a continuing program of instruction related to their content curriculum that builds on the basic skills they have acquired and teaches the higher level critical and creative reading-reasoning processes appropriate to the tasks assigned them.

Assumption two: Skills taught in reading classes transfer automatically to the reading of content-area textbooks. One need not look far to find reports of secondary and college teachers bemoaning their respective learners' inability to comprehend required reading materials in the sciences, the social sciences, literature, and mathematics. What they fail to recognize is that reading is not simply a process that occurs automatically through application of the segmented sets and sequences of reading skills taught in the elementary schools. A growing body of evidence indicates that

> reading comprehension occurs as a complex interaction among all the knowledge systems operating within the reader—conceptual, social, linguistic, etc.—and all the linguistic systems operating within the text—grapho-phonic, syntactic, and semantic. (Nelson and Herber, 1981)

Meaning resides in the experience of the reader as well as in the content of the text. The related knowledge and experience that the reader brings to the text influences, to a great extent, what the reader is able to interpret from the text (Adams and Bruce, 1980; Adams and Collins, 1979; Anderson, Spiro, and Montague, 1977; Kamil, 1978; Rumelhart, 1977; Santa and Hayes, 1981; Spiro, Bruce, and Brewer, 1980).

Elementary school reading programs recognize the importance of background knowledge in reading when they use basal readers containing vocabulary, concepts, and values that are familiar in pupils' experience. Stories about home, family, friends, pets, play, etc. abound in elementary readers. By the end of the elementary grades, with good instruction, most pupils can successfully use their reading skills to recognize common vocabulary and to reconstruct familiar meanings. The mistake lies in the assumption that these skills transfer automatically to the reading of textbooks containing uncommon vocabulary, unknown concepts, and unfamiliar values. That some students make this transfer with apparent ease is testimony to their reading and reasoning powers; that many have difficulty should be no surprise to educators (Nelson and Herber, 1981).

Students who have limited knowledge of the technical vocabulary, the organizing principles, and the significant concepts related to a particular discipline will be limited in their ability to read and comprehend text material in that discipline no matter how well the basic reading skills were learned. Thus, at the secondary level, reading is best taught in the context of the content in which it is required. It is the content-area teacher who is in the best position to provide instruction (1) that builds positively on basic reading skills instead of recycling them, (2) that prepares students for reading assignments, (3) that guides students' reading of content materials, and (4) that helps students to integrate new ideas and meanings into a conceptual framework to support comprehension of the more complex and sophisticated reading tasks of the discipline.

Assumption three: Student deficit rather than program deficit. Though all of the preceding discussion speaks to this assumption as well, it is worth stating that the inclusion of increasingly larger numbers of secondary school students in remedial and corrective reading classes, when there is no evidence of a generalized deficiency in the basic reading skills, should prompt an immediate reexamination of program needs. It is our conviction that if all secondary school students had the benefit of reading instruction in every classroom where reading is required, and if reading strategies were taught simultaneously with the content of the subject being taught, there would be little need to use the word "deficit" in relation to either students or programs. Content-area reading instruction acknowledges and accepts the skills that students bring from the elementary grades and builds positively on them. It acknowledges that students will experience difficulty in transferring and adapting their skills to manage content reading tasks, and it builds the higher level inferential reading and reasoning skills essential for appropriate response to sophisticated concepts and materials.

Studies of teaching reading in content areas, while equivocal because of the many constraints imposed by field-based research, generally support the value of such instructional strategies. For example, students improve in their concept attainment (Herber, 1964), in their acquisition of technical vocabulary (Barron and Melnick, 1973), in their comprehension skills (Berget, 1973; Sanders, 1977), and in their ability to organize information and perceive relationships implicit in materials read (Earle, 1973; Alvermann, 1980).

Evaluations of programs for teaching reading in content areas in secondary schools reveal that when instruction becomes accessible to all students, the number of corrective and remedial reading classes is drastically reduced. Sometimes corrective classes are omitted entirely with remedial classes retained only for the relatively few, genuinely handicapped readers in the schools (Herber, 1962; Davis et al., 1971; Herber, 1978).

Assumption four: The best use of secondary reading personnel is in organizing and managing remedial and corrective reading classes. This assumption—as follows from the discussion of the previous assumptions—should be questioned on three grounds: (1) need; (2) efficiency; (3) economy. We have argued in this chapter and elsewhere (Nelson and Herber, 1981) that most students who seem to need corrective reading instruction in middle and secondary schools really don't, and that those who do need corrective instruction, don't need the kind they are getting. Most students need, can, and should be offered reading instruction in regular content-area classrooms by content-area teachers. The true need for, and the appropriate use of, reading specialists' time and expertise is in helping content teachers to provide this instruction. For those few students who need special help, reading specialists can provide remedial and corrective instruction that parallels and supports what students are learning in their content-area classes.

By working through other teachers, reading specialists can reach and influence the learning of many more students than if they were to spend all their time working directly with students in remedial or corrective classes. Thus, a more efficient use of the reading specialists' expertise and time is available to school districts who choose to establish programs for teaching reading in content areas.

If the use of the reading specialists' time becomes more efficient, it also becomes more economical. The per pupil cost relative to reading personnel is dramatically reduced because the number of students influenced by the specialist is dramatically increased. The need for equipment and materials for use in special reading classes is also reduced because reading is taught through the curriculum-related resources used in content-area classes. These represent considerable savings to school districts which establish programs for teaching reading in content areas.

Implications for Organization and Management

As already noted, most secondary school reading programs consist of remedial and/or corrective reading classes organized for special groups of students, the criteria for which have been generally dictated by categorical funding. Occasionally, one also finds developmental reading classes and some attempts to provide reading instruction in content areas as a supplement to the remedial and corrective classes. The assumptions on which these programs appear to be based are not supportable when one considers the research and authoritative opinion regarding the needs of students, the nature of the reading process, and the efficacy of reading strategies.

We propose that the most appropriate organization of secondary reading programs would be just the opposite of what now generally exists. The main emphasis—the basic program—would be on teaching reading in content areas. Potentially all teachers and all students would be involved in the program. Reading and reasoning processes which are natural to the study of each discipline would be taught along with the relevant content of that discipline. Using instructional strategies outlined and illustrated elsewhere (Herber, 1978; Earle, 1976; Lunstrum and Taylor, 1978; Thelen, 1976; Robinson, 1978; Vacca, 1981), content teachers would simultaneously teach their course content and related reading/reasoning processes to all their students. We make this recommendation with confidence because we see this kind of instruction occurring in a variety of school districts and we know that it works.*

Reading classes for special groups of students would be organized only as supplements to this basic program and only as their need was clearly established. Clinical classes would be organized to provide help for students with specific learning disorders requiring specialized aid. Supplemental classes would be organized for students whose needs were not being fully met in the basic program and who would benefit from additional instruction in content-related reading and reasoning skills.

Conceptually, this organization makes a great deal of sense to most educators. Practically, the organization requires management related attitudes, skills, and support that are a severe test to the decision makers in a school. Where educators accept the management challenge, excellent programs are produced. This management challenge involves the following: (1) nurturing conditions; (2) staff development; (3) facilitating personnel.

*The authors are directors of the Network of Secondary School Demonstration Centers for Teaching Reading in Content Areas funded by the National Basic Skills Improvement Program, U.S. Department of Education (Grant # G008001963).

Several conditions are essential to the nourishment and prosperity of this program. First, there must be an unswerving commitment to the program by all administrators who control budget and who plan the use of teachers' time. Second, administrators must be willing to make supportive decisions that are consistent with their commitment: providing time for teachers to have access to one another for the study of teaching strategies; supporting curriculum study and refinement that are a natural outgrowth of the teachers' study of their own teaching; recognizing that student change follows teacher change and if sufficient time is not allowed to support the latter, the former will not occur. By their commitment and support, administrators and other decision makers manage the conditions which facilitate this program and make it prosper.

Staff development is central to this program. Teachers need to learn how to provide reading instruction as a natural part of their curriculum. Most content-area teachers have a reasonable repertoire of instructional strategies which they regularly use. By a reorganization of some of these strategies, by the addition of some new strategies, by the application of special materials which support the old and new strategies, teachers can adapt their teaching so as to emphasize reading skills along with course content. Specifically, the staff development program emphasizes instruction that includes the following (Nelson and Herber, 1981, p. 12–13):

1. Strategies that tap students' experience related or analogous to new concepts to provide conceptual frameworks for integrating new ideas with prior experience
2. Strategies that build new concepts or examine conflicting values before students are expected to comprehend them in reading
3. Strategies that provide students experience with the technical or uncommon vocabulary of the content area before they are expected to recognize that vocabulary in their reading
4. Feed-forward strategies that emphasize predicting and anticipating meanings on the basis of prior experience
5. Strategies that guide and support students' reading at literal, interpretive, and applied levels of comprehension
6. Strategies that build positively on students' skills instead of recycling them
7. Strategies that provide opportunities for interaction among students for pooling of experience; discussion of ideas; clarification of concepts; multiple recitation of vocabulary, facts, concepts, and values; and for taking advantage of the benefits of peer-tutoring
8. Strategies that guide and support creative reasoning in, through, and beyond the text material

For teachers to learn these strategies requires a staff development program based on materials and activities that explain and illustrate the instructional strategies, that provide opportunity for participants to practice the strategies and to receive feedback, that support the development and use of related curricular materials, and that encourage the refinement of their instructional skills over a long term. Further, the staff development program needs to be organized around a consistent information source so that as new generations of teachers become participants, what they learn will be consistent with what previous generations of participants have learned. The Network of Secondary School Demonstration Centers for Teaching Reading in Content Areas demonstrates a model program for this sort of staff development (Nelson, 1981).

Three main categories of personnel are involved in the management of this program: (1) administrators; (2) reading specialists; and (3) content-area teachers.

The superintendent is the key to successful implementation of a program for teaching reading in the content areas. The administrative staff in the central office and the administrators in the schools reflect the superintendent's priorities and his or her commitment to those priorities. If the superintendent *wants* this program, it will become a reality. If he or she does not believe in it, it will not become a district program and, at best, will be only a supplement or addendum to whatever *is* the priority. The superintendent need not have an intimate knowledge of the instructional strategies and materials in order to support the program. Knowing that it is effective for teachers and students and observing this effect in classrooms can be a sufficient knowledge base. The superintendent's primary role in this program is to provide the means by which the program can be established: time (for teachers to study the strategies and to create curriculum materials) and money (to provide the time for teachers to have access to one another in this study of teaching).

Building principals are also crucial to the success of such a program. Shoemaker and Fraser (1981) reviewed several well-known studies of schooling and implications for the roles of the principal. While most of the research they reviewed focuses on elementary schools, there is good reason to believe that the same conclusions hold for secondary schools. Shoemaker and Fraser identified four themes that emerged from their survey: "(1) assertive achievement-oriented leadership; (2) orderly, purposefully peaceful school climate; (3) high expectations for staff and pupils;

and (4) well-designed instructional objectives and evaluation system" (p. 180). We believe that these themes suggest administrative qualities essential to the management of a program that is organized around reading instruction in content areas. These are qualities that value and facilitate *instruction* in the fullest sense of the word. Our experience is that when principals with such qualities work with their teachers to organize a program for teaching reading in content areas, that program *is* implemented and it *is* beneficial to teachers and students alike.

The management role of reading specialists is to facilitate the work of the content-area teachers and to provide any specialized instruction in reading that is needed to supplement the basic program. They manage the staff development program for content-area teachers. This involves appropriate use of information sources, demonstrations of instructional strategies, observations of teachers' demonstrations, analysis of and advice on teachers' construction of instructional materials, participation in curriculum revision, and participation in program evaluation. Contrary to what some reading specialists fear, this program does not jeopardize their jobs because other teachers are teaching reading. Rather, the program merely changes their role to that of helping other teachers to teach reading. Thus the reading specialists' expertise is extended—through others—to all students rather than limited to only a selected few.

Classroom teachers have two management roles to play. They participate in the staff development program and become involved in a study of teaching that incorporates a simultaneous emphasis on reading, reasoning, and course content. While they are aided in this learning by reading specialists and administrators, in many respects their learning is self-managed. For learning to take place and to have an effect on classroom instruction, it must be driven by a personal desire to change. The attitudes and actions of participants are those of self-managed learners: they know what they need; they know how to find it; it is made available to them; they choose to receive it; and they make certain they learn it.

What teachers learn are strategies for improving students' learning of course content and related reading and reasoning processes. They manage these strategies in their classrooms as they help their students learn to read to learn.

Conclusion

Research related to the organization and management of secondary reading programs suggests that what now exists in most schools is not adequate to meet the need. What is needed is not just more of the same but actually the inverse of what now exists.

Now, programs are organized around remedial and corrective reading classes, supplemented occasionally by reading instruction in content areas. We propose that programs be organized around reading instruction in content areas, supplemented—as appropriate to students' needs—by remedial and corrective instruction in reading classes.

This proposed organization of secondary programs is easily manageable if it has administrative support. It is efficient in its use of teachers' time. It is economical in its per pupil cost. It is comprehensive in its inclusion of students. It is productive in its development of students' learning. It is stimulating in its support of the study of teaching and the improvement of instruction.

References

Adams, M., and Bruce, B. *Background knowledge and reading comprehension* (Reading Education Report No. 13). Champaign: University of Illinois, Center for the Study of Reading, January 1980. (ERIC Document Reproduction Service No. ED 181 431; 44p.)

Adams, M., and Collins, A. A schema-theoretic view of reading. In R. Freedle (Ed.), *New directions in discourse processing*. Norwood, N.J.: Ablex, 1979.

Alvermann, D. *Effects of graphic organizers, textual organization, and reading comprehension level on recall of expository prose* (Doctoral dissertation, Syracuse University, 1980). *Dissertation Abstracts International*, 1981, *41*, 3963A-3964A. (University Microfilms No. 8104509)

Anderson, R., Spiro, R., and Montague, W. E. *Schooling and the acquisition of knowledge*. Hillsdale, N.J.: Lawrence Erlbaum, 1977.

Artley, S. A study of certain relationships existing between general reading comprehension and reading comprehension in a specific content area. *Journal of Educational Research*, 1944, *37*, 464-473.

Barron, R. F., and Melnick, R. The effects of discussion upon learning of vocabulary meanings and relationships in tenth grade biology. In H. L. Herber and R. F. Barron, *Research in reading in the content areas: Second year report*. Syracuse, N.Y.: Syracuse University, Reading and Language Arts Center, 1973.

Berget, E. Two methods of guiding the learning of a short story. In H. L. Herber and R. F. Barron, *Research in reading in the content areas: Second year report*. Syracuse, N.Y.: Syracuse University, Reading and Language Arts Center, 1973.

Davis, A., Daughtrey, E., Brinson, V., and Hall, K. *A study of the effectiveness of teaching reading in the content areas of English, mathematics, science, and social studies*. Norfolk: Norfolk, Virginia, Public Schools, Department of Secondary Education, 1971.

Earle, R. A. The use of vocabulary as a structured overview in seventh grade mathematics. In H. L. Herber and R. F. Barron, *Research in reading in the content areas: Second year report.* Syracuse, N.Y.: Syracuse University, Reading and Language Arts Center, 1973.

Earle, R. A. *Teaching reading in science* (Reading Aids series). Newark, Del.: International Reading Association, 1976.

Farr, R., and Blomenberg, P. Contrary to popular opinion. *Early Years,* May 1979, 52–53, 68.

Farr, R., Fay, L., and Negley, H. *Then and now: Reading achievement in Indiana (1944–45 and 1976).* Bloomington: Indiana University Press, 1978. (ERIC Document Reproduction Service No. ED 158 262; 146p.)

Farr, R., Tuinman, J., and Rowls, M. *Reading achievement in the United States: Then and now.* [Report for Educational Testing Service (Contract DEC-71-3715 U.S.O.E.)]. Washington, D.C.: U.S. Government Printing Office, 1974. (ERIC Document Reproduction Service No. ED 109 595; 174p.)

Gates, A. The nature and function of reading in the content areas. In J. A. Figurel (Ed.), *New frontiers in reading.* Newark, Del.: International Reading Association, 1960.

Herber, H. L. *Teaching reading through seventh grade science content.* Unpublished manuscript sponsored by the Division of Research, N.Y. State Department of Education, 1962. (ERIC Document Reproduction Service No. ED 023 564; 30p.)

Herber, H. L. Teaching reading and physics simultaneously. In J. A. Figurel (Ed.), *Improvement of reading through classroom practice: Proceedings of the ninth annual convention of the International Reading Association* (Vol. 9). Newark, Del.: International Reading Association, 1964. (ERIC Document Reproduction Service No. ED 146 547; 347p.)

Herber, H. L. *Teaching reading in content areas.* Englewood Cliffs, N.J.: Prentice-Hall, 1970, 1978.

Herber, H. L. *An instructional model for teaching reading in content areas: Network report no. 1.* Syracuse, N.Y.: Syracuse University, A Network of Secondary School Demonstration Centers for Teaching Reading in Content Areas, 1981.

Kamil, M. Models of reading: What are the implications for instruction in comprehension? In S. Pflaum (Ed.), *Aspects of reading education.* Berkeley, Calif.: McCutcheon Publishing, 1978.

Karlin, R. *Teaching reading in high school* (3rd ed.). Indianapolis: Bobbs-Merrill, 1977.

Lundstrum, J., and Taylor, B. *Teaching reading in the social studies.* Newark, Del.: International Reading Association and ERIC/RCS, 1978. (ERIC Document Reproduction Service No. ED 157 008; 96p.)

Micklos, J. The facts, please, about reading achievement in American schools. *Journal of Reading,* 1980, *24,* 41–45. (ERIC No. EJ 231 928)

National Assessment of Educational Progress. *Three national assessments of reading: Changes in performance, 1970–1980* (Reading Report No. 11-R-01). Denver, Colo.: Education Commission of the States, April 1981. (ERIC Document Reproduction Service No. ED 200 898; 91p.)

Nelson, J. *A Staff Development Program for Teaching Reading in Content Areas: Network Report 2.* Syracuse University: Network for Secondary School Demonstration Centers for Teaching Reading in Content Areas, 1981.

Nelson, J., and Herber, H. *A positive approach to assessment and correction of reading difficulties in middle and secondary schools: Network report no. 3.* Binghamton, N.Y.: A Network of Secondary School Demonstration Centers for Teaching Reading in Content Areas, State University of New York, 1981.

Robinson, H. A. *Teaching reading and study strategies: The content areas.* Boston: Allyn and Bacon, 1975, 1978.

Rumelhart, D. E. Toward an interactive model of reading. In S. Dornic (Ed.), *Attention and performance VI.* Hillsdale, N.J.: Lawrence Erlbaum, 1977.

Sanders, P. L. The effects of instruction in the interpretation of literature on the responses of adolescents to selected short stories. In H. S. Herber and R. L. Vacca (Eds.), *Research in reading in the content areas: The third report.* Syracuse, N.Y.: Syracuse University, Reading and Language Arts Center, 1977.

Santa, C., and Hayes, B. (Eds.). *Children's prose comprehension: Research and practice.* Newark, Del.: International Reading Association, 1981. (ERIC Document Reproduction Service No. ED 198 492; 193p.)

Shoemaker, J., and Fraser, H. W. What principals can do: Some implications from studies of effective schooling. *Phi Delta Kappan,* 1981, *63*(3), 178-182. (ERIC No. EJ 255 029)

Spache, G. D. *Diagnosing and correcting reading disabilities.* Boston: Allyn & Bacon, 1976.

Spiro, R. J., Bruce, B. C., and Brewer, W. F. *Theoretical issues in reading comprehension.* Hillsdale, N.J.: Lawrence Erlbaum, 1980.

Thelen, J. *Improving reading in science* (Reading Aids series). Newark, Del.: International Reading Association, 1976. (ERIC Document Reproduction Service No. ED 116 181; 60p.)

Vacca, R. T. *Content area reading.* Boston: Little, Brown, 1981.

11 Specialized Services

Barbara C. Palmer, Virginia M. Brannock
Florida State University

In this chapter we look, in some depth, at the research related to specific programs or services (largely remedial in nature) set up to improve the reading of high school students. Like many good things in life, specialized reading services are based largely on faith. Little research evidence exists to suggest their lasting value. Many of these programs and services are described in the literature; few are presented in the framework of carefully-controlled research. In this chapter we highlight existing reports and then extract commonalities from the successful programs.

Historical Perspective

Some of the early calls for improved reading services were published more than half a century ago. Whipple (1925) reported, in the Twenty-fourth Yearbook of the National Society for the Study of Education, that the first step toward improving instruction in reading should be to secure accurate information about the status of reading in a school system and to determine desirable changes.

Twelve years after Whipple's call for a comprehensive reading program, Center and Persons (1937) completed their report of reading improvement in Theodore Roosevelt High School in New York City. They very thoroughly described how they tested 7,174 students using the Terman Group Test of Mental Ability, the New Stanford Reading Tests, the Haggery Reading Test, and the Iowa Advanced Reading Test. They found "large percentages of pupils in each grade reading below the accepted norm for the grade ..." (p. 14). It is interesting to read, now, about the background of the reading instruction.

> The depression, which may have been responsible for some of the reading difficulties of students and the reading problems

159

of high schools, was also responsible for a plan in Theodore
Roosevelt High School which provided remedial instruction
for hundreds of boys and girls. . . .

In December, 1934, a group of Civil Works Administration
teachers was offered to the English Department for assignment to remedial work. These teachers were for the most part
college graduates; some of them had Master's degrees. Many
of the older ones had, before the depression, held positions in
public and private schools. The majority had majored in English and related subjects, such as journalism and public speaking. However, there were teachers who held degrees in French,
German, science, law, sociology, and education. These teachers
has sufficient background and general education for the instruction as it was planned, but they lacked specific training
in the teaching of silent reading.

Therefore, from the very first day and throughout the
experiment, a daily conference of one hour has been devoted to
the training of these teachers. (p. 15)

Center and Persons also provided a detailed account of what the
instructors did to improve the reading skills and general scholar-
ship of the students in the reading program. They broke their
analyses down in various ways and, in general, reported favorable
results.

Through the years there have been a number of reports about
reading improvement in the secondary school, but little research.
The Forty-seventh Yearbook of the National Society for the Study
of Education, *Reading in the High School and College* (Henry,
1948), included the views of many of the pioneers in reading education. Many of the problems have been discussed from time to
time in such journals as *The Bulletin of the National Association of
Secondary-School Principals* and the *High School Journal.* A
number of monographs have been published by the International
Reading Association. As useful and informative as many of these
publications have been, little is based on research; however, much
of the sage advice seems related to the current scene.

Effects of Specialized Programs

In the remainder of this chapter, we present the effects of specialized programs—short-term and long-term—and then discuss
aspects of successful programs which might be useful to consider
for future research and practice.

Short-Term Effects

Aaron, Call, and Muench (1975) described the positive effects of one program with adolescents at a state youth development center. The program was computer-managed and individually prescribed. These youths, who were considered behaviorally disordered and delinquent, had a mean chronological age of 16.36, a mean reading score of 4.9, and a mean IQ of 81.69. With a mean attendance of 120.9 days in the program, the mean gain in total reading was one year and three months. Additionally, an attitude questionnaire evidenced a positive change in attitude toward school. The researchers attributed the success of the program to student control of planning, immediate learning feedback, a high level of on-task behavior, amount of time spent in actual reading, and a totally individualized program.

Simon et al. (1976) described a project with tenth graders who were four or more years below grade placement in both oral reading and reading comprehension. In a comparison of three groups of poor decoders, one group received a combination of taped echoic response method and segmented print materials; one group received the taped echoic response method and the same printed material in nonsegmented form; and one group was placed in a diagnostic prescriptive reading program. The tapes provided models of expert oral reading for imitation and word identification. For the first group, the polysyllabic words were spatially segmented to aid in word identification. At the end of a twelve-week-period of instruction, the Gilmore Oral Reading Test was administered. The group using segmented words had gained 8.7 months; the group using tapes and nonsegmented print had gained 6.4 months; while the group in the diagnostic prescriptive program had gained 1.6 months. On the Metropolitan Reading Test total reading, the group using the segmented print made the greatest gains, but the differences were not statistically significant. The researchers felt that the taped echoic response segmented print model provides students with (1) multisensory inputs of visual, auditory, and vocal stimuli; (2) an undistracted learning environment with individual carrels, cassette recorders, and earphones; (3) a degree of active participation; and (4) word-identification in a context of whole language.

Penty (1961) reported on a diagnostic prescriptive remedial reading program in grades seven, eight, and nine. Most students were excused from English or social studies class to attend the twice-weekly one-hour sessions. Students in one school were able to remain in the reading group for a year or more, if necessary; however, only twelve weeks' help was permitted many students in the second school. For that reason, retesting was done at twelve week intervals. Emphasis was given in setting purposes for improving reading and increasing self-confidence. Students were given help in groups of six, and a variety of methods was employed including visual, auditory, and kinesthetic. Practice was given in reading various types of content. In addition, the SQ3R study method was employed. The average gain in reading ability of the seventy-two students enrolled in the programs each twelve weeks was eight months in vocabulary and one year and two months in comprehension.

Steirnagle (1971) reported the progress of the Title I reading programs in El Paso, Texas. In the year 1967-68, there were twenty-one remedial students in grades nine through twelve in this program. With a September pretest score of 5.9, the group had gained three years and eight months when they were posttested in May. Eighty-two students were in the program the following year and gained one year, one month. Students who were accepted for the program were diagnosed for reading disabilities; then their instruction, practice, and reinforcement were individually prescribed.

Landis, Jones, and Kennedy (1973) reported on a curricular modification of secondary school reading which meets subject matter learning needs and remedial needs of learning disabled students. Content-area teachers restructured English, mathematics, and science courses to enable students with reading problems to succeed. When multisensory media experiences were provided to teach content-area material, textbooks were no longer the primary means of obtaining information. The reading specialist worked with students individually and in groups to develop word recognition, comprehension, and study skills on the basis of need. Although the method of presentation was changed, the courses were not "watered down." The researchers believed that relieving the urgency and pressure of content-area reading resulted in an increased interest in reading and an improved student self-concept.

A structured tutoring system (Metra-Basic Reading for Secondary Students) was introduced in seven secondary schools of the Department of Defense Dependent Schools (DODDS) located on American military installations in Japan, Korea, Okinawa, and the Philippines (Eckel, 1980). The professional staff, who received thorough instruction in the Metra System, trained volunteers to serve as reading tutors. These tutors were students in the secondary schools and, in one location, adult volunteers. The Metra-structured tutoring system provided a set of materials to work through but emphasized teaching techniques, positive reinforcement, and tutor-learner rapport. The 129 students in the program began with an average reading grade level of 4.4. They averaged a reading level of 6.8 on the posttest. The largest gains occurred in word attack. The average word attack grade for entering students on the pretest was 3.4; the posttest average was 11.2. The tutors had a significant gain in their reading ability as a result of being a tutor. The tutors averaged 7.5 on the pretest and 11.3 on the posttest. As a result of this pilot study, the Metra-structured tutoring system was expanded to thirty-two DODDS schools.

Sinatra (1973) used a point reinforcer system in a summer program for thirty-six students in grades eight through ten who were reading at a fourth to sixth grade level. A mean gain in reading level of one year, four months was achieved with twenty-one days of instruction. However, since eleven students dropped out before completing the program, it appears that the point system did not provide a strong enough incentive to maintain students' interest in the program.

Long-Term Effects

Few researchers conducted follow-up surveys two or more years after remediation ceased. And those that were conducted, according to Silberberg and Silberberg (1969) in a review of research in remedial reading, "almost invariably demonstrate that the beneficial effect of this remediation 'washes out' in a relatively short time after terminating remedial reading" (p. 34).

Rasmussen and Dunne (1962) studied the effect, over time, of placement in a corrective reading program and the dropout rate. The program began with fifty-nine seventh graders who were admitted on the basis of average intelligence, a reading disability two or more grades below reading norms, parental consent, and teacher recommendations. The program stressed improvement of study skills, participation, and reading for fun. A variety of interesting graded materials was purchased for each classroom. Students were encouraged to believe they were capable of improving their skills.

To measure the effectiveness of the program statistically, twenty of the fifty-nine students were matched with twenty similar students who were in the seventh grade a year earlier and had not received corrective reading instruction. Students were matched by intelligence, reading age score, parents' education, and amount of school absences. At follow-up three years later, the reading scores of both groups were compared. Students in the corrective reading classes made more improvement than those who had not had remediation, but the difference was small and not statistically significant. However, during this period nine out of the twenty control students had dropped out of school. It may be that the corrective program played a role in a higher retention rate for those receiving corrective instruction.

Evans (1968) evaluated the effects of a junior high special reading program for seventh and eighth grades by conducting follow-up testing one and two years later. The treatment varied with schools and teachers, but generally the program emphasized basic reading skills, comprehension, and vocabulary.

From the 193 students enrolled in the special classes, Evans was able to match sixty-seven students on the basis of sixth grade Iowa reading scores, average IQ, and junior high school attended with sixty-seven similar students who had not been enrolled in special classes. Thirty-nine of the pairs were retested one year later, and all sixty-seven pairs were retested in the tenth grade. On each of the two follow-up tests, the difference favoring those enrolled in the remedial program was found to be statistically significant, but extremely small. No difference was found between the students who had one semester of instruction and those who had two or more.

In another study, Evans compared ninety-five remedial reading students with seventy-six students who had received no remedial instruction. This comparison group was selected randomly from untreated students in the eleventh grade. A t-test showed no significant differences between groups on the Iowa Test of Educational Development which was given to them as ninth graders and again as eleventh graders. A test comparing remedial students with randomly selected students who may not have needed remediation would appear to be inequitable.

From these studies, Evans concluded that the present methods and content of the special reading courses surveyed were not meeting the needs of students. He felt that because students did not make substantial progress, the continued expenditures of time and money to provide remedial reading instruction is unwarranted.

Shaver and Nuhn (1971) reported the results of a tutorial program in reading and writing for the fourth, seventh, and tenth grade levels. Students were selected on the basis of discrepancy between performance and potential as measured by the California Test of Mental Maturity and the Sequential Tests of Educational Progress (STEP). At each grade level, students with the greatest discrepancies were randomly assigned to either a one-to-one or a one-to-three tutorial arrangement, or to the control group. Tutoring by auxiliary adult personnel took place one hour per day throughout the regular school year. In a two-week workshop, tutors were trained in diagnosing the student's reading and writing deficiencies, improving the student's self concept, and providing specific assistance in an accepting atmosphere in which success could be experienced. After one year in the program, the STEP test was administered, and it was found that the tutored groups had made significantly greater gains than the control group. Repeated testing with the STEP two years later revealed that the mean gains were sustained by those at the seventh and tenth grade levels, but not at the fourth grade level. At follow-up, no significant differences between the two tutorial arrangements were found. Shaver and Nuhn also found that students tutored as seventh and tenth graders had significantly higher English grades, and there were scattered effects on their grades in social studies and science.

Fiedler (1972) described a reading clinic established in a large comprehensive high school which provided individual diagnosis and remediation for students whose reading level was two or more years below expectancy. Most of the students were instructed as freshmen and had no additional help. After an average of twenty-five hours of remediation, students were retested and showed an average gain of 1.7 years in vocabulary and 2 years in comprehension.

To ascertain the effects of the reading program on attitude, Fiedler compared the responses from an interest inventory related to reading given on a follow-up inventory when they were seniors. Fiedler, who considered change in attitude a legitimate goal of remedial reading, found that in the comparison, twenty-two of the students expressed positive changes in their attitudes toward reading.

Newman (1969) interviewed and retested thirty-four of fifty-one high school dropouts who had received an average of thirteen months' instruction in high school remedial reading classes. The retesting occurred three years after the students had received the remedial instruction. Ranging in age from twenty to twenty-three years of age, all of the former students lived in a lower socioeconomic area. Most parents had an elementary education, and fathers worked in a trade requiring semiskilled or unskilled labor.

Twenty-four of the dropouts had been in classes for slow learners prior to high school, and six had been classified as mentally retarded. As a group they experienced many failures in high school; only two achieved all passing marks. Five had been reported as severe behavior problems, and many had been rated as unsatisfactory in citizenship. Most reported they had left school because of unsatisfactory school experiences.

As a result of their remediation while in high school (although their reading level mean was 3.3), each group showed gains exceeding normal expectancy. The gains suggested unrealized potential within the supportive atmosphere of the reading class and the possibility that even greater improvement could have taken place if remediation were provided on a school-wide basis. At follow-up three years later, the group which was reading below third grade level showed a mean gain of .7 years. Those above third and below fifth had gained .3 years while those reading above fifth grade level had lost .5 years. Newman stated,

> The dropouts in this study probably were potential dropouts long before they had reached high school. Their reading retardation was in evidence in the early elementary grades and became rather conspicuous in junior high. By the time they had reached high school, their mean reading retardation had increased to six years. It would seem that the greatest gains occurred during remediation. Subsequent to remediation, about three years later, they seem to make little progress, probably because they do so little reading. (p. 351)

Guy's (1976) "Relationship between Student Participation in a Secondary School Reading Program and Selected School Performance Variables" supported previous findings that short-term compensatory education does not produce significant long-term effects on objective measures of achievement or on school-related behavior.

This review of the literature shows that short-term, stopgap remedial reading programs of brief duration do not seem to make a great deal of difference in an individual's lifetime reading skills. Furthermore, no matter how innovative the program or how effective the method of instruction, it is unrealistic to assume that "band-aid approaches" have a significant or permanent effect on reading skills improvement.

Possible Commonalities for Success

In "A Critical Review of Approaches to Remedial Reading for Adolescents," Otto (1979) concluded that "what little research has been done with regard to secondary level remedial reading pro-

grams suggests that a whole language approach is beneficial."
This conclusion is evident as one examines the studies of programs
that seem to produce effective results. When attention is focused
on establishing a reading improvement program or service with
an emphasis on helping students understand our language, better
results are achieved. Miller (1974) reports in "A Psycholinguistic
Basis for Reading Improvement in the Secondary School" on constructing a model for a secondary school reading program. Her
conclusions, in a nutshell, were that secondary schools should
establish reading programs based on psycholinguistic theories
of reading instruction, consultants should be hired to work with
content-area teachers, evaluation should focus on affective as well
as cognitive areas of growth, including success in school subjects,
and there should be follow-up studies periodically.

To further support the need for language improvement in reading improvement programs in the secondary school, the reader
can examine the results of studies done by Mavrogenes (1977) and
Hoyt (1973). Mavrogenes assessed the performance of twenty
reading-disabled secondary school students who took Carol Chomsky's Tests of Five Stages of Language Development. She found
that eighteen of the twenty had a low level of linguistic competence
and observed that most of meaning miscues occurred during the
reading of complex language structures. She noted the importance
of strengthening the language competence as well as the reading
skills of similar students in secondary schools.

Hoyt (1973) examined the "Effects of an Individualized Reading
Program and Communication Skills through Authorship on the
Language and Reading Experience of Reluctant Readers at the
Secondary Level." Ninth grade students who had been identified
as reluctant readers were randomly assigned to one of four classes
upon entering the tenth grade. Hoyt concluded that combining an
individualized reading program with the development of communication skills produced gains in word meaning and paragraph
meaning in these reluctant readers at the secondary level.

By having a reading program based in language development,
it seems that there are changes not only in reading skills but also
in the attitudes of readers in secondary schools. Van Voorhees and
Scoblete (1975) reported a study involving two groups, one of disabled readers and one of better but unmotivated readers, receiving
one period of instruction in English and one in social studies four
days a week while a reading specialist worked intensively with
small groups of disabled readers. Teachers met for planning on
the fifth day. Students worked in multilevel texts. The researchers
reported, according to student questionnaire responses, improved

attitudes toward reading and individuals; teachers reported a lessening of racial and ethnic tensions; and posttesting indicated a 60 percent gain in reading ability.

The Madison Area Project in Syracuse (1964) also focused on combining reading improvement with personal development. The program was designed to increase academic achievement; increase the acquisition of social skills; motivate students to excel in academic and nonacademic pursuits; develop positive vocational attitudes, skills, and self concepts; develop a consistent program of public relations to inform and involve the community; and evaluate the program. A sequential approach to curriculum was developed in language arts, mathematics, science, reading, and social studies. Remedial reading clinics and a curriculum materials development center were created. School volunteers freed teachers from routine clerical work so that they could use their time and talents more fully. Closed circuit television was also used in the Madison Area Project. Tests given at the end of the second year were analyzed for personality grouping, sex, classroom grouping, ability groupings, grade, teacher, and change score.

At one time parents were left out of the educational process; such days, for better or worse, are gone, as reflected in part by Bigler (1974) in "Parental Use of Household Literature to Reinforce Secondary School Reading Instruction." Involved were twenty secondary school students who were reading one to three grade levels below grade placement. Bigler first delineated and defined the skills needed by secondary school students, then designed activities to practice and reinforce these skills, and carried out field testing to determine if parents could use these activities successfully. The activities designed to improve vocabulary, word recognition, comprehension, and rate were geared to household materials such as newspapers, magazines, phone books, junk mail, recipes, sewing patterns, maps, and catalogs. She concluded that guidelines could be devised to help readers improve their skills through household literature; parents could use those guidelines to their own satisfaction; and both teachers and parents reported improvements in the attitudes and reading skills of the students involved.

Combining community involvement, student aspirations, and a language-based reading improvement program, Hickerson (1973) focused on the "Application of a Reading Model to the Reading Syllabi of the Ten Largest U.S. Secondary School Districts." Her purpose was to design a comprehensive and effective model for a secondary reading syllabus to be used in the educational institutions as controlled by the culturally-different communities. The model was designed upon the recommendations of experts representing varying points of view on philosophy, sociology, psychology, linguistics, and language arts as well as on the findings of what was available in the literature. Her major philosophical conclusion drawn from the findings was that an effective reading program must emphasize the individual as a citizen gaining power within a community decision-making body of peers. Rather than treating the student as an isolated member of a powerless culturally-different community, the reading program must serve as a vehicle for transmitting the central concept of literacy embedded in the representative community.

Conclusion

What can we conclude about the status of specialized reading services in the secondary schools? The sparse research available seems to suggest that band-aid kinds of services which focus only on skills do not seem to be very effective in the long run. The trend now is to broaden the base of specialized reading services to include language and human development, content areas in the curriculum, and involvement of parents and the community. Some of these things have been going on from time to time in various places, but now, instead of being done sporadically, there seems to be a movement. Embedding specialized reading services into the curriculum, as suggested by Nelson and Herber in chapter 10, seems to be a healthy development. Such a movement echoes some of the advice given to us by many of the pioneers in the field of reading so many years ago.

References

Aaron, R. L., Call, L. T., and Muench, S. A language arts program for disturbed adolescents. *Journal of Reading*, 1975, *19*, 208–213. (ERIC No. EJ 127 480)

Bigler, M. A. G. Parental use of household literature to reinforce secondary school reading instruction (Doctoral dissertation, University of Michigan, 1974). *Dissertation Abstracts International*, 1975, *35*, 7146A–7147A. (University Microfilms No. 75-10133)

Center, S. S., and Persons, G. L. *Teaching high school students to read: A study of retardation in reading.* Champaign, Ill.: National Council of Teachers of English, 1937.

Eckel, J. A secondary tutorial program in U.S. Department of Defense dependent's schools in the Pacific. *Journal of Reading*, 1980, *23*, 687-690. (ERIC No. EJ 227 604)

Evans, H. An evaluation of the effects of junior high school special reading instruction upon subsequent reading performance (Doctoral dissertation, University of Illinois, 1968). *Dissertation Abstracts International*, 1969, *30*, 202A. (University Microfilms No. 69-10696)

Fiedler, M. Did the clinic help? *Journal of Reading*, 1972, *16*, 25-29. (ERIC No. EJ 063 991)

Guy, M. J. W. Relationship between student participation in a secondary school reading program and selected school performance variables. (Doctoral dissertation, University of North Dakota, 1976). *Dissertation Abstracts International*, 1977, *37*, 4262A-4263A. (University Microfilms No. 76-30304)

Henry, N. B. *Reading in the high school and college* (Forty-seventh Yearbook of the National Society for the Study of Education). Chicago: University of Chicago Press, 1948.

Hickerson, P. L. R. Application of a reading model to the reading syllabi of the ten largest U.S. secondary school districts (Doctoral dissertation, University of Southern California, 1973). *Dissertation Abstracts International*, 1973, *33*, 6791A-6792A. (University Microfilms No. 73-14411)

Hoyt, J. R. Effects of an individualized reading program and communication skills through authorship on the language and reading experience of reluctant readers at the secondary level. (Doctoral dissertation, University of Idaho, 1973). *Dissertation Abstracts International*, 1974, *34*, 4564A. (University Microfilms No. 74-04063)

Landis, J., Jones, R. W., and Kennedy, L. D. Curricular modification for secondary reading. *Journal of Reading*, 1973, *16*, 374-379. (ERIC No. EJ 070 443)

Madison area project: Syracuse action for youth. Cambridge, Mass.: Harvard Graduate School of Education, 1964. (ERIC Document Reproduction Service No. ED 002 458; 4p.)

Mavrogenes, N. A. *The language development of the disabled secondary reader.* Paper presented at the twenty-second annual convention, International Reading Association, Miami Beach, 1977. (ERIC Document Reproduction Service No. ED 141 763; 24p.)

Miller, E. F. A psycholinguistic basis for reading improvement in the secondary school (Doctoral dissertation, University of Southern California, 1974). *Dissertation Abstracts International*, 1974, *35*, 1964A. (University Microfilms No. 74-21490)

Newman, H. *The reading habits, attitudes, and achievements of high school dropouts.* New York: Odyssey Press, 1979.

Otto, J. A critical review of approaches to remedial reading for adolescents. *Journal of Reading*, 1979, *23*(3), 244-250.

Penty, R. C. Remedial reading pays in junior high schools. *Education*, 1961, *80*, 277-280.

Rasmussen, R. G., and Dunne, H. W. A longitudinal evaluation of a junior high school corrective reading program. *Reading Teacher*, 1962, *15*, 95-106.

Shaver, J., and Nuhn, D. The effectiveness of tutoring underachievers in reading and writing. *The Journal of Educational Research*, 1971, *65*, 107-112. (ERIC No. EJ 049 703)

Silverberg, N. E., and Silverberg, M. C. Myths in remedial education. *Journal of Learning Disabilities*, 1969, *2*, 209-217. (ERIC No. EJ 002 567)

Simon, L. H., Hansen, R. A., Ketsteen, I., and Porterfield, R. A remedial program for poor decoders in an inner-city high school. *Journal of Reading Behavior*, 1976, *8*, 311-319.

Sinatra, R. Summer reading program on a point reinforcer system. *Journal of Reading*, 1973, *16*, 395-400. (ERIC No. EJ 070 445)

Steirnagle, E. A five year summary of a remedial program. *Reading Teacher*, 1971, *24*, 537-542. (ERIC No. EJ 035 676)

Van Voorhees, S., and Scoblete, F. *Eleventh-grade core program.* Paper presented at the twentieth annual convention, International Reading Association, New York City, 1975. (ERIC Document Reproduction Service No. ED 105 423; 6p.)

Whipple, G. M. (Ed.). *Report of the national committee on reading* (Twenty-fourth Yearbook of the National Society for the Study of Education). Bloomington, Ill.: Public School Publishing Co., 1925.

12 Computer Literacy

Harry Singer
University of California—Riverside

Mariam Jean Dreher
University of Maryland

Michael Kamil
University of Illinois at Chicago

Chapters 1-11 have focused on the reading process, reading strategies, instructional strategies, and assessment. In this chapter we discuss how technology, particularly the computer, may become a potent force in each of these areas. Emphasis is placed on teacher education as a vital factor in the development of computer literacy.

Historical Perspective

Technological innovations in society and school have increased at a rapid pace in the twentieth century. This rate of increase can be appreciated by a time-line perspective beginning with the development of language in some distant time as the basic and primary means of communicating information. The next major development occurred in the Near East some 3,000 to 4,000 years ago with the invention of the alphabet, a system of signs for representing consonants and vowels in written communication. About 400 B.C. Socrates used a questioning method for eliciting latent ideas and getting persons to make admissions leading to the formulation of propositions in an argument (Stein, 1973). The Socratic method is still advocated as a major procedure for teaching students to become aware of their knowledge, examine their basic belief systems, and acquire new knowledge (Collins, 1977). If the questions become internalized, they can lead individuals to be active in the process of learning (Singer and Donlan, 1980, 1982). Other early innovations include the instructional uses of chalk and blackboards and pens and paper as tools for extending memory.

A major development that revolutionized instruction occurred about 1440 when Johannes Gutenberg invented a type mold that solved a problem in the development of movable type for his printing press. Gutenberg's printing of the German Bible demonstrated that he had solved the major technical problems for printing. Thereafter presses using movable type flourished and provided the books that enabled the Protestant Reformation to pursue its ideal of having people find their own salvation by reading the Word themselves, without any intermediary. The combination of the Gutenberg press and the Protestant idea played a prominent role in a literacy revolution that is still continuing to have an impact on the classroom.

About 400 years after Gutenberg, the rate of inventions influencing classroom instruction accelerated. Photography emerged with Daguerre's announcement in 1839 of the daguerrotype process, the first practical photographic method. Edison's invention of the phonograph occurred in 1878. Marconi's wireless appeared in 1895, and De Forest's invention of the vacuum tube in 1907 made radio broadcasting possible. Over the period from 1900 to 1930 moving pictures accompanied by sound became a reality.

Pressey's programmed instruction appeared in the 1920's, but attracted little attention until the 1960s when it was further developed. Although programmed instruction promised to have a great impact in instruction, it failed to live up to its promise in part because of lack of adequate software or programs. But the knowledge gleaned from research on progammed instruction in the 1960s (E. Baker, 1973) was not for naught because it is now being applied to programming computers.

Television started in the 1930s, became widely available in the 1950s, and has had enormous success as a medium for instruction, particulary in programs for children, such as Sesame Street and the Electric Company (Carroll and Chall, 1975), and in selected programs for older students. Schools bought video equipment in the 1960s under federal grants. Although initial enthusiasm has waned, 72 percent of all teachers in 1977 had TV available, but only 59 percent used it, mostly in the form of public television. At the high school level, teachers generally employed videotapes. However, only 30 percent of the nation's teachers had access to videotape recording and playback equipment. Teachers, especially English, science, and foreign language teachers, also inform students of television programs to view at home and even use them for out-of-class assignments. Among the programs they ask students to view are literary/historical classics, such as the Masterpiece Theater series, the National Geographic specials, and TV shows broadcast in non-English languages. In 1980, the Public Broadcasting System catered to such use of TV by developing programs for inschool and at-home viewing (Dranov, Moore, and Hickey, 1980).

A time delay between publication of materials and getting them to students was vastly reduced when photography and xerography were coupled together by the Xerox corporation. Photocopying machines then appeared in schools throughout the nation in the 1960s. This technological innovation has had widespread applications not only in rapid reproduction of printed materials but also in quick production of transparencies for use in overhead projectors. Tape recorders also made their presence known in the classroom in the 1960s. They were integrated with filmstrips to form machines for synchronized presentations of visual and auditory stimuli. In 1963, O. K. Moore essentially connected audiotapes to an electric typewriter and created a talking typewriter for teaching reading (Steg, 1977).

Although the computer dates back to the 1800s, its modern, completely electronic form began with the ENIAC, which was developed at the University of Pennsylvania in 1945. It contained 18,000 vacuum tubes and occupied a large air-conditioned room. The invention of the transistor in 1947 made it possible to reduce heat, eliminated tube replacement problems, and made commercial production and sales possible (Mason and Blanchard, 1979). Later developments of printed circuits and silicon chips made hand-held computers possible in the 1960s and microcomputers and minicomputers in the 1970s. Development of simpler languages such as BASIC (Beginners All-Purpose Symbolic Instruction Code), LOGO, and most recently SMALL-TALK for programming and interacting with computers in the late 1970s, and further reduction in their costs have made microcomputers available in schools and homes. Indeed, the rate of increase in use of computers indicates we are on the verge of an educational revolution (Splittgerber, 1979; Suppes, 1978).

Videodiscs, which can contain 54,000 pictures on one side of the disc, enough for approximately twenty-seven minutes of film, are one of the latest additions to the time line. The videodisc system consists of a television set, a videodisc player unit, and a computer for making the system interactive with the user. The army uses it for showing soldiers how to repair equipment, training through simulation techniques, and, in general, circumventing the reading of manuals and other documents. But the army still maintains its basic reading instruction program (Morris, 1981). Another late addition is the almost unbelievable Kurzweil computer (Cushman, 1980) which reads printed materials aloud and will stop on command to reread or spell any word it has read.

All of these inventions have had an impact on teaching and learning inside and outside of classrooms. Each of the major inventions, such as texts, films, radio, television, programmed instruction, and computer-assisted instruction were hailed as technological innovations that would replace teachers, but such prophecies were never realized. The teacher is still the dominant instructional force within the classroom, but uses the inventions to assist in instruction. Doing what no machine can do, teachers use judgment for adapting instruction to individual differences and make decisions about modifications in instruction as new information becomes available. Of course, when teachers decide to modify or change their instruction, then the computers can also be updated. Thus, the computer can extend the productivity of the teacher.

We will not document the impact of each of the innovations in the classroom. Research on these innovations in the classroom has indicated that students can learn from machine-based instruction often as well as they can from teacher-based instruction and sometimes even better because the machines are infinitely patient, readily adaptable to individual rates of learning (Lumsdaine, 1963; Kulik, Kulik, and Cohen, 1980), and provide correction without embarrassment (Magidson, 1977). However, even with the multiplicity of machines available for presenting materials through the visual and auditory senses, for extending memory through the use of recording devices, and for carrying out computations accurately and rapidly, the main tool of instruction for the last 500 years has been and still is the textbook (Cole and Sticht, 1981).

The availability of texts and the extension of literacy has gradually changed instruction. From an historical perspective of some 500 years, we can perceive that a vast change has occurred in instruction (Singer, 1981a; Smith, 1965). Students today not only learn from teachers but also from texts (Ausubel, 1960; Herber, 1978; Pearson and Johnson, 1978; F. Robinson, 1961; H. Robinson, 1978; Rothkopf, 1982; Royer and Cable, 1967; Singer, 1982a; Stauffer, 1969; Tierney and LaZansky, 1980).

Research has also produced some changes in instruction. Investigators over the past thirty-five years have been busy discovering how students learn from text and how teachers can improve upon instruction in teaching students to read and learn from text (Singer, 1982a, b, c; Singer and Donlan, 1980). But, like other technological innovations, the influence and spread throughout the public school systems of research-fostered innovations in reading and learning from text have been slow, albeit steady.

Many of the strategies for learning from text have been put into computer-assisted instructional programs. These programs have been described very well in *Computer Applications in Reading* (Mason and Blanchard, 1979). New programs for computer applications are being developed at a fast rate. Also computers with limited applications—for example, for teaching spelling or for displaying English/foreign language equivalent terms—are being manufactured and put on the market at an increasingly rapid rate.

In the remainder of this chapter we describe computer programs that appear to be appropriate for high school. Then we describe what we think is a newer and more exciting concept for schools, the development of *computer literacy*. Finally, we describe some preservice and inservice programs for teaching teachers how to develop computer literacy.

Computer Applications in Secondary Schools

The first computer-based reading program was initiated in the Brentwood Elementary School in East Palo Alto in 1963 under the direction of Richard Atkinson and a grant from the Carnegie Corporation (Atkinson and Hansen, 1966). Although the Stanford Project terminated after it demonstrated that students could learn to read under computer-assisted instruction at their own rate of learning, the PLATO Project (Programmed Logic for Automatic Teaching Operation) is still going strong in many sites throughout the U.S. and Canada.

The principal uses of computers are computer-assisted instruction (CAI) and computer-managed instruction (CMI). Computer-assisted instruction is based on programmed instruction and consists of three types: tutorial, a self-contained program with machine-made decisions; drill and practice programs, designed to supplement teacher-based instruction; and dialogue programs, in which students converse with the computer and control the information sequence (Mason and Blanchard, 1979; Blanchard, 1980). Computer-managed instruction consists of teachers using computers for diagnostic, prescriptive, and evaluative tasks for retrieval of information to plan units or lessons, for research on student learning, and for determining the effectiveness of materials and instructional strategies (Thompson, 1980). Although the initial applications of computers were based on Skinnerian learning theory, today's interactive programs and equipment include computers with keyboard, color video-monitors, and videodiscs all integrated into one system (Michalopoulos, 1976). It is also possible today to use a voice-synthesizer with such a system to transform print on the screen into audio form! This system makes it possible to instruct through simulation and imitative learning, something the army is currently doing (Morris, 1981). Indeed, a scenario can be described of a student interacting with such a system for all direct instruction and the teacher doing only the planning and serving as an advisor (Glaser and Cooley, 1973).

A variety of applications have already been developed for each subject in the curriculum and for each level of education. For example, in English, computers are being used as word processors: students compose on them, teachers correct the compositions, and students then revise their work. Computer-assisted instruction is also available for teaching punctuation, parts of speech, vocabulary, critical reading, and reading in the content areas. The major publishers are also developing programs for all areas of the curriculum (Polin, 1981). A small sample of specific uses of the computer would include determination of reading and readability levels; a course in high school physics; generation of cloze text materials; survival skills, such as balancing a checkbook; preparation for minimal competency exams; instruction in Latin vocabulary; record keeping and grading facilities; basic skills course for adults and children; phonics programs; bilingual reading instruction; composition in music; and inservice education. [Rather than present details of individual programs, a list of materials that provide information on computer hardware (equipment) and software (programs) is appended at the end of this chapter.]

The Outlook

When it comes to the use of computers in elementary schools, the results have been extremely favorable. Vinsonhaler and Bass (1972) and Edwards et al. (1975) reported nearly unanimous agreement among studies on the effectiveness of computer-supplemented instruction at the elementary school level. However, Kulik, Kulik, and Cohen (1980) assessed the effects of CAI at college levels to be modest, but positive. By extrapolation, the effects in middle and secondary schools should be somewhere in between. Meta-analyses now under way should provide a clearer answer (H. Walberg, personal communication).

However, the rapidly increasing number of microcomputers in schools will provide a solid testing ground for computer instruction of all sorts. As teachers begin to adapt to computers and integrate them into the curriculum they should contribute even more effectively to the instructional program (Johnson-Taylor, 1981).

Computers are already in widespread use throughout society. This use is very visible in airline terminals, banks, supermarkets, space exploration, and entertainment centers. Adults as well as youths are becoming accustomed to them. Hence, it is increasingly imperative for schools to develop computer literacy.

Computer Literacy

Computer literacy, like text literacy, can vary from a minimal level, consisting essentially of ability to operate a computer, to a maximal level, which includes knowledge of one or more computer languages and ability to program the computer. One of the most succinct statements about computer literacy appeared as part of a statement in the *Mathematics Teacher* (Board of Directors, 1978):

> an essential outcome of contemporary education is [the development] of computer literacy. Every student should have first-hand experiences with both the capabilities and the limitations of computers through contemporary application. Although the study of computers is intrinsically valuable, educators should also develop an awareness of computers both in interdisciplinary problem solving and as an instructional aide. (p. 468)

While it is vital that educators become computer literate (S. Robinson, 1981), it is even more important that children be exposed to computers as early as possible. One example that has successfully worked with elementary school children is LOGO (Solomon, 1976). In this program, children become immersed in a "computer culture." They learn how to manipulate and use computers by designing their own programs. Other computer literacy programs for younger students have been described by Holzman and Glaser (1977), Charp and Altschuler (1976) and Kibler and Campbell (1976). A commercial venture, Creative Programming, also has been successful with young children (Gleason, 1981).

One of the most thorough development efforts for computer literacy has been undertaken through the Minnesota Educational

Computer Consortium (MECC). Johnson et al. (1980) generated a comprehensive program for computer literacy that consists of sixty-three objectives grouped in several categories. *Hardware* objectives include knowing what the components of a computer are and how hardware differs from software. Objectives related to *programming* require individuals to be familiar with techniques necessary to have computers perform desired tasks. Another set of objectives is related to *applications* of computers in a variety of fields. *Impact* objectives deal with a wide range of career goals, computer crime, and other concerns about computers in society. Finally, *affective* objectives deal with developing positive values toward computers and computer usage. These objectives and other material are available from the Minnesota Educational Computer Consortium.

Computer literacy will have to be continually redefined as progress is made in both hardware and software. For example, computer literacy for the ENIAC computer required knowing how to hand-wire boards for each program. Such a skill could not even be applied to most modern machines. Until recently, using computers required a knowledge of key punching to obtain cards for the computer to use. Microcomputers rarely even have the option of using cards as input. Present-day state-of-the-art programs for writing CAI/tutorial materials require almost no programming knowledge. Materials are generated by the computer program on the basis of information obtained by the computer program in a conversation-like interaction between the user and machine. Already some school districts are providing a course in computer literacy. For example, the Philadelphia School System taught an introductory course in computer literacy to 11,000 junior high school students in one year (Charp, 1978).

This constantly changing definition of computer literacy will not obviate the need for such literacy. The key to success will be the use we make of what is undoubtedly the vital commodity of the future: information. Burke has observed that "unless changes are made in the way information is disseminated, we will soon become a society consisting of two classes: the informed elite and the rest. The danger inherent in such a development is obvious" (1978, p. 294). The development of widespread computer literacy will be the best assurance that we can avoid an information schism in contemporary society.

Teachers also need to develop computer literacy. Many are doing so through preservice and inservice education courses that are beginning to spring up in schools of education in universities across the globe.

CAI Instruction for Teachers of Reading

A number of colleges and universities have formulated computer-assisted instruction (CAI) lessons for use in their teacher education programs. For example, at Purdue University simulation and tutorial lessons have been developed for use in secondary reading education courses. Discussions of several other CAI programs for teacher education can be found in Mason and Blanchard (1979). These include lessons on how to teach reading in the content areas (Florida State University), how to score word recognition tests (University of Delaware), how to diagnose reading problems (Northwestern University), and how to teach phonics (Pennsylvania State University).

Teachers who are exposed to CAI as students become familiar with operating a terminal or microcomputer and with some of the capabilities that computers have. Familiarity with CAI lessons may be considered a first step toward becoming literate. However, exposure to CAI lessons during teacher education courses is only adequate for enabling teachers to aid their students in becoming computer literate if computer literacy is defined very narrowly. But most definitions of computer literacy go beyond just learning to use CAI lessons (e.g., Hirschbuhl, 1980; Johnson et al., 1980; MacKinnon, 1980; Watts, 1981). Therefore, teachers who have only been exposed to CAI as students still need the additional knowledge about computers they can get in preservice and inservice courses.

Preservice Computer Literacy Programs for Teachers

Molnar charged that "a student who graduates without being exposed to computers has had an incomplete education" (1978, p. 37). In order to ensure that their students' education is not incomplete, some colleges and universities have developed programs which provide teacher education students with computer experiences. For example, as part of their mathematics methods course, all elementary credential candidates at the University of Delaware are exposed to computers and have the opportunity to explore computers in depth if they wish (William Moody, personal communication, 1981). In addition, University of Delaware students who take an introductory computer science course may enroll in an "Introduction to Computer-Based Instruction" course. This introduction includes learning about computer hardware and software, instructional theory and design, and authoring instructional materials for computers (Richard Venezky, personal communication, 1981). Another example of preservice education for teachers is a no-prerequisite course, "Introduction to Microcomputers in Instructional Settings," offered at the University of Maryland. This course involves learning about instructional uses of computers, becoming familiar with the components of a computer system and a computer language, and writing a program of use in instruction (David J. Lockard, personal communication, 1981).

Although these types of courses are offered at a number of institutions they are generally electives in which only some pre-service teachers are involved. Thus, it is still very likely that most teachers enter the field without having attained computer literacy. For example, a 1975 nationwide survey of colleges of education indicated that only 6.8 percent offered comprehensive computer education programs (J. Baker, 1976).

Inservice Programs for Teachers

Inservice programs have been designed to fill the gaps in teachers' knowledge about computers. For example, in 1980 the Pennsylvania Department of Education began a Computer Literacy Project. Its goal was to develop a "funadmental computer literacy course . . . that would be appropriate for students age 12 to 112 and would incorporate computer awareness and computer usage with a brief study of computer applications and a look at positive and negative social implications of computers" (Kirchner, 1981, p. 43). Experts on computer education designed fifteen forty-five-minute lessons that included actual computer use in each lesson. The resulting course was offered for the first time in the spring of 1981 to twenty-five teachers from across the state. These teachers, whose computer experience ranged from none to considerable, received the fifteen lessons over three days. The training was designed to allow the teachers to offer the same course to their students. The teachers were given lesson plans, worksheets, and other materials needed so that they could provide computer literacy courses. The first wave of trained teachers offered courses to students ranging from fourth graders to adults. Pennsylvania also planned to train teachers to instruct other teachers so that computer literacy can be offered in all interested school districts (Kirchner, 1981).

Another example of teacher inservice education was the Leadership Training Program conducted by the Mathematical Sciences Teaching and Learning Center at the University of Delaware. The Leadership Training Program, funded by the National Science Foundation, was designed to prepare math and science teachers from each school district in Delaware to provide inservice instruction to other teachers throughout the state. Twenty-four junior and senior high school teachers who were already experienced with computers were selected to participate in nine monthly workshops. These workshops were followed by a week-long summer institute in June. Participants prepared inservice units, reviewed and evaluated microcomputer courseware, and compiled a *Handbook for Delaware Teachers on Using Microcomputers.* Using the products of the Leadership Training Program, the teachers then served as resource personnel and began offering their own inservice programs in the fall.

A variety of seminars on the PLATO computer-based education system have been offered by the Office of Computer-Based Instruction at the University of Delaware. These seminars—free to University of Delaware faculty, staff, and students, and to Delaware teachers—range from general orientations to more complex programming and lesson design. Also offered was a three-week summer institute for teachers sponsored by the National Science Foundation which subsidizes the participants' expenses. This institute was not confined to Delaware teachers and did not require any previous computer knowledge. It was designed to give teachers skills in instructional design and programming, and to familiarize them with computer-based educational materials in biology, chemistry, economics, mathematics, physics, and psychology. Teachers worked on both the PLATO system and the Apple II microcomputers.

In the fall of 1981, the Office of Computer-Based Instruction and the University of Delaware also offered two-day institutes on microcomputers for administrators and other school decision makers. These institutes, also sponsored by the National Science Foundation, were intended to provide school decision makers with the information needed to make wise choices in purchasing and administering computer-based educational materials (Morris Brooks, personal communication, 1981).

Loyola University developed a microcomputer literacy program for the faculty of two New Orleans high schools. The program consisted of five two-hour lectures and additional worktime on microcomputers. After learning the basics of microcomputer operation, the teachers learned what types of CAI programs are available and what each can do. They then learned how to write simple instructional programs and how to modify existing programs to make them match a teacher's classroom objectives. The content of each of the five lectures was described by Lopez (1981).

In addition to the example programs we have reviewed, there are a number of other sources of suggestions about what should be included in inservice computer literacy courses. Johnson et al. (1980) listed extensive and specific computer literacy objectives in both the cognitive and affective domains. Jackson (1975) outlined objectives for computer inservice education at even a broader level. Marsh (1976) described her course for teachers in Australia. She spent half the course on computer analysis of research data; the other half involved learning a computer language and exploring topics such as computer-assisted instruction, simulation, and computer-managed instruction. Diem (1981) briefly explained an inservice computer course that could be offered as a one-week summer seminar. In addition, Diem recommended that school districts hire a programmer with whom teachers can consult about designing their own courseware.

The teacher education courses we have reviewed provide useful examples for future efforts in teaching educators about computers. Certainly all of the example courses are aimed at making teachers computer literate.

If these and other courses are successful, then perhaps future surveys of computer education activities will find different results than those of Bukoski and Korotkin (1976). They surveyed public secondary schools in 1975 and found that 26.7 percent of the schools made some instructional use of computers. Although this figure was up from 12.9 percent in 1970, it still does not reflect the growing use of computers in American life and the continued calls for computer literacy. Further, Bukoski and Korotkin found that in 1975, "as it was in 1970, instructional computing within a school is still the responsibility of one or two individuals who have committed their own time, talent, and energy to the introductions of the computer into their school's educational program" (1976, p. 22). In addition, the most common instructional use of computers was in mathematics. This 1975 survey indicated a rather narrow base of computer use and knowledge in schools. Perhaps campaigns to educate teachers about computers, such as those we have described, will help broaden the base of computer literacy in schools.

Because current efforts are relatively small scale, calls to action on computer literacy continue to be heard (e.g., Dickerson and Pritchard, 1981; Hirschbuhl, 1980; Kibler and Campbell, 1976; MacKinnon, 1980; Molnar, 1978; S. Robinson, 1981; Spivak and

Varden, 1980; Watts, 1981). Among those to have recognized teachers' need to deal with technological innovations is the National Education Association (NEA), which established a Special Committee on Instructional Technology. The committee issued its report in July 1981. It recommended that NEA begin a "technology awareness campaign," that teachers be involved from the beginning in planning and using technology in the schools, and that teachers be given adequate inservice training on technological advances (NEA, 1981).

Another important recommendation made by the NEA committee was that teachers should work more closely with those who manufacture and design instructional hardware and software (NEA, 1981). NEA's concern for quality materials was shared by others such as Joseph (1979) who argued that education "is largely dependent on what industry supplies rather than education deciding what is needed to be developed" (p. 13). Currently, however, teachers have the opportunity to change the situation. For example, Bell (1980) stressed that English teachers can move to the forefront of courseware design. She noted that little courseware is available for secondary English classes. If English teachers would make themselves computer literate, Bell believes that they would be in a perfect position for guiding the development of computer educational materials for English. In reading the situation is much the same. Thompson (1980) reported that most of the available CAI programs in reading are of the drill and practice type. Computer literate teachers would be aware of the many other modes of CAI and would be able to design or guide the development of future courseware.

The International Reading Association (IRA) has already recognized the growing concern with computers. In 1981, IRA formed a Committee on Computer Technology and Reading. This committee has been instructed to find out what is being done with computers and microcomputers in teaching reading. The committee is also to suggest what policies, programs, and publications IRA should pursue on computer technology and reading. IRA's involvement with computers indicates a recognition that computers are no longer solely the concern of math and science teachers. Thus, we anticipate that reading educators will be moving to the forefront in developing computer literacy and adapting computers for widespread use in instruction. A new era of computer literacy has begun.

Conclusion

A range of inventions and innovations have affected secondary instruction, but usually with a considerable time lag. Most notable has been the slow spread of text literacy. After some five hundred years, some 99 percent of students graduating from American high schools have attained text literacy at a minimal level (Harris and associates, 1970). However, this level was recently raised from a sixth to about a ninth grade level of reading difficulty. Students now have to demonstrate they are literate by reading unfamiliar material and answering inferential and applied questions in order to pass a minimal competency test (Resnick and Resnick, 1977; Singer 1981b).

The latest development in an accelerated rate of inventions over the past century that have affected instruction in secondary schools is the computer, not only for computer-assisted instruction but also for development of computer literacy. By computer literacy, we mean a range of competencies from minimal ability to simply interact with and use computers, much as a person who learns to drive a car, to a maximal ability to actually write programs, which is analogous to knowing how an automobile works and even how to repair or construct an engine.

Development of simpler programming languages, such as SMALL-TALK, may facilitate acquisition of a maximal level of computer literacy in more students and at an earlier age. As costs of computers continue to decrease, we can expect more schools to obtain them. Moreover, with the advent of preservice and inservice courses for teaching teachers how to develop computer literacy in their students, we can anticipate that teachers will be instructing more and more students in computer literacy. Judging from the vast sums of money expended by students on computer games, we can anticipate that some of these students will be highly motivated to develop maximal levels of computer literacy. As they do, the problem of having a corps of trained people for producing the necessary software to maximize computer-assisted instruction will be solved.

References

Atkinson, R. C., and Hansen, D. Computer-assisted instruction in initial reading; The Stanford project. *Reading Research Quarterly*, 1966, *2*(1), 5–25.

Ausubel, D. The use of advance organizers in the learning and retention of meaningful verbal material. *Journal of Educational Psychology*, 1960, *51*, 267–272.

Baker, E. The technology of instructional development. In R. Travers (Ed.), *Second handbook of research on teaching*. Chicago: Rand McNally, 1973.

Baker, J. C. *Computers in the curriculum. Fastback 82*. Bloomington, Ind.: Phi Delta Kappa, 1976. (ERIC Document Reproduction Service No. ED 133 166; 45p.)

Bell, K. The computer and the English classroom. *English Journal*, 1980, *69*, 88–90. (ERIC No. EJ 238 448)

Blanchard, J. S. Computer-assisted instruction in today's reading classroom. *Journal of Reading*, 1980, *24*, 430–434. (ERIC No. EJ 225 383)

Board of Directors. Computers in the classroom. *Mathematics Teacher*, 1978, *71*(5), 468.

Bukoski, W. J., and Korotkin, A. L. Computing activities in secondary education. *Educational Technology*, 1976, *16*, 9–23. (ERIC No. EJ 131 315)

Burke, J. *Connections*. Boston: Little, Brown, 1978.

Carroll, J., and Chall, J. *Toward a literate society*. New York: McGraw-Hill, 1975.

Charp, S. Computers and the learning society: Hearings before the Subcommittee on Domestic and International Scientific Planning, Analysis and Cooperation of the Committee on Science and Technology (Report No. 47). Ninty-fifth Congress, First Session, October 27, 1977. Washington, D.C.: U.S. Government Printing Office, 1978. (ERIC Document Reproduction Service No. ED 162 643; 698p.)

Charp, S., and Altschuler, H. A decade of usage of computers for instructional purposes. *Technological Horizons in Education*, 1976, *3*, 10–30.

Cole, J. Y., and Sticht, T. *The textbook in American society*. Washington, D.C.: Library of Congress, 1981.

Collins, A. Processes in acquiring knowledge. In R. C. Anderson, R. Spiro, and W. E. Montague (Eds.), *Schooling and the acquisition of knowledge*. Hillsdale, N.J.: Lawrence Erlbaum, 1977.

Cushman, R. C. The Kurzweil reading machine. *The Wilson Library Bulletin*, 1980, *54*(5), 311–315.

Dickerson, L., and Pritchard, W. H., Jr. Microcomputers and education: Planning for the coming revolution in the classroom. *Educational Technology*, 1981, *21*, 7–12. (ERIC No. EJ 240 911)

Diem, R. A. Developing computer education skills: An inservice training program. *Educational Technology*, 1981, *21*, 30–32.

Dranov, P., Moore, L., and Hickey, H. *Video in the 80s*. White Plains, N.Y.: Knowledge Industry Publications, Inc., 1980.

Edwards, J., Norton, S., Taylor, S., Weiss, M., and Dusseldorp, R. How effective is CAI? A review of the research. *Educational Leadership*, 1975, *33*, 147–153.

Glaser, R., and Cooley, W. W. Instrumentation for teaching and instructional management. In R. Travers (Ed.), *Second handbook of research on teaching.* Chicago: Rand McNally, 1973.

Gleason, G. Microcomputers in education: The state of the art. *Educational Technology*, 1981, *21*, 7–18. (ERIC No. EJ 244 284)

Harris, L., and Associates. Survival literacy study. *Congressional Record*, 1970, November 18, E 9719–9723.

Herber, H. L. *Teaching reading in content areas.* Englewood Cliffs, N.J.: Prentice-Hall, 1978.

Hirschbuhl, K. The need for computer literacy and computer applications in the nation's classrooms. *Journal of Educational Technology Systems*, 1980, *9*(3), 183–191.

Holzman, T., and Glaser, R. Developing computer literacy in children: Some observations and suggestions. *Educational Technology*, 1977, *17*, 5–11. (ERIC No. EJ 166 381)

Jackson, A. In-service education for teachers of computer science. In R. Colman and P. Lorton (Eds.), *Computer science and education.* New York: Association for Computing Machinery, 1975.

Johnson, D., Anderson, R., Hansen, T., and Klassen, D. Computer literacy—What is it? *Mathematics Teacher*, 1980, *73*, 91–96.

Johnson-Taylor, R. (Chair). *Report of NEA Special Committee on Instructional Technology.* Washington, D.C.: National Education Association, July 1981.

Joseph, E. C. *Long-term electronic technology trends: Forecasted impacts on education.* Paper presented to Congress of the United States, House of Representatives, Committee on Education and Labor, Subcommittee on Elementary, Secondary, and Vocational Education, April 25, 1979. (ERIC Document Reproduction Service No. ED 179 878; 18p.)

Kibler, T., and Campbell, P. Reading, writing and computing: Skills of the future. *Eductional Technology*, 1976, *16*, 44–46. (ERIC No. EJ 145 193)

Kirchner, A. M. One state's approach to computer literacy. *Technological Horizons in Education*, 1981, *8*(4), 43–44.

Kulik, J., Kulik, C., and Cohen, P. Effectiveness of computer-based college teaching: A meta-analysis of findings. *Review of Educational Research*, 1980, *50*, 525–544. (ERIC No. EJ 239 578)

Lopez, A. M. Computer literacy for teachers: High school and university cooperation. *Educational Technology*, 1981, *21*, 15–18. (ERIC No. EJ 247 520)

Lumsdaine, A. A. Instruments and media of instruction. In N. L. Gage (Ed.), *Handbook of research in teaching.* Chicago: Rand McNally, 1963.

MacKinnon, C. F. Computer literacy and the future: Is it possible to prevent the computer from doing our thinking for us? *Educational Technology*, 1980, *20*, 33–34.

Magidson, E. M. One more time: CAI is not dehumanizing. *Audio-visual Instruction*, 1977, *22*, 20–21. (ERIC No. EJ 172 233)

Marsh, B. Teaching teachers about computers: A course description. In R. Colman and P. Lorton (Eds.), *Computer science and education.* New York: Association for Computing Machinery, 1976.

Mason, G. E., and Blanchard, J. S. *Computer applications in reading.* Newark, Del.: International Reading Association, 1979. (ERIC Document Reproduction Service No. ED 173 771; 115p.)

Michalopoulos, D. A. A video disc oriented educational system. In R. Colman and P. Lorton (Eds.), *Computer science and education.* New York: Association for Computing Machinery, 1976.

Molnar, A. R. The next great crisis in American education: Computer literacy. *Technological Horizons in Education,* 1978, *5,* 35–39. (ERIC No. EJ 187 471)

Morris, H. Videodisc replaces paper. Demonstration presented at the annual conference of the California Reading Association, Anaheim, November 1981.

NEA Special Committee on Instructional Technology. *Report: Presented to the 60th Representative Assembly of the National Education Association.* Washington, D.C.: National Education Association, 1981.

Pearson, P. D., and Johnson, D. *Teaching reading comprehension.* New York: Holt, Rinehart and Winston, 1978.

Polin, G. (Ed.). *Apple Education News,* June 1981.

Resnick, D. P., and Resnick, L. B. The nature of literacy: An historical exploration. *Harvard Educational Review,* 1977, *47*(3), 370–385. (ERIC No. EJ 167 146)

Robinson, F. P. Study skills for superior students in secondary school. *The Reading Teacher,* 1961, *15,* 29–33.

Robinson, H. A. *Teaching reading and study strategies: Content areas.* Boston: Allyn and Bacon, 1978.

Robinson, S. P. Teachers and computers. *Journal of Computer-Based Instruction,* 1981, *7*(4), 106–110.

Rothkopf, E. Z. Adjunct aids and the control of methemagenic activities during purposeful reading. In W. Otto and S. White (Eds.), *Reading expository text.* New York: Academic Press, 1982.

Royer, J. M., and Cable, G. W. Facilitated learning in connected discourse. *Journal of Educational Psychology,* 1967, *58,* 56–61.

Singer, H. Teaching the acquisition phase of reading development: An historical perspective. In O. Tzeng and H. Singer (Eds.), *Perception of print.* Hillsdale, N.J.: Lawrence Erlbaum, 1981.(a)

Singer, H. *The great educational earthquake of 1981: Reallocation of resources in California high schools to meet minimal competency requirements—Was the reallocation necessary?* Paper read at the annual conference of the California Reading Association, Anaheim, November 1981.(b) (ERIC Document Reproduction Service No. ED 211 933; 18p.)

Singer, H. Hypotheses on reading comprehension in search of classroom validation. In M. Kamil (Ed.), *Thirtieth yearbook of the National Reading Conference.* Washington, D.C.: The National Reading Conference, 1982.(a)

Singer, H. The substrata-factor theory of reading: Its history and conceptual relationship to interaction theory. In L. Gentile, M. Kamil, and J. Blanchard (Eds.), *Reading research revisited*. Columbus, Ohio: Merrill, 1982.(b)

Singer, H. *A century of landmarks in research on reading.* Paper read at the annual convention of the American Educational Research Association, New York, March 1982.(c)

Singer, H., and Donlan, D. *Reading and learning from text.* Boston: Little, Brown, 1980.

Singer, H., and Donlan, D. Active comprehension: Problem solving schema with question generation for comprehension of complex short stories. *Reading Research Quarterly*, 1982, *17*, 166-186.

Smith, N. B. *History of American reading instruction.* Newark, Del.: International Reading Association, 1965.

Solomon, C. Leading a child to a computer culture. In R. Colman and P. Lorton (Eds.), *Computer science and education*. New York: Association for Computing Machinery, 1976.

Spivak, H., and Varden, S. Classrooms make friends with computers. *Instructor*, 1980, *90*, 84-86. (ERIC No. EJ 220 471)

Splittgerber, F. L. Computer based instruction: A revolution in the making? *Educational Technology*, January 1979, 20-26. (ERIC No. EJ 203 457)

Stauffer, E. G. *Directing reading maturity as a cognitive process.* New York: Harper and Row, 1969.

Steg, D. R. Intervention through technology: The talking typewriter revisited. *Educational Technology*, 1977, *17*(10), 45-47.

Stein, J. (Ed.). *The Random House dictionary of the English language.* New York: Random House, 1973.

Suppes, P. *The future of computers in education. Computers and the Learning Society. Hearing before the Subcommittee on Domestic and International Scientific Planning, Analysis and Cooperation of the Committee on Science and Technology* (Report No. 47). Ninety-fifth Congress, First Session, October 27, 1977. Washington, D. C.: U.S. Government Printing Office, 1978. (ERIC Document Reproduction Service No. ED 162 643; 698p.)

Thompson, B. J. Computers in reading: A review of applications and implications. *Educational Technology*, 1980, *20*, 38-41. (ERIC No. EJ 232 552)

Tierney, R. J., and LaZansky, J. The rights and responsibilities of readers: A contractual agreement. *Language Arts*, 1980, *57*, 606-613. (ERIC No. EJ 233 977)

Vinsonhaler, J., and Bass, R. A summery of ten major studies on CAI drill and practice. *Educational Technology*, 1972, *12*, 29-32. (ERIC No. EJ 071 745)

Watts, N. A dozen uses for the computer in education. *Educational Technology*, 1981, *21*, 18-22.

Appendix: Information about Computer Hardware and Software.

Books

Frederick, F. *Guide to microcomputers.* Washington, D.C.: Association for Educational Communication and Technology, 1980. (ERIC Document Reproduction Service No. ED 192 818; 159p.)
A good general reference for almost all aspects of microcomputers and applications.

Doerr, C. *Microcomputers and the 3 R's.* Rochelle Park, N.J.: Hayden Book Company, 1979.
Doerr presents a survey of applications and uses of microcomputers in schools, dealing with all subjects and including a number of program listings.

Mason, G. and Blanchard, J. *Computer applications in reading.* Newark, Del.: International Reading Association, 1979. (ERIC Document Reproduction Service No. ED 173 771; 115p.)
This is a thorough, though now a bit dated, summary of the uses of computers in teaching reading.

Wood, R. K., and Worley, R. D. So you want to buy a computer? *Instructor,* 1980, *89,* 86–90.
A consumer's shopping guide to buying a computer. Compares eight different computers, including Apple II, Atari 800, TRS-80, and Texas Instruments 99/4. Also defines terms and provides a computer directory.

Review in Professional Journals

Blanchard, J. Computer-assisted instruction in today's reading classroom. *Journal of Reading,* 1980, *20,* 430–434. (ERIC No. EJ 225 383)

Bukoski, W., and Korotkin, A. Computing activities in secondary education. *Educational Technology,* 1976, *16,* 9–23.

Gleason, G. Microcomputers in education: The state of the art. *Educational Technology,* 1981, *21,* 7–18. (ERIC No. EJ 244 284)

Mason, G. Computerized reading instruction: A review. *Educational Technology,* 1980, *20,* 18–22. (ERIC No. EJ 234 640)

Thompson, B. Computers in reading: A review of applications and implications. *Educational Technology,* 1980, *20,* 38–41. (ERIC No. 234 640)

Computer Education Journals

Classroom Computer News
P.O. Box 266
Cambridge, Massachusetts 02138

Courseware Magazine
4919 N. Millbrook #222
Fresno, California 93726

The Computing Teacher
c/o Computing Center
Eastern Oregon State College
La Grande, Oregon 97850

Educational Computer
P.O. Box 535
Cupertino, California 95015

Educational Technology
140 Sylvan Avenue
Englewood Cliffs, New Jersey
07632

School Microware Reviews
Dresden Associates
P.O. Box 264
Dresden, Maine 04342

Other Sources of Information

Minnesota Educational Computer
Consortium
2520 Broadway Drive
St. Paul, Minnesota 55113

MicroSIFT
Northwest Regional Educational
Laboratory
710 2nd Avenue, S.W.
Portland, Oregon 97204

CONDUIT
P.O. Box 338
Iowa City, Iowa 52240

Project LOCAL
500 Nahaton Street
Westwood, Massachusetts 02090

International Systems and
Courseware Exchange
Swen Larsen, Dean
World University
Barbosa esq. Guayama
Hato Rey, Puerto Rico 00917

Epilogue: New Students, New Teachers, New Demands

Margaret Early
Syracuse University

Perhaps *what research reveals* is too strong a phrase. Perhaps, so far as classroom practice is concerned, this review of research brings less revelation than affirmation. It affirms what thinking teachers have known, or suspected, about the reading process and about reading materials and how students learn, or fail to learn, in the complex setting in which teachers work every day. What this review reveals, we hope, is how *researchers* work, what directions they have taken in recent years, how cautious they are about recommending changes in practice on the basis of their findings, and how much they need teachers' advice as to the directions of future research as well as their reactions to current findings. In the drama of school life, researchers are part of the supporting cast; teachers and students take the starring roles. So this "epilogue" shifts the spotlight to the principal players.

To cast research in a supportive role in no way demeans it. Teachers, and especially administrators, need to have their assumptions verified. For example, it is reassuring to learn from the present review that research supports those teachers and administrators who have been acting for many years now upon the following principles:

> Most students in secondary schools continue to need help in using reading as a means of learning.
>
> The best setting for learning how to learn from a history textbook (for example) is the history class. Most reading instruction belongs in the so-called content courses of the secondary school curriculum—and in English classes. (I view English as more process than content, more aligned with the arts than with "subject matter.")

Some students in high school, especially those who are still in the early stages of reading acquisition, need special help beyond the content classes. Teachers trained in how to teach beginning reading skills to adolescents must provide this help.

To be successful, high school reading programs require: (1) administrative support; (2) teachers who appreciate the role of language in all kinds of learning but especially learning which derives in any way from text; (3) specialists who can assist teachers in their continuing efforts to help students not only to assimilate ideas but to refine learning strategies.

How much students read in school and outside directly affects their ability to comprehend.

Prior knowledge affects comprehension and teachers can help students to become aware of, and to apply, what they already know.

The structure as well as the language of the text affects comprehension, and teachers can help students to use structure as an aid to understanding and remembering what they (the students) consider important.

When teachers and students agree on what is important and have similar purposes for reading a particular text, teachers can perhaps judge most accurately students' comprehension of that text. However, when teachers alone set purposes, they influence the nature of students' comprehension, sometimes limiting and distorting what students might learn from text. In most instances, "setting purposes" boils down to the questions the teachers ask, or that textbook editors pose.

If comprehension is the state of having all one's questions answered, the range and quality of comprehension depends on the range and quality of one's questions. Students, to be independent, must learn to ask their own questions as they read and not simply seek answers to other people's questions. To be sure, "success" in academic terms may depend on how closely students' questions match their teachers' questions.

Raising questions is only one of several ways that readers respond to what they have read. Other responses must also be cultivated, especially those which express affective reactions, such as a journal entry, a poem or picture, mime or drama, debate or discussion.

The reader's purposes in approaching a text are governed by the nature of the text, whether it is a poem, for example, or a political tract, or a scientific explanation, and also by the context in which the reading takes place, how others react to the reading (as in a classroom), and how the student's purposes are affected by teachers, peers, parents, the community, and broader societal influences.

Especially at secondary levels, reading and writing are joined together almost as if they made up a single tool of learning. There are other reasons for reading and writing besides absorbing ideas, but the fact that this reason is so emphasized in secondary schools extends the old slogan to: Every teacher is a teacher of reading *and* writing.

The principles I've just reiterated are ones that strike me as important to teachers of English and most other secondary school personnel. They sample rather than summarize the research presented in the preceding twelve chapters. They are there to remind the reader of what this book contains and to introduce this "epilogue" whose purpose is to suggest the context within which teachers read reports of current research.

The High School as the Common School

The "new" researcher in reading says you can't study the process of reading as if the interaction between reader and text took place in an isolation booth. Today's teachers say you cannot talk about classroom practice in the abstract as if it were unaffected by changes in society and in federal, state, and local regulations on education and by changes in students and teachers themselves. When teachers read research reports, they think of the students in their classes, the minutes of class time, the school calendar, their schedules, the administrative set up, their faculty colleagues, the pressures from parents and boards of education and union representatives. Of all these factors—and others—that impinge on classroom practices, students as individuals but also as part of the ethnic/social class mix are undoubtedly the most powerful.

To generalize about students, or about teachers, is to flout the basic concept of modern education: individual differences. (Research does so all the time, of course.) Nevertheless, to assess the potential influence of research findings on classroom practices, we must think about who is attending high school today. Almost everyone in the age group is. When the first edition in this series on research in high school reading appeared in 1957-58, less than 60 percent of youth who had been in fifth grade seven years earlier remained to graduate from high school. In 1980, nearly 80 percent of the age group graduated from high school and half of them continued into postsecondary education (Grant and Eiden, 1980).

In the late 1960s, when the second edition in this series was published, high school enrollments were approaching their peak. In the 1980s, while the percentage of youth attending high school will be the highest ever, the numbers will have declined by 15 percent from 1975. One effect is that we have fewer classroom teachers, not smaller classes.

Retaining almost all of the teenage cohort through twelfth grade has converted the high school into the common school, the last stop in formal education for half the population but a preparatory experience for the other half. The secondary school today is what the grammar school was in earlier decades of this century, and just as the latter shifted its emphasis from content to process when most of its graduates continued into high school, so the secondary school is now making its primary goals teaching students to read and write well enough to cope with learning in postsecondary courses.

New Students and New Teachers

Even though many high schools, especially in rural and suburban areas, have remained relatively stable in their ethnic and socio-economic characteristics over the last twenty years, the fact that most of the age group stays in high school forces all teachers to examine their expectations about the range of abilities, attitudes, and achievement which may be "normal." New students in secondary schools include "exceptional children," who in 1931 constituted less than 1 percent of those attending school and today make up 10 percent; immigrants whose literacy in English and sometimes also in their first language is severely limited; adolescents from working class and welfare homes who might have dropped out if unemployment were not so high. These three groups represent the additional "new" population in high school.

New in another sense are the students of the eighties whose personal and political views and career expectations are quite different from those of youth a decade ago. Although today's youth may be more concerned about material success than were the children of the counter-culture, they are not, for that reason, more interested in academic learning. The high cost of adolescent living means that earning money is a high priority for many teenagers for whom going to school is just one more item on a crowded agenda. There are many competing curriculums, not only part-time jobs but sports, electronic games, TV and movies, rock groups and records, sex, social life, "hanging out" at the shopping malls. Add to these distractions from academic studies adolescents' worries about their bodies, their self-image, their chances of making it, and one can understand why teenagers guard their time and energy very carefully against the demands of teachers. In response, many teachers tend to lower their demands, and homework, for instance, has become an unaccustomed activity for at least a third of the students.

Concern for how the presence of "new" students in the high school may affect teachers' expectations and what they choose to teach has led many educators at both college and secondary levels to reexamine goals and curricula which may have been more appropriate to the mid-century high school than they are to today's common school. Is a common curriculum possible? Can every student learn the skills and knowledge essential for living in today's society? If the high school years are simply one piece of a life-long learning continuum, can we make better use of those years for some students by breaking away from traditional time allotments and subject matter? Such questions heighten our awareness that neither research nor trial-and-error practices have solved the myriad problems of teaching to individual differences. In the high schools of the fifties, where the range was much narrower, these problems persisted and "solutions" were damaging to students, especially those at the lower end of the range of achievement and ability. Today the "solutions" that teachers grasp at in attempting to meet a far wider range of differences jammed into a system designed for a select population may be even more damaging to students with average and better-than-average abilities.

"New" teachers face these challenges. Many of them have taught for many years, but as they change their goals and teaching styles to fit the new common school they too become "new." In many high schools, and in many classes in most high schools, teachers who were once subject matter specialists only are becoming generalists whose first concern is for how students learn and whose second concern is for the information and ideas to be assimilated. As teachers work with each other to specify the goals they hold in common as well as the distinctions which characterize their content fields, they are viewing teaching as less of a private act, more of a common endeavor. Among the new breed of secondary teachers, both specialization and privacy are on the wane.

How and what students learn in high school has to be affected by the distractions to which their teachers are subject. Many of the same distractions that compete for students' learning time cut into teachers' preparation time. Added to these are commitments to unions, to professional advancement, to marital, familial, and civic obligations. No one can predict the chances for improving literacy in the high school without looking to the quality of teachers who will replace the recruits of the fifties and sixties. Given the sharp decline in the number of college entrants, especially women, who elect teaching as a career and given, too, the discouraging comparisons on SAT scores between education majors and students entering management, engineering, the physical sciences (for example), concern runs high for the quality of teaching in the next decade.

The Texts

Recent research has pointed to the difficulties readers encounter in using structural codes as aids to comprehension, and has led to recommendations for making textbook prose more explicit in its hierarchical ordering. Although textbooks are revised regularly and publishers are responsive to teachers' demands, several generations of students may enter and leave high school before research findings move teachers to demand "improved" textbook prose. Such was the case with readability studies made in the forties and fifties which did not make a real impact on high school texts until the seventies. So in the long meanwhile, teachers have to adjust their instruction to make texts accessible to readers. In doing so, most teachers won't attempt to rewrite or to reorganize textbooks; instead they make much less use of them for students' initial learning, more often assigning textbook passages that permit students to rehearse ideas with which they are already familiar.

But English teachers don't have the same problems with textbooks that their colleagues in the content fields encounter. They assign textbook prose much less often than they ask students to read established writers whose style and structure cannot—should not—be tampered with. So for English teachers instruction in how to read is quite a different process from what is appropriate to other content teachers. Their motivations are different. They are less concerned with having students learn how to learn from textbooks; instead they want their students to be able to read the literature of the past as well as the present and to be aware of many purposes for reading in addition to acquiring information. Most of the research studies reported in this monograph have more relevance for teaching learning from texts than responding to literature. That's all right because English teachers are often both the "reading teacher" and the teacher of literature, and in any case they want to know how content teachers teach reading and how administrators and teachers organize reading programs. Still, they have to sift research findings carefully to sort out what applies to learning from nonliterary text that does not apply to the reading of literature.

While English teachers tend to view reading as most useful for revealing past events, ideas, and experiences, leaving to electronic media the reporting of immediate experience, they are, of course, interested in the language, ideas, and media students will use in the future. They, too, are interested in technological innovations. When they are wearing their "reading teacher" hats, their interest in texts of all kinds extends to instructional materials packaged as courseware for computers as well as in more conventional print forms. They want to know what research finds about the effectiveness of both kinds of materials, but they have learned not to ask too much of research.

The Limitations of Research

Britton said that teaching has often been transformed by the social scientists' taxonomies, the powerful theories that they generate, and the research studies that support them, but he acknowledged, as I've just done, that "such effects take time, and meanwhile teachers must go on teaching. Working by hunch, they have to beg many of the questions that basic research has barely begun to tackle" (Britton, 1974, p. 2). With respect to research in reading as it affects secondary teachers, this warning rings especially true. The recent decade has seen great advances in the amount and quality of research on the reading process of high school students and has yielded information on reading habits and preferences. Systematic inquiry into what happens in secondary classrooms and in reading programs has lagged behind studies of students' reading of particular texts, but it is growing.

Whether focused on reading process or teaching practices, recent research tends to be more descriptive than analytic. Many studies emphasize the idiosyncratic nature of reading, especially when the reader is intent on meaning and can be unmindful of the mechanics of decoding. Many studies emphasize the powerful effects of particular texts upon readers' comprehension. Other kinds of studies place observers in particular classrooms to record students' and teachers' language and practices. Nevertheless, researchers stand at a distance from their subjects and risk generalizations based on their findings in ways that teachers cannot. It is no exaggeration to say that for the teacher every student is exceptional and this or that generalization from research cannot apply to him or her. Not only individuals are unique, of course; so are situations. What may be true for this classroom may be at odds with the way things are down the hall or across town or in another county.

So much of the research is usually not directly applicable to classroom practices. Findings from research are most useful to teachers when they suggest reasons why a particular approach succeeds with this student but has little effect on these others. Then research helps teachers to understand why they believe as they do and why they use certain practices and reject others in pursuit of their objectives. In short, research should not dictate practice; it should contribute to the belief systems that teachers develop from their own observations of students.

The Usefulness of Theory

People who teach and who think about teaching very often enunciate theories which influence other teachers whenever they recognize in these theories truths that match their own experiences. Very often these theories have such deep and pervading influence on teachers' thinking and practice that psychologists and psycholinguists also draw upon them as they construct models to be tested through research. A prime example in the field of reading, especially the reading of literature, is Louise Rosenblatt's transactional theory, which is referred to in one essay after another in this collection. For more than forty years, beginning with the first edition of *Literature as Exploration,* teachers of English have been indebted to Rosenblatt for centering attention on the reader's contribution to the two-way transaction through which a "reading" of a literary work emerges. In 1978, she collected and developed more fully in *The Reader, the Text, the Poem* several essays that had appeared in the preceding decade. Perhaps more than the earlier work, this new volume reached researchers in reading who found they were echoing what Rosenblatt had written in 1978.

Of special significance to all teachers, not English teachers alone, is Rosenblatt's clarification of what the reader does in evoking from the printed text the experience of the literary work. In making this clear, she differentiated between what happens in reading a poem and what happens when the reader draws upon past experience to call forth meaning from, say, a scientific text. The chief difference is the reader's focus of attention during the "reading-event." When the text is literary or aesthetic, the reader's attention is on what is happening to her or him *during* a transaction with the text. With other kinds of text, "the reader's attention is focused primarily on what will remain as the residue *after* the reading—the information to be acquired, the logical solution to a problem, the actions to be carried out" (p. 23).

In distinguishing one kind of reading from the other, Rosenblatt contributed not only a new concept but a new and useful label for it. To designate the kind of reading where the reader's concern is with what he or she carries away from it, Rosenblatt suggested the word "efferent," derived from the Latin "to carry away" and not used before with this or similar referents. The transactional theory permits us to think in terms of the *reader's* purposes as well as the author's presumed purposes. So when we say a reading-event (what is evoked from the printed page) is aesthetic or efferent, we refer to the reader's focus of attention. We are freed from the strained classification of "literary" or "informational." The reader's focus on any text may run along a continuum from aesthetic to efferent and usually hovers near the middle (p. 37).

To attempt to distill Rosenblatt's thinking into two paragraphs would be inexcusable were it not that even so inadequate an allusion serves two purposes: (1) to illustrate my point that a carefully conceived theory, even before it is affirmed by research data, influences classroom practices; and (2) to represent rather more fully than preceding essays have done the congruence of Rosenblatt's ideas with current and future research in reading.

The Role of the English Teacher

Most of the contributors to this monograph work in a corner of the educational establishment labeled "reading," and their communiques on current research are directed to all secondary teachers. The fact that this monograph is sponsored in part by an organization of English teachers carries a message of such significance that it almost goes without saying. But here it is: Reading research in the last two decades has found its place in the wide arena of language studies, making use of what is known and what is being discovered about language acquisition and development, the relationships to thinking, and its uses in learning.

This movement in reading research adds strength to a parallel movement in teaching and curriculum development which puts English teachers at its center. Because language—the English language in most American high schools—is the chief medium of learning in school and outside, English teachers have taken a new view of their responsibilities. No longer is the responsibility for extending and refining the literacy of all students theirs alone. But they have an added task. They take a leading role in promoting their colleagues' willingness and competence to teach reading and writing to every student in every high school subject where learning depends to any extent upon these abstract modes of language.

References

Britton, J. Language and the nature of learning: Individual perspective. In J. Squire (Ed.), *The teaching of English* (Seventy-sixth Yearbook of the National Society for the Study of Education). Chicago: NSSE, 1977.

Grant, W., and Eiden, L. (Eds.). *Digest of education statistics.* Washington, D. C.: National Center for Education Statistics, 1980. (ERIC Document Reproduction Service No. ED 202 085; 269p.)

Rosenblatt, L. M. *Literature as exploration* (3rd ed.). New York: Noble and Noble, 1976 (now distributed by Modern Language Association).

Rosenblatt, L. M. *The reader, the text, the poem.* Carbondale: Southern Illinois University Press, 1978.

Contributors

Allen Berger is professor of Language Communications, University of Pittsburgh, and editor of *English Education*. He is founding editor of a number of periodicals and his poetry has appeared in leading newspapers. He has served as consultant to the U.S. Department of Justice, the Federal Trade Commission, and the National Assessment of Educational Progress. His professional interests include reading and writing for high school and college students, reviewing books and tests for national publications, and translating research for school teachers and administrators.

Virginia M. Brannock is a doctoral candidate in reading and language arts at the Florida State University, where she has taught language arts and is currently teaching children's literature. She is a former public school teacher.

Robert F. Carey is assistant professor in the Language Education Department (Reading Program Area) at Indiana University. He teaches graduate and undergraduate courses in reading research and linguistics and conducts research in the socio-psycholinguistic aspects of reading. A frequent speaker at national conferences, he is presently writing on naturalistic research methodology and on semantics and reading.

Mariam Jean Dreher is assistant professor of Education at the University of Maryland, College Park. She teaches graduate and undergraduate courses in reading education and research. Previously, she was an elementary teacher and a Title I resource teacher. Her research interests include reading comprehension, memory, and cognitive processes.

Margaret Early is professor of Education, associate dean for Academic Affairs at Syracuse University, and a member of the faculty of the Reading and Language Arts Center. She teaches graduate courses in reading as well as literature and language. She has special interests in secondary reading and in English education. President of NCTE in 1974, she has also served NCTE as chair of the Committee on Research, as a trustee of the Research Foundation, and as a member of the Commission on Reading. She has served on the Board of Directors of IRA and as coeditor of the *Journal of Reading*. She is past president of NCRE.

Thomas H. Estes is associate professor of Reading in the McGuffey Reading Center of the University of Virginia. He is coauthor of *Reading and Learning in the Content Classroom* and author of the *Estes Attitude Scales* as well as of numerous NCTE, IRA, and NRC publications.

S. Lee Galda is assistant professor of Language Arts and Children's Literature at the University of Georgia. She received the 1981 NCTE Promising Researcher Citation for her dissertation (New York University) on response to literature.

Jerome C. Harste is professor of Reading Education at Indiana University. His research interests include written language growth and development, language arts and reading teacher education, text production and comprehension, and the context of literacy and literacy learning. He is a member of NCTE's Commission on Reading, a frequent speaker at annual meetings, and series editor with Lynn Rhodes of "Making Connections" in *Language Arts*.

Harold L. Herber is professor of Education and director of the Reading and Language Arts Center at Syracuse University. A former member of the Board of Directors of IRA and former director of the Commission on Reading of NCTE, he now directs—along with Joan Nelson—the Network of Secondary School Demonstration Centers for Teaching Reading in Content Areas. He is author of *Teaching Reading in Content Areas*.

Peter Johnston is assistant professor in the Reading Department at the State University of New York at Albany. Previously he was with the Center for the Study of Reading at the University of Illinois at Urbana-Champaign. His research interests include comprehension assessment, strategic behaviors in teaching and learning, and metacognition.

Michael Kamil is associate professor of Education at the University of Illinois at Chicago. He has been editor of the *National Reading Conference Yearbook* and has written numerous articles and chapters on reading research and theory. Currently he is editing (with L. Gentile and J. Blanchard) a volume on reading research. He is also interested in the applications of microcomputers in educational settings and teaches computer literacy for educators.

Judith A. Langer is a visiting scholar at the School of Education, University of California—Berkeley, a research consultant to the Bay Area Writing Project, and coinvestigator with Charles Fillmore and Paul Kay on a study of reading comprehension tests. She is also conducting research concerned with aspects of reading and writing processes and the relationship between child knowledge, child language, and performance in reading and writing.

Joan Nelson is professor of Education at the State University of New York at Binghamton, and is codirector of the Network of Secondary School Demonstration Centers for Teaching Reading in Content Areas, a project funded by the U.S. Department of Education in support of staff development, curriculum development, and school-based research in reading comprehension. Her interests include translating research findings into practical strategies for instruction and the design of school-based research.

William D. Page is professor of Education at the University of Connecticut at Storrs. His publications include *Help for the Reading Teacher* (NCRE and ERIC/RCS, 1975) and, with Gay Su Pinnell, *Teaching Reading Comprehension* (NCTE and ERIC/RCS, 1979). He serves on the editorial board of the *Reading Research Quarterly*, as chair of the Research Award Subcommittee to select the outstanding reading dissertation of the year for IRA, and is a research fellow of NCRE.

Barbara C. Palmer is associate professor of Education at Florida State University. She has published numerous journal articles and coauthored several books, including *Test Lessons in Reading Figurative Language* and *Reading by Doing: An Introduction to Effective Reading*. She served as chair for the Migratory Children and Reading Committee of IRA and coordinated the compilation of *Migrant Education*.

P. David Pearson is professor in the Department of Elementary and Early Childhood Education at the University of Illinois at Urbana-Champaign, where he also holds an appointment at the Center for the Study of Reading. He is coauthor (with Dale D. Johnson) of *Teaching Reading Comprehension* and *Teaching Reading Vocabulary*. With S. Jay Samuels, he edits *Reading Research Quarterly*. His research interests include strategies teachers use to accommodate student difficulties with content-area reading material.

Anthony R. Petrosky is associate professor of Language Communications at the University of Pittsburgh. He coauthored the National Assessment of Educational Progress report, *Reading, Thinking, and Writing*. He currently serves as chair of the NCTE Committee on Research.

H. Alan Robinson is professor of Education and coordinator of Doctoral Reading Programs at Hofstra University. He has served as a member of the Board of Directors and as president of IRA. He is also a past president of NCRE and a former member of the NCTE Commission on Reading. He is currently a member of the Comparative Reading and Long Range Planning Committees of IRA. He has authored and coauthored a number of books focused on reading in the secondary school. His interests include cognitive psychology, linguistics, and content-area reading.

Harry Singer is professor of Education at the University of California— Riverside, and the director of the Reading and Learning for Text Project for the University of California and California State University systems. He is past president of NRC and has served as chair of Citations and Awards for IRA. Author of numerous journal articles, chapters, and books, he is coauthor with Dan Donlan of *Reading and Learning from Text.*

Sharon L. Smith is director of the Indiana University Learning Skills Center and assistant professor in the Language Education Department (Reading Program Area). Besides research and program development in learning skills, she teaches graduate courses in college reading. She is former director of The Young Authors Program in Indianapolis and is coauthor of a text in secondary reading. Her research interests include naturalistic approaches to examining learning environments in a large university and use of unprobed retellings to assess comprehension.

Robert J. Tierney is associate professor at Harvard University and adjunct associate professor at the Center for the Study of Reading, University of Illinois at Urbana-Champaign. A teacher-consultant and researcher, in both the United States and Australia, he has taught at various grade levels (elementary through college) and has written articles on educational theory, research, and practice. Author of *A Guide for Improving Instruction,* he is also coauthor of a number of classroom reading programs.

Joseph L. Vaughan, Jr. is professor of Reading Education at East Texas State University. He serves on the NCTE Commission on Reading, NRC, and IRA. He has published numerous articles on secondary reading instruction, initiated publication of the monograph series *Research on Reading in the Secondary Schools,* and presently organizes an annual symposium on secondary reading research. Besides research on attitude assessment and learning strategies, he is currently pursuing a longitudinal study into characteristics of adolescent readers.